Reference Guides to Rhetoric and Composition
Series Editor, Charles Bazerman

REFERENCE GUIDES TO RHETORIC AND COMPOSITION
Series Editor, Charles Bazerman

The Series provides compact, comprehensive and convenient surveys of what has been learned through research and practice as composition has emerged as an academic discipline over the last half century. Each volume is devoted to a single topic that has been of interest in rhetoric and composition in recent years, to synthesize and make available the sum and parts of what has been learned on that topic. These reference guides are designed to help deepen classroom practice by making available the collective wisdom of the field and will provide the basis for new research. The Series is intended to be of use to teachers at all levels of education, researchers and scholars of writing, graduate students learning about the field, and all who have interest in or responsibility for writing programs and the teaching of writing.

Parlor Press and The WAC Clearinghouse are collaborating so that these books will be widely available through low-cost print editions and free digital distribution. The publishers and the Series editor are teachers and researchers of writing, committed to the principle that knowledge should freely circulate. We see the opportunities that new technologies have for further democratizing knowledge. And we see that to share the power of writing is to share the means for all to articulate their needs, interest, and learning into the great experiment of literacy.

EXISTING BOOKS IN THE SERIES
Invention in Rhetoric and Composition (2004, Lauer)
Reference Guide to Writing across the Curriculum (2005, Bazerman, Little, Bethel, Chavkin, Fouquette, and Garufis)
Revision: History, Theory, and Practice (2006, Horning and Becker)
Writing Program Administration (2007, McLeod)
Community Literacy and the Rhetoric of Local Publics (2008, Long)
Argument in Composition (2009, Ramage, Callaway, Clary-Lemon, and Waggoner)
Basic Writing (2010, Otte and Mlynarczyk)
Genre: An Introduction to History, Theory, Research, and Pedagogy (2010, Bawarshi and Reiff)

Basic Writing

George Otte and Rebecca Williams Mlynarczyk

Parlor Press
West Lafayette, Indiana
www.parlorpress.com

The WAC Clearinghouse
http://wac.colostate.edu/

Parlor Press LLC, West Lafayette, Indiana 47906

© 2010 by Parlor Press and The WAC Clearinghouse
All rights reserved.

Printed in the United States of America

S A N: 2 5 4 - 8 8 7 9

Library of Congress Cataloging-in-Publication Data

Otte, George.
  Basic writing / George Otte and Rebecca Williams Mlynarczyk.
    p. cm.
  Includes bibliographical references and index.
   ISBN 978-1-60235-174-5 (pbk. : alk. paper) -- ISBN 978-1-60235-175-2 (hardcover : alk. paper) -- ISBN 978-1-60235-176-9 (adobe ebook) -- ISBN 978-1-60235-177-6 (epub ebook)
  1. English language--Rhetoric. 2. English language--Grammar--Problems, exercises, etc. 3. Report writing. I. Mlynarczyk, Rebecca. II. Title.
  PE1408.O77 2010
  808'.042--dc22
                    2010008778

Series logo designed by Karl Stolley. Copyediting by Jessica Williams. This book is printed on acid-free paper.

Parlor Press, LLC is an independent publisher of scholarly and trade titles in print and multimedia formats. This book is available in paperback, cloth, and Adobe eBook formats from Parlor Press on the World Wide Web at http://www.parlorpress.com. For submission information or to find out about Parlor Press publications, write to Parlor Press, 816 Robinson St., West Lafayette, Indiana, 47906, or e-mail editor@parlorpress.com.

The WAC Clearinghouse supports teachers of writing across the disciplines. Hosted by Colorado State University's Composition Program, it brings together four journals, three book series, and resources for teachers who use writing in their courses. This book will also be available free on the Internet at The WAC Clearinghouse (http://wac.colostate.edu/).

Contents

Acknowledgments ix

Series Editor's Preface xi
   Charles Bazerman

Introduction xv

1 *Historical Overview* 3
   The 1960s 4
   The 1970s 7
   The 1980s 18
   The 1990s 27
   2000 and Beyond 37

2 *Defining Basic Writing and Basic Writers* 41
   Early Definitions 42
      Basic Writing as a Fix-It Station 43
      Basic Writing as a Back Formation of First-
         Year Composition 44
      A Sense of Mission and Purpose 47
   Adjustments and Revisions 50
      Cognitivist Definitions 50
      Contextual Definitions 51
      Prescribing Without Defining 54
      Initiation as a Goal 55
      Problems with Initiation as a Goal 59
   A Point of Crisis 61
      The Vulnerability of Basic Writing 63
      The Crisis as Reflected in the Journal of Basic Writing 64
   Climate Change for Basic Writing 67
      Responding to Calls to Eliminate Basic Writing 67
      "Our Apartheid" 69
      Context-Contingent Definitions 70
      "Basic Writing at a Political Crossroads" 71
   Capitulating on Definition 73

3 *Practices and Pedagogies*   78
    Error   80
        Teaching Complication 1: The Need for Complexity   82
        Teaching Complication 2: The Need for Tolerance   83
        Teaching Complication 3: The Need (Still) for Correctness   84
        Teaching Complication 4: The Need for Process Analysis   85
        Teaching Complication 5: The Need for Interpretation   86
        Teaching Complication 6: The Need for Negotiation   88
        Teaching Complication 7: The Need for (and Lack of) Consensus   89
    Assessment   90
        Teaching to the Test   91
        Teacher Resistance to Institutionally Imposed Testing   94
        State-Mandated Testing   97
    Teaching   99
        The Importance of Process   100
        Cognitive Schemes and Their Limitations   101
        A Grab Bag of Instructional Strategies   103
        Facts, Artifacts and Counterfacts: A Redefined Teaching Project   105
        The Politics of Identity   110
        Literacy as a Social Practice   114
        Experiments in Mainstreaming   117
        The Fragmentation of the Teaching Enterprise   118

4 *Research*   122
    Error   123
        Insights from Linguistics   123
        Error Analysis   125
        Upholding the Standard   127
        Changing Attitudes toward Error   128
        Error Recognition   129
    Assessment   132
        Foundational Work in Mass Testing   133
        Disillusionment with Holistic Assessment   135
        Not How to Test, But Whether   138
        Alternatives to Established Assessments   139
        High Schools as Gatekeepers   141
    Process   142
        Writing Process(es)   144
        Thinking Process(es)   145
        Cognition or Discourse Conventions?   148

        Academic Literacy   *151*
    Attitudes and Identities   *156*
        The Conflict Within, the Conflict Without   *158*
        Case Studies of Conflict and Struggle   *160*

5 *The Future of Basic Writing*   *163*
    Political Portents   *164*
        Questioning the Value of Remediation   *164*
        Real-World Repercussions   *167*
    Basic Writing Under Siege from Within   *168*
        Arguing for Abolition   *168*
        The Great Unraveling   *170*
    Basic Writing Revised   *172*
        Public Policy and Basic Writing   *172*
        Alternative Program Structures   *174*
    Basic Writing for the Twenty-First Century   *179*
        Anticipating the Need   *179*
        Examining Costs and Benefits   *182*

Appendix: Basic Writing Resources   *189*

Works Cited   *197*

Index   *221*

About the Authors   *223*

Acknowledgments

Like all books, this one owes much to many not named on the cover. We invoke the indulgence shown authors on acknowledgment pages to give the chief among those many their due. We would like to thank our families for their patience, love, and support during the writing and revising of this book. George is especially grateful to wife Dee, who, as always, assessed much and censured little, but always resisted when it counts; he would also like to note daughter Amanda's review of parts of this text as she finished her college career and emerged a teacher with a special interest in educational policy. Rebecca wishes to thank her husband Frank for his steadfast support of many writing projects over the years, this one most recently; she is grateful as well to those who encouraged her with their enthusiasm and offered important insights during the final phases of revision—daughter Susanna, sister Carol, and the members of her writing group, Pat Juell, Susan Babinski, and Jane Isenberg. We would also like to thank each other: co-authorship is in many ways more challenging than single authorship, but our work together has also made it more rewarding, and the book better for it.

We owe a special debt of gratitude to Charles Bazerman, the series editor for the Reference Guides to Rhetoric and Composition. This book has benefited greatly from his astute guidance. We offer thanks to David Blakesley, editor of Parlor Press, and Mike Palmquist, editor of the WAC Clearinghouse, for their support and expertise as the book moved into production—on schedule. Their responsiveness and professionalism are much appreciated. Jessica Williams, a doctoral student at Purdue University, copyedited the manuscript with care and attention to detail, for which we thank her.

We are deeply grateful to the basic writing scholars whose work is cited in this book, many of whom we came to know before and during our work as editors of the *Journal of Basic Writing*. It has been a privilege to work alongside such humane and dedicated colleagues. They have taught us the tensions that animate so much of this book.

Finally, we acknowledge the many inspiring students, teachers, and administrators we have worked with during our long careers at the City University of New York. Collaborating with those who daily demonstrate the importance of open access to higher education has fueled our continuing commitment, while walking with them on the many paths blazed by BW instruction ratifies our refusal to oversimplify the complex endeavor known as basic writing.

Series Editor's Preface

Charles Bazerman

I have a very personal connection with this volume. I began teaching at Baruch College of City University of New York when the second cohort of open admissions students had arrived. My position was defined specifically to meet the needs of these students new to the university, poorly prepared to meet traditional entrance standards. Three years before I met the younger siblings of these students as I taught elementary school in the Bedford-Stuyvesant section of Brooklyn. I was to spend the next twenty years of my career devoted to the task of making university education accessible to open admissions students by developing the writing skills necessary for success. I worked with colleagues across the City University of New York (CUNY), including Mina Shaughnessy, Ken Bruffee, Bob Lyons, Dick Larson, Harvey Wiener, Sondra Perl, Richard Sterling, Blanche Skurnick, Lynn Troyka, Karen Greenberg, and many others. We shared ideas for teaching, formed research projects, and fought institutional battles to keep alive the spirit of open admissions and the mission of CUNY to provide opportunity for all of New York's diverse students.

I knew that mission because almost forty years before I began teaching, my immigrant father had begun studies in City College, Downtown Branch, in the very same building where I was to work. When I was a child, he took me to see the building and his graduation honors inscribed on an honor roll at the entrance. On our home bookshelves were the books my father had used for his freshman composition class years before.

At the very same spot as Baruch College and its prior incarnation as Downtown City, in 1847 the Free Academy of the City of New York was founded by President of the Board of Education Townsend Harris. This first institution for public higher education would provide access to free higher education for generations of immigrants and working class youth based on academic merit alone. The basic writing mission at CUNY formed the very grounds of my American and academic experience.

The project of basic writing addresses a fundamental question of equity and opportunity: What are we to do, as a society, with the fact that large parts of our population reach the age for higher education with only limited writing skills, inadequate for the challenges of the university or the contemporary workplace? This situation may be blamed on many things: failed policies, failed school systems, misguided pedagogies, class, race, family, perceived job prospects, dialect and language, culture and technology, individual motivation and discipline, social anomie, developmental trauma and difficulties, or whatever other ills might be identified in society, economy, or individuals. Whatever cluster of causes may come together in each individual case, they all fit within a larger picture of our society becoming more literate, requiring larger numbers of highly literate citizens and workers, raising the literate demands on even the most prepared, and providing attractive opportunities only to those who are prepared to communicate effectively in writing with knowledge gained from reading. For a century and a half higher education has been opening its doors ever wider to provide opportunities and produce the intelligence needed for prosperity, governance, and social harmony. That educational project has meant that colleges and universities have been drawing and will continue to draw in students at the margins of preparation. It is a matter of equity and societal self-interest to provide these students the tools to succeed along with their better prepared colleagues.

Basic writing as an educational imperative sits at the frontier of expanding university opportunity. While the Free Academy may have been founded on the corner of 23rd Street and Lexington Avenue in New York City, its vision of access and mobility has spread not only through New York and the United States but also throughout the globe. As access to higher education has been expanding in every nation, the educational systems have been struggling with how to meet the literacy needs of new populations entering the university. Writing education is on the global increase, much of it directed toward what we would consider basic writing. As I finish this preface, I am at a campus in rural Brazil consulting with faculty dealing with these same issues; they seek the same access and social change we sought in New York but with even more limited resources and greater constraints. This book provides many lessons of value to every region as they engage pedagogy, policies, and institutional politics to meet the needs of students and provide real opportunity. The mission of basic writing seems to be always in a state of struggle, but because it is at the edge of social change and growth, and that may be the greatest lesson, we have no choice but to persist in this struggle.

Introduction

The story of basic writing in the United States is a rich one, full of twists and turns, powerful personalities and pivotal events. Framed by historic developments—from the open admissions movement of the 1960s and 1970s to the attacks on remediation that intensified in the 1990s and beyond—this account will trace the arc of these large social and cultural forces.

But this narrative will also capture the insider's perspective. Basic writing (BW) is a field acutely conscious of itself, imbued with a sense of being called into existence to accomplish a mission. Its self-awareness has always been shaped by its vulnerability to social forces that helped to call it up and have since threatened to shut it down. That vulnerability, in turn, helps to explain why this academic enterprise was never fully accepted within the academy. As academic fields go, basic writing has always seemed unusually new, exposed, and challenged to justify itself.

All this creates problems as well as prospects for anyone telling the story—or stories. The plural is necessary, as is the realization that these multiple stories overlap and complicate each other. There are defining characteristics of basic writing (perhaps first and foremost its quest for self-definition) that pull in different directions. It is a field remarkable for deriving so much of its sense of what it is about, at least early on, from one especially forceful seminal figure, Mina Shaughnessy. Yet it is also a field that, in its latter days, is marked by iconoclastic, decanonizing efforts to break that spell. It is a field that, like so many, is to a great extent defined by its research, and yet, because the marginalization of its students is mirrored in the marginalization of its faculty, it is also a field in which teaching practice can seem unusually disengaged from (even oblivious to) research. It is a field with a strong political as well as pedagogical mission, yet one that seems far more buffeted by political forces than capable of effecting political change.

Such tensions and divergences can get their due only if the story of BW is told as a number of overlapping stories, letting what might seem a mere footnote in one assume a critical role in another. Allowing some central concern like teaching or research to come to the fore means traveling the same ground with an eye out for a different emphasis each time. What, then, is the whole picture? It might help to think of the chapters that follow as transparent overlays, maps to be laid upon other maps so that the full topography shows through.

Chapter 1, "Historical Overview," is the most purely narrative—a brief history of basic writing in which personalities and events are allowed to dominate the stage. Chapter 2, "Defining Basic Writing and Basic Writers," is a kind of exercise in pop epistemology—a field's sense of itself and how that changes in terms of actions and reactions as it struggles to define itself. Chapter 3, "Practices and Pedagogies," traces the evolution of basic writing as it attempted to fulfill its overarching mission—meeting the needs of the students in its classrooms in pedagogically sound ways. Chapter 4, "Research," surveys the territory through the lens of the scholarly work that informed and described and often critiqued the central teaching mission. Chapter 5, "The Future of Basic Writing," sums up, as best we can, the state of basic writing—and basic writers—in the early years of the twenty-first century. Finally, we include an appendix, "Basic Writing Resources": an annotated list of useful websites, listservs, and materials available online.

Do these chapters add up to the whole story? It would be foolhardy to claim that this account of basic writing is, if not the only one, then the one that matters. It would be no less foolish to deny that it is the account of basic writing as it matters to us. And so it is probably wise to engage in some personal (but far from full) disclosure with each of us speaking as individuals for a moment.

GEORGE: Like many compositionists of my generation, I was a self-styled literature scholar in graduate school pulled into composition in the early 1980s not only to teach it but also to administer a large writing program—and to do that even as an untenured professor. Knowing (at least) how little I knew, I tried to educate myself. A friend, a sociolinguist, told me the book to start with was Mina Shaughnessy's *Errors and Expectations*. I did not stop there, of course, and the next thing I knew (that next thing being a couple years down

Introduction   xvii

the road), I realized that I was indeed committed to the teaching (and even administration) of writing; what's more, I was determined to pursue that commitment somewhere within the City University of New York (CUNY). So that is where I have been since the mid-1980s, directing writing programs for a decade and a half, chairing the CUNY Association of Writing Supervisors for a full decade, coediting the *Journal of Basic Writing* for seven years. In that time, conferences and correspondence (to say nothing of reading published work) gave me so much contact with BW teachers and scholars beyond CUNY that I actually know most of the people named in the stories that follow. That can be as much a liability as a qualification, I suppose, but it does make a difference. Seeing (if only with the mind's eye) the faces of people I am writing about, often ranged on opposite sides of a controversy, has made me want all the more to give them their due. Similarly, as someone who testified for the preservation of basic writing at colleges it was removed from in the late 1990s (including my own), I am acutely aware of the forces behind such changes, though no less aware that such changes have been far from universal.

REBECCA: My story within CUNY also reaches back many years. In 1974, with the qualifying credential of a master's degree in literature, I accepted a part-time position as a writing tutor at Brooklyn College's New School of Liberal Arts, a discipline-based preparatory program developed to deal with the vast influx of open admissions students. With the budget cuts of the mid-1970s, I was "promoted" from writing tutor to adjunct instructor of writing workshops for this same student population—a population that captivated my interest as a teacher and beginning researcher.

In 1980 I moved on to CUNY's Hunter College, where I taught (still as a part-timer) basic writing courses for native speakers and later for English as a Second Language (ESL) students, a growing demographic at CUNY at the time. My fascination with and respect for the writing of my BW and ESL students eventually resulted in a coauthored textbook, *In Our Own Words: Student Writers at Work*, featuring essays by these students rather than the usual professional samples.

In 1989 I began doctoral studies at New York University, focusing on the challenges and rewards of working with basic writers—both native speakers of English and multilingual students. In 1993, having completed the PhD, I accepted a full-time, tenure-track position in the English Department of CUNY's Kingsborough Community College, where I have worked ever since as a classroom teacher and writing program administrator. In 2007 I also became a Professor of English at the CUNY Graduate Center, where I work with PhD students in the Rhetoric and Composition area group. Since 2003 I have served as coeditor of the *Journal of Basic Writing*, and so, like George, I often feel a personal as well as a professional connection with the ongoing story of basic writing in America.

We hope that this book, with its historical perspective, will be of use to a wide audience of readers including scholars and practitioners of basic writing as well as students enrolled in graduate courses in composition and rhetoric or writing studies—particularly those in the growing number of master's degree programs in BW but also doctoral students in seminars focusing on the history of pedagogy and research in composition. Because some of the most influential research in composition since 1970 has related to basic writing, the extensive review of the literature contained in this book will be of interest to a diverse audience concerned with the important trends that have shaped the teaching and researching of composition in the United States. Since basic writing began—and continues to exist—in a highly politicized climate, the book is also relevant for leaders in education, college and university administrators, and elected or appointed state and federal officials.

Available in multiple forms, this book is designed to be used in multiple ways. Professors of graduate courses in composition may choose to assign just one chapter (available without charge to their students in PDF form through the WAC Clearinghouse). University administrators may want to skim through a chapter or two while traveling to attend a meeting focused on the future of basic writing at their institution; they might choose to store the book on their laptop as an Adobe e-book (available from Parlor Press). Doctoral students doing research in basic writing may want to purchase a hard copy of the entire book (also available from Parlor Press) for current and future reference. Our treatment of the subject here, looking at the field of basic writing through different lenses in different chapters, recognizes that the book will be read differently—in part or in its entirety—by different readers.

Ultimately, the onus on a guide like this is to seem both comprehensive and concise. And so we have attempted a delicate balancing act: between fidelity to the past and present relevance, between local and (presumptively) global knowledge, and between personal judgment and (apparent) objectivity. Our chief means of finding balance is to circle back on the same general story, being on the lookout for different themes or seeing the same themes from different perspectives. What we hope emerges is a gestalt of basic writing that will give people interested in its history or self-definition or pedagogy or research a sense of the important trends and patterns. In this exercise of mapping, we have tried to make directions clear (if not simple) without denying the undeniable blurring and dissensus and differential development that characterizes the field, always mindful of its greatest irony: that something called basic writing should so often find itself snagged on the complexities it uncovers.

Basic Writing

1 Historical Overview

For most scholars and teachers, the story of basic writing is tied to a specific historical moment—the open admissions movement of the 1970s at the City University of New York (CUNY). This seismic shift in university policy grew out of the social and political volatility of the late 1960s. And it resulted in the memorable teaching program led by the charismatic teacher-scholar Mina Shaughnessy at CUNY's City College. Any overview of basic writing needs to begin with an account of how this outgrowth of the fairly new field of composition, which came into its own in the 1960s, emerged as an important subfield in the 1970s.

Of course, the presence of unskilled writers in college classrooms was not a completely new phenomenon. What was new was the heightened focus on the needs of such students. Michael G. Moran and Martin J. Jacobi make this point in their introduction to *Research in Basic Writing: A Bibliographic Sourcebook.* Surprised that "it took so many years for scholars to turn their attention to the problem of extremely weak student writers," they ask what changed so that "basic writing is now an important discipline within the larger area of rhetoric and composition" (1). Their answer: "Attitudes toward these students changed during the 1960s and 1970s" (1). Despite all the talk from basic writing scholars about a new kind of student, what really made BW possible was a new kind of attention.

In the opening pages of their introduction to *Landmark Essays on Basic Writing,* Kay Halasek and Nels P. Highberg give a useful overview of "the early moments in the history of basic writing" going back to the nineteenth century (xi–xiv), but the first essay in the collection is Adrienne Rich's account of open admissions at City College. People like Shaughnessy and Rich represent a critical shift of attention and sympathy, acting as catalysts of BW's emergence, however far back its origins might be traced. Precisely because other historians of composition have duly traced distant roots and foreshadowings (see, for

3

example, Berlin, *Writing*; Brereton; Connors, *Composition-Rhetoric*), a focused treatment of basic writing needs to know its limits. Though some scholars have found the precursors of BW in institutional and curricular developments many decades earlier, we focus here not on century-distant predecessors of basic writing at Harvard or Wellesley but instead on that time when basic writing became aware of itself, achieving self-definition as a considered answer to an urgent need.

In this chapter, we provide an overview of the history of basic writing as it has developed over the decades. Given BW's origin in the crucible of political and educational pressures of the 1960s, it comes as no surprise that its definition has been highly contested, its past repeatedly remapped.

The 1960s

The 1960s, in the popular mind, is the classic period of unrest and upheaval, much of it concentrated in colleges and universities. Partly, this concentration resulted from the weight of numbers. Ever since World War II, when the GI Bill allowed many returning service personnel to enter college who never would have otherwise, college enrollments had been rising steadily, mounting throughout the 1960s and into the 1970s. This was a time of dramatic enrollment growth, faculty hiring, and curricular change. But this unprecedented growth brought problems as well, particularly to institutions unable to support further growth. One flashpoint was City College of the City University of New York (CUNY), where free tuition made the demand for higher education especially great. In the past, raising admissions standards had kept enrollments in check—but at a cost: higher admissions standards brought into question the right to "equal educational opportunity," which, as Kenneth Howe has shown in *Understanding Equal Educational Opportunity,* was a critical principle in public education in the second half of the twentieth century.

New York had found a safety valve of sorts in the legislative mandate that, in 1966, created the SEEK Program. The acronym stood for Search for Education, Elevation, and Knowledge, and the program's purpose was to provide higher education opportunities to economically and educationally disadvantaged students. As it later turned out, the SEEK Program opened the door and laid the groundwork for open admissions.

With open admissions, the door became a floodgate. Enrollments of first-year students at CUNY nearly doubled in the very first year (1970), jumping from 20,000 to 35,000. Almost half of these students entered under the new open admissions standards. City College and the other CUNY colleges were not ready for open admissions and its consequences, rushed into the change in admissions policy by student demonstrations and campus unrest. Located in Harlem, City College in particular had come to seem a bastion of white privilege in a largely black neighborhood. Calls to make it less exclusive and excluding became increasingly strident. Accounts of this stridency vary, however. One alumnus (and opponent of open admissions) states flatly that "the 1970 introduction of open admissions was . . . in response to race riots" (Berman), while Adrienne Rich, discussing the seizure of City College's South Campus by the Black and Puerto Rican Student Community in April of 1969, recounts "the faculty group's surprised respect for the students' articulateness, reasoning power, and skill in handling statistics—for the students were negotiating in exchange for withdrawal from South Campus an admissions policy which would go far beyond SEEK in its inclusiveness" (6). Yet in the wake of such negotiations came the torching of City College's Great Hall, which seems to have been a decisive event. Seymour H. Hyman (who was Deputy Chancellor at the time) recalls the fire: "'I was telling people about what I felt when I saw that smoke coming out of that building, and the only question in my mind was, How can we save City College? And the only answer was, Hell, let everybody in'" (qtd. in Maher, *Shaughnessy* 40). An overstatement, this was nevertheless symptomatic of a significant shift in policy. Open admissions, planned by the Board of Higher Education (now the CUNY Board of Trustees) for gradual phase-in to full implementation in 1975, was renegotiated with the protesting students in May of 1969. Minutes from the Board meeting of July 9, 1969, note that students' demands were met for the most part.

Much has been made of this acquiescence to students' demands, then and now. For many, it meant "caving in" and worse. The response of one City College professor at the time, effectively signaled by the title of his book *The Death of the American University: With Special Reference to the Collapse of the City College of New York,* was to declare that "there can and must be no retreat, no craven capitulation to the anarchists, Communists, and know-nothings who would bring down society" (Heller 12). As recently as 1999, a report on open admissions for the Mayor's Advisory Task Force on the City University of New York used the telling heading "Policy by Riot" in its account of this time ("CUNY: An Institution Adrift" 19).

Yet presumed immediate causes are usually part of a more complex chain of causes and effects. Especially critical in this case was a looming budget crisis. As documented in *Right Versus Privilege: The Open-Admissions Experiment at the City University of New York,* the Black and Puerto Rican Student Community (BPRSC) made common cause with white student organizations in response to announced budget cuts. The coalition produced demonstrations of CUNY students at the state legislature in Albany many times the size of any back at CUNY (and well before the seizure of the South Campus). What's more, the budget cuts the BPRSC feared would reduce opportunities for minority students were so serious that the college president himself announced his resignation in protest, only to have twenty-seven department chairs announce theirs as well in a dramatic gesture of support (Lavin, Alba, and Silberstein 10–11).

Open admissions, then, was no sudden, student-led coup, though it is important to see it as a real change shaped by radical egalitarianism as well as fiscal exigency. It is equally important to realize that City College already had a structure in place for the writing instruction of the new students that the hurried-up policy of open admissions brought in. Since 1965, even before the SEEK program, the college had offered a Pre-Baccalaureate Program, and the director of the SEEK Program had some trouble getting out of the habit of referring to it as the "Pre-Bac" Program (Maher, *Shaughnessy* 92). Her name was Mina Shaughnessy.

Like the social circumstances surrounding her program, Shaughnessy's personal circumstances seem especially significant. An extraordinarily successful and committed teacher passionate about both writing and literature, she lacked a PhD, and her teaching prior to her appointment at City College had been in part-time positions, chiefly at Hofstra University on Long Island and Hunter College, another CUNY campus in Manhattan. Impressive recommendations from Hofstra and Hunter and a successful interview earned her an appointment as lecturer in City College's Pre-Baccalaureate Program in April of 1967, starting in September of that year. Just how profound an impression she had made as an applicant became apparent over that summer when the director of the Pre-Bac program suffered a heart attack and Shaughnessy was asked to assume the directorship. Anxious about the challenge she was taking on, she could scarcely gauge the much greater challenges to come. The SEEK program (so renamed) that Adrienne Rich and Shaughnessy taught in and that Shaughnessy directed had classes capped at fifteen students and was a relatively modest enterprise in the 1960s, though Shaughnessy did meet with resistance from the tenured (and mostly male) professors who felt the students served by her program signaled a lowering of standards and a misdirection of effort (Maher, *Shaughnessy* 88–90). But such grumbling was only a mild intimation of the seismic rumblings to come.

The 1970s

With open admissions came a dramatic shift in scale and intensity. During the summer of 1970, while most faculty were away, Shaughnessy hired over forty teachers for her program (Maher, *Shaughnessy* 101). Just months after threatened budget cuts produced massive protests, Shaughnessy was recruiting for a program that many of her colleagues saw as an unfortunate diversion of resources. Not so long before that, the focus had been on raising standards at City College (partly as a check on burgeoning enrollments), something of a national trend, one documented by Albert Kitzhaber (18). Only a few years later, there was an abrupt reversal. The pressure of rising enrollments hadn't disappeared any more than the concern over standards had, yet a dramatic policy change had suddenly swung the gate open wide, allowing students into college who never would have had a chance to attend only a short time before.

Why had this happened—and not just at City? It was a question Shaughnessy herself struggled with in the opening pages of "Basic Writing" (1976), the bibliographic essay she wrote for Gary Tate's collection *Teaching Composition*. This question was related to another: what was she to call the new field? The memorable opening of her essay situated her on a frontier: "The teaching of writing to severely unprepared freshmen is as yet but the frontier of a profession, lacking even an agreed upon name" (177). And the evocation of a new frontier was not something she did lightly: she was convinced that the kind of instruction she was speaking of was really quite new, leading her to reject terms like "remedial" or "bonehead" English—though the latter term

> catches something of the quality of the course and the attitudes that shaped it. But this type of course was waning, along with Freshman English, when the new remedial population began to appear in the sixties. In 1964, the first year of the War on Poverty, the headings "cultural deprivation" and "cultural differences" appeared for the first time in *Education Index*. By the next year, they were among the most heavily itemed headings in the *Index*. We can date the "new" remedial English from then. (178)

More important than her choice of terminology that still grounds the field and gives it an identity (people call it basic writing because she did) is Shaughnessy's sense of social change giving rise to the "new"—above all to "the 'new' students who entered colleges under the open admissions revolution of the sixties" (178).

In her teaching and writing, Shaughnessy conveyed her sense of a new population of student writers brought forward by shifts of social perspective and responsibility. For Shaughnessy, blaming the students for supposed deficiencies was feckless and unjust; errors and other nonstandard features were the result of social inequities, not personal failings. As Deborah Mutnick has written, "More than the scholars who followed in her footsteps, Shaughnessy consistently shifted the focus of her research and writing on the problems of Open Admissions from the students to the teachers, administrators, and society in general" ("On the Academic Margins" 185).

At the time, however, City College was not the only CUNY campus to develop programs to meet the needs of the new student population, and Shaughnessy was not the only one working to develop exciting new programs. The 1970s were a time of pedagogical innovation throughout the university. Dynamic programs of a different focus and pedagogy were developed at Queens College under Robert Lyons, later assisted by Donald McQuade. Acclaimed poet Marie Ponsot, also working at Queens, emphasized the imagination in working with open admissions students. Brooklyn College developed an innovative program called the New School of Liberal Arts (NSLA), originally housed in downtown Brooklyn. NSLA was a high-level academic program for traditional as well as "underprepared students" that included additional counseling and workshops in academic reading and writing for open admissions students. On the main campus of Brooklyn College, English professor Kenneth Bruffee was doing groundbreaking work on peer tutoring and collaborative learning. At Lehman College, new pedagogies and programs were being developed under the leadership of Richard Larson, Richard Sterling, and Sondra Perl. At Baruch College, experiments in computer assisted instruction (CAI) were taking place. At Hunter College, faculty in the Developmental English Program, under the leadership of Ann Raimes, were developing policies and practices for the new students and also sowing the seeds for what later became known as WAC (Writing Across the Curriculum). At the same time, faculty at CUNY's five community colleges were also developing programs to meet the needs of the new students who were pouring into their classrooms.

In the mid-1970s, the CUNY Open Admissions Conference fostered a strong community spirit, which led to the formation of the CUNY Association of Writing Supervisors (CAWS), initially led by Robert Lyons and Harvey Wiener with Kenneth Bruffee as a third. CAWS gave rise to study and research groups; it also began to sponsor an annual conference and put out a newsletter, CAWSES. A variety of approaches emerged at different CUNY campuses, some of them rather distant from Shaughnessy's efforts at City College, creating a strong hothouse atmosphere.

But these efforts developed throughout the decade. At its beginning, in 1970, Shaughnessy was faced with immediate practical problems. She had teachers to train and a program to run. She did not assume that she had a controlling theory or even an effective roadmap for how to proceed. Her own teaching approach had always been to puzzle through things, looking for patterns and possibilities. Ultimately, that would be the method behind *Errors and Expectations,* the groundbreaking book she published in 1977. For now, it was how she invited teachers in her program to work. She eventually codified her sense of appropriate pedagogical preparation and action, summing it up in the phrase "Diving In," the title of her talk at the Modern Language Association (MLA) convention in 1975. A decade later, Robert Lyons described Shaughnessy's approach as program administrator, a role he succeeded her in:

> Instead of establishing a required curriculum for the writing program, she encouraged teachers to follow their hunches and share their insights with one another, and she encouraged them as well to engage in a wide range of research projects: studies of derailments in student prose, contrastive studies of first language interference in nonnative speakers, and examinations of perceptual problems that affect some students' ability to proofread. She also sponsored a different kind of project that sent English teachers as auditors into introductory courses in disciplines unfamiliar to them, such as biology and psychology. Their efforts to grasp the concepts governing these subjects made them more aware of the particular intellectual assumptions and the distinctive languages appropriate to these disciplines. Transforming teachers into learners, a constant in Shaughnessy's pedagogy, but here done quite literally, made the teachers comprehend the situation of students new to all kinds of academic discourse. (176)

Lyons's account of Shaughnessy's program is worth quoting at some length because almost all the critical elements of her legacy are there: embracing an inductive approach, urging collaboration and note-sharing, validating and using classroom-based research (especially with the teacher as researcher asking why students do what they do), and exploring the importance of language uses and academic strictures within the academy.

Shaughnessy's attention to language use in academic contexts is, from some perspectives, the most problematic aspect of her legacy. As Lyons himself notes, "Those who knew her and shared her concern for basic writers were often irritated by the degree of deference she showed to the forms of the academy . . ." (174). Accepting established standards as goals can be a strategic as well as a principled move, a way of stressing that increasing access need not entail a lowering of expectations. Though this was transparently Shaughnessy's intention, individual intentions can be bent in being institutionalized. And Shaughnessy's success and influence were not long in helping to reshape her institution. By 1975, when she gave her "Diving In" address at the MLA convention, Shaughnessy was no longer a teacher or even a BW program director but an associate dean of the City University, overseeing the development of assessment tests in writing, reading, and mathematics. This change of venue and position also gave her the time and scope to do two things that would round off her legacy in the few years no one knew at the time were all she had: the writing and publication of *Errors and Expectations* and the launching of the *Journal of Basic Writing*.

It's hard to overemphasize the enormous importance of *Errors and Expectations: A Guide for the Teacher of Basic Writing* (1977). Jane Maher's biography devotes pages to the glowing reviews the book received when it came out—including reviews in *The Atlantic Monthly*, the *The Chronicle of Higher Education*, *The Nation*, and *The New York Times* (197–99). This attention was quite unlike any ever before afforded a study of student writing. And the attention didn't stop there. In the mid-1980s, Carol Hartzog's national survey of writing programs found Shaughnessy's book far and away the most influential text in the eyes of *all* program directors—not just BW program directors. In 1997, Nancy Myers cited *Errors* as the one scholarly book reliably recommended for canonical status in rhetoric and composition studies. In 1999, it was the first of five texts treated in a special review section of *Teaching English in the Two-Year College* titled "Books That Have Stood the Test of Time" (Knodt 118). There are also countless personal testimonials to the power and influence of the book; in a special issue of *Language and Learning Across the Disciplines* devoted to the history of Writing Across the Curriculum (WAC), for instance, Thomas A. Angelo closes his contribution by saying, "The first and most personally meaningful book I've read on writing remains Mina Shaughnessy's *Errors & Expectations*. . . . In twenty years, no other book has had more impact on my teaching" (71). What is most compelling about the way the book was initially received and continues to register is that it is seen as a book "on writing," not some subset thereof, and it exerts its influence well beyond basic writing to composition, English studies, WAC, pedagogy, literacy, and language studies. But what explains not only its initial impact but also its enduring and widespread appeal?

Those early reviews reflect Shaughnessy's sense that a profound social change had brought a new population to the attention of colleges and those who teach in them. As Benjamin DeMott said in his review of her book in *The Nation*, "Her work was the kind of work you would do if you were really going to take democracy seriously" (645). Another reason for the book's appeal is the almost irresistible invitation for the reader to identify with the role Shaughnessy enacts in the Preface, that of someone dumbfounded by the new students on her doorstep who nevertheless learn to cope, even succeed:

> I remember sitting alone in the worn urban classroom where my students had just written their first essays and where I now began to read them, hoping to be able to assess quickly the sort of task that lay ahead of us that semester. But the writing was so stunningly unskilled that I could not begin to define the task nor even sort out the difficulties. I could only sit there, reading and re-reading the alien papers, wondering what had gone wrong and trying to understand what I at this eleventh hour of my students' academic lives could do about it.
>
> Looking at these papers now, I have no difficulty assessing the work to be done nor believing that it *can* be done. (vii)

This transformation from confounded to confident would seem magical had Shaughnessy not supplied samples of the student writing she was referring to along with the thinking she brought to bear on it. Suddenly, for teachers in a world defined much more by textbooks than by studies of writing, here was someone who spoke as one of them, puzzling over real student texts and making sense of them.

Her ability to dispel what she called the "'mystery' of error" (according to Robert Lyons, her book was originally titled *The Logic of Error* ["Mina Shaughnessy" 183]) was complemented by an ability to think and feel along with the students, to enter into both the affective and cognitive dimensions of error:

> The "mystery" of error is what most intimidates students—the worry that errors just "happen" without a person's knowing how or when. . . . Freedom from error is finally a matter of understanding error, not of getting special dispensation to err simply because writing formal English is thought to be beyond the capabilities or interests of some students. (127–28)

This demystification of error is a complex task, but Shaughnessy conveys the invincible conviction that, for the students' sake, it must be done, and it can be done. Seeing how it could be done led the reviewer in *The Chronicle of Higher Education* to say that Shaughnessy had brought to bear on student writing the kind of "intelligence that literary scholars have traditionally been trained to lavish on T. S. Eliot, James Joyce, and Ezra Pound"; her urgency that it must be done made him reckon her book a "force that can redirect the energies of an entire profession" (Hungiville 18).

For all this, there remains the focus on error, with its ramifications for the new field. Just how would and should the profession's energies be (re)directed? Shaughnessy was clear that error was only an important initial focus—not the be-all and end-all of basic writing. Still, one has to start somewhere, and (a choice made all the more consequential by her early death) error seemed to her the place to start. She explained why in her introduction to the first issue of the *Journal of Basic Writing* (*JBW*), the in-house journal she ushered into being in 1975 with an entire issue devoted to error. Characteristically, she opens with the sense of a new student population:

> A policy of admissions that reaches out beyond traditional sources for its students, bringing in to a college campus young men and women from diverse classes, races, and cultural backgrounds who have attended good, poor, and mediocre schools, is certain to shake the assumptions and even the confidence of teachers who have been trained to serve a more uniform and prepared student population. ("Introduction" 1)

In introducing the new journal, she seems almost apologetic about the perceived necessity of foregrounding errors, as much as they figure in the initial impressions of teachers (to say nothing of placement assessments readers). "Error," she confesses,

> may seem to be an old place to begin a new discussion of writing. It is, after all, a subject English teachers already know about. Some people would claim that it is the English teacher's obsession with error that has killed writing for generations of students. Yet error—the unintentional deviation from expected patterns—dominates the writing of many of the new

students, inhibiting them and their readers from concentrating on what is being said. And while no English teacher seems to have difficulty counting up and naming errors, few have been in the habit of observing them fruitfully, with the intent, that is, of understanding why intelligent young adults who want to be right seem to go on, persistently and even predictably, being wrong. (3–4)

In introducing the articles in this first issue of *JBW,* Shaughnessy notes that the issue's "opening and concluding articles take up some of the social and pedagogical issues that hover about the subject of error" (4). The first article, Sarah D'Eloia's "Teaching Standard Written English," begins by unapologetically and unequivocally announcing the conviction that "teaching 'basic' writing is synonymous with teaching standard written English" (5). Its counterweight is the concluding article, Isabella Halsted's "Putting Error in Its Place," which approvingly cites the 1974 Conference on College Composition and Communication position paper "Students' Right to Their Own Language" and argues that "a major problem our students (and we ourselves) have is fixation on Error" (77). Certainly, D'Eloia's and Halsted's positions were not the extremes they could be taken to; moderated by Shaughnessy's gravitational pull, they were brought into closer orbit around her center. Shaughnessy, as Glynda Hull has noted, occupied a kind of critical middle ground in those early days, staking out

> a position [that] can be seen as a sidestep, even a sleight of hand, since it shifts our attention from the overwhelming question of whether we ought to sanction through our roles as teachers the existence of a privileged language, particularly when privileged means only arbitrarily approved scribal conventions. But it can also be seen as a compelling argument, both to provide instruction on error and to include editing among those aspects of writing worth our study. ("Research" 167)

Shaughnessy had her own ways of registering what she might be sidestepping, as when (at the end of *Errors and Expectations*) she allows that college, for the students she cares so much for, can have a negative aspect despite its proffered rewards, "threatening at the same time to take them from their distinctive ways of interpreting the world, to assimilate them into the culture of academia without acknowledging their experience as outsiders" (292). And, of course, it is not just *what* a teacher focuses on but *how*. Hull grants Shaughnessy not only a compelling argument for a focus on error but also a compelling method: a determination "to study error from the point of view of causation" ("Research" 173). This resolve to investigate the whys of what writers did opened up new vistas for basic writing: once the question was what was happening in the writer's mind, the answers could not stop with treatments of error, and so studies of process, cognition, and resistance ultimately came to take center stage.

But, at the time, there were also more practical concerns to be dealt with. The original pioneer in what she memorably labeled the frontier (she concluded as well as began the bibliographic essay "Basic Writing" with that figure) spent her last years not only making a beginning for the field, notably with *Errors and Expectations* and the *Journal of Basic Writing* but also fighting off what looked like its end. Maher's biography of Shaughnessy makes especially compelling reading in its discussion of her last years as a university administrator. It was a time of fiscal crisis for New York as the city was near bankruptcy, and fledgling programs were especially vulnerable to cuts. An attempt to bring enrollments down included proposed entrance exams, which Shaughnessy opposed as "the end of the University's Open Admissions policy" (from her memo to the Board of Higher Education, qtd. in Maher, *Shaughnessy* 177); as an alternative, she began work on a never-realized project of collaboration with high schools that would ensure better preparation for college. The inaugural issue of *Resource,* the newsletter of the Instructional Resource Center she created and directed, began, "As I write this, we are still uncertain about the kind of University the budget cutters will finally allow us, and the survey of CUNY Skills programs which we began runs the risk of being more historical than we originally planned" (qtd. in Maher *Shaughnessy* 179).

That was May 1976. The month before, as the keynote speaker at the first conference of the CUNY Association of Writing Supervisors (CAWS), she had given a more detailed and poignant picture of what the budget cuts might mean, had indeed already meant:

> These are discouraging times for all of us, most particularly for the teachers who have been working with unprepared students on basic skills. Both stu-

dents and teachers are already discovering that they are expendable, and the programs they have helped to build over the past five years to remedy the failure of the public schools (and the society of which those schools are an extension) now begin to shake and fracture under the blows of retrenchment.

We experience the crisis most directly on our individual campuses:

- Our staffs are shrinking and our class size increasing.
- Talented young teachers who were ready to concentrate their scholarly energies on the sort of research and teaching we need in basic writing are looking for jobs.
- Each day brings not a new decision but rumors of new decisions, placing us in the predicament of those mice in psychological experiments who must keep shifting their expectations until they are too rattled to function.
- Our campuses buzz like an Elizabethan court with talk of who is in favor and who is out. And we meet our colleagues from other campuses with relief: "Ah, good," we say (or think to ourselves)—"you're still here."
- We struggle each day to extract from the Orwellian Language that announces new plans and policies some clear sense of what is finally going to become of the students whom the university in more affluent times committed itself to educate. ("The Miserable Truth" 263–64)

Things would get worse, considerably worse. The need to curtail enrollments (and so expenses) was achieved not by entrance exams but by the charging of tuition, something the Board of Higher Education voted through in June 1976. An account of this time, LaVona L. Reeves's "Mina Shaughnessy and Open Admissions at New York's City College" (2002), succinctly outlines the immediate consequences: "In the fall of 1976, enrollment had declined 17 percent, making it necessary for several thousand faculty members to be laid off. As usual, the last to be hired were the first to be fired, and many of the newer minority teachers lost their jobs, despite massive student protests" (123).

Such was the turmoil that surrounded Shaughnessy as an administrator, and it made the publication of *Errors and Expectations* in the same academic year all that much more the "godsend" Reeves calls it (123). The honors and attentions bestowed on Shaughnessy and her book had to be gratifying, given the circumstances, but they did not change those circumstances. Only weeks after the release of the book, Shaughnessy was diagnosed with kidney cancer, first misdiagnosed as a stress-related ulcer (Maher, *Shaughnessy* 200). By December 1977, she was diagnosed as having a brain tumor. By November of the following year, she was dead.

The memorializing of Mina Shaughnessy, beginning with an event in December 1978 at which Adrienne Rich, Irving Howe, and others spoke, went on for some time. She was eulogized by Janet Emig in the February 1979 issue of *College Composition and Communication* and by E. D. Hirsch and others at an MLA conference special session at the end of that year. As late as 1985, Robert Lyons, summing up the "most widely respected authority on basic writing in this country," stated, "In a field often marked by controversy and division, her work was invariably accorded attention and respect" (171–72). Lyons tellingly preceded his remarks with the admission that "I still find it difficult to accept her absence and to regard her as a writer and teacher to be appraised rather than solely as a colleague to be mourned" (171). By force of personality as well as intellect, marshaling support and sympathy for the students who mattered so much to her and for the instruction she believed would save them, Mina Shaughnessy had an influence on basic writing, one that the field is still learning to reckon with. In the years that were to come, Shaughnessy's legacy was revered by some but found to be stiflingly enduring by others, as is suggested by the title of an essay published two full decades after her death: Jeanne Gunner's "Iconic Discourse: The Troubling Legacy of Mina Shaughnessy." But in the decade following the one she dominated, critiques of her were in fact rare, though winds of change certainly swept the BW landscape.

Maxine Hairston's "The Winds of Change," based on her speech at the 1978 convention of the Conference on College Composition and Communication and published in 1982, heralded a paradigm shift in composition, including a turn of attention from product to process. Much of the impetus for this shift came from BW research, not least of all from what Glynda Hull called the resolve "to study error from the point of view of causation" (173). In addition to Shaughnessy's own work, which had been preceded by her good friend Janet Emig's seminal study *The Composing Processes of Twelfth Graders* (1971), there were several especially noteworthy research projects and publications as the 1970s came to an end. A particularly clear-cut case of a causal approach to error was Muriel Harris's 1978 *College English* article "Individual Diagnoses: Searching for Causes, Not Symptoms of Writing Deficiencies." That same year saw the completion of Sondra Perl's important dissertation "Five Writers Writing: Case Studies of the Composing Processes of Unskilled College Writers," which quickly spawned a series of articles: "The Composing Processes of Unskilled College Writers" (1979), "Understanding Composing" (1980), and "A Look at Basic Writers in the Process of Composing" (1980). In addition to providing the case studies Shaughnessy had called for, Perl backed up Shaughnessy's claim that basic writers were not without established writing patterns and processes; the problem was that these processes tended to be far from efficient or proficient, full of disruptions in the flow of thought, ironically creating and compounding errors partly out of a debilitating attempt to eliminate them.

The 1980s

The process movement, which had its roots in the 1970s, flourished in the 1980s. Early in the decade, critical work in BW on the writing process was highlighted in themed issues of journals like the Fall/Winter 1981 issue of the *Journal of Basic Writing* devoted to revision and the "Language Studies and Composing" issue of *College Composition and Communication* published in May of that same year. Attention soon widened to show how the process of writing was also the process of thinking about writing. Why not make the process of thought itself a focus of study, particularly in application to basic writers? At the end of her bibliographic essay, Shaughnessy had noted that "no effort has as yet been made to determine how accurately the developmental model Piaget describes for children fits the experience of the young adults learning to write for college" ("Basic Writing" 206).

This was, in effect, an invitation that many would accept. An important early example was Mike Rose's 1980 essay "Rigid Rules, Inflexible Plans, and the Stifling of Language: A Cognitivist Analysis of Writer's Block." Not the first—Linda Flower had already published "Writer-Based Prose: A Cognitive Basis for Problems in Writing" in *College English* in 1979—but Rose's was the rare treatment of such ideas by a teacher/researcher with graduate training in developmental psychology. Significantly, Flower teamed up with John R. Hayes, a cognitive psychologist, as her coauthor in other articles: "Problem Solving Strategies and the Writing Process" (1977), "The Dynamics of Composing: Making Plans and Juggling Constraints" (1979), "The Cognition of Discovery: Defining a Rhetorical Problem" (1980), and "Problem Solving and the Cognitive Processes of Writing" (1981). Another early "cognitivist"—her "Cognitive Development and the Basic Writer" had been published in *College English* in 1979—was Andrea A. Lunsford, the person picked to do the "Basic Writing Update" that followed Shaughnessy's bibliographic essay "Basic Writing" in the revised and expanded 1986 edition of Gary Tate's anthology of bibliographic essays, *Teaching Composition*. Lunsford began as a researcher in basic writing (it had been the focus of her dissertation), eventually becoming one of the foremost scholars in composition (she became chair of the Conference on College Composition and Communication in 1989). At this point, her major focus was cognitive development, and she may have produced the best summation of its perceived relevance to basic writing and to composition generally in "Cognitive Studies and Teaching Writing" in the 1985 MLA overview *Perspectives on Research and Scholarship in Composition*.

Though the tide would turn against it—Mike Rose would be speaking of "cognitive reductionism" in the late 1980s ("Narrowing the Mind")—efforts to place (and move) basic writers along a scheme of cognitive development proliferated in the first part of the decade. As titles like "Building Cognitive Skills in Basic Writers" (Spear) and "Cognitive Immaturity and Remedial College Writers" (Bradford) suggest, work of this kind partook in the two great tasks BW teachers and researchers had set for themselves: to define what they should do and to define whom they should do it to.

The latter project was the more pressing one. Just who was the basic writer? What were the distinguishing features? Answers were needed to warrant the appropriate pedagogical strategies and to set the appropriate goals. And though answers in terms of recent preoccupations were certainly being offered—Lee Odell's "Measuring Changes in Intellectual Processes as One Dimension of Growth in Writing" (1977) is one example—the most powerful answers were coming from something that apparently preceded (and superseded) both research and practice in BW: mass mandated, standardized assessment.

Richard Lloyd-Jones, in his 1986 essay "Tests of Writing Ability," makes it easy to see why it's hard to find much intellectual excitement in such assessment:

> The assessment of writing abilities is essentially a managerial task. It represents an effort to record quantitatively the quality of the writing or writing skills of a group of people so that administrators can make policies about educational programs. Tests are given and scores are assigned to individual performances of people as parts of large groups. As a rule the scores then are used in the aggregate. (155)

The caution with which Lloyd-Jones generalizes is telling: writing assessments and the uses they were put to were eventually found to be almost as various as the institutions that deployed them. Little could be counted on beyond the tendency of such assessments to mark underprepared or weak students for BW placement. Questions about how effectively and accurately they did this caused concern and controversy, as did questions about what to do with the students so marked.

Some found BW scholarship less helpful for this purpose than the practical guides for instruction that began to appear, chief among them Alice Trillin's *Teaching Basic Skills in College* (1980), Harvey Wiener's *The Writing Room* (1981), and Marie Ponsot and Rosemary Deen's *Beat Not the Poor Desk* (1982)—all, significantly, authored by CUNY faculty. Wiener's introduction gives some of the sense of such books' motives and methods:

> This is a book of ideas for beginning teachers who must teach beginners of a special sort—those who are just starting to learn the writer's craft in any serious and comprehensive way. It is a book about traditional composing tasks taught to "remedial" or "developmental" students, happily called *basic writers* (BW) now at many enlightened colleges and high schools, which have accepted Mina Shaughnessy's thoughtful tag. Such students are working to *qualify* for instruction in the usual sequence of courses. (3)

As Wiener suggests, BW instruction was proliferating well beyond CUNY, as were questions about how BW instructors ought to proceed—and, not least of all, how they ought to define their roles within their institutions (especially as members of a college community that marked them as "pre-college" in terms of whom and what they teach).

The marginal status of basic writing teachers—a perennial problem—meant they desperately needed a sense of common cause and community that scholarship and even practical guides could not give them. They got it in the Conference on Basic Writing (CBW). As Karen Uehling recounts in her history of CBW, Charles Guilford, interested in starting a Special Interest Group (SIG) of the Conference on College Composition and Communication (CCCC), posted a sign-up sheet on the message board at the 1980 CCCC convention in Washington, D.C. Soon there were four sheets filled with signatures, and CBW had its start (48). In addition to meetings at the annual CCCC conventions, CBW sponsored its own national conferences in 1985, 1987, 1989, and 1992 as well as a newsletter, an electronic journal (BWe), and an active listserv (CBW-L), all of which further the organization's goal "to provide a site for professional and personal conversations on the pedagogy, curriculum, administration, and social issues affecting basic writing" ("Conference on Basic Writing").

Another venue for a national conversation about basic writing was the *Journal of Basic Writing*. Initially an in-house publication supported by CUNY's Office of Academic Affairs and called simply *Basic Writing*, it gradually developed a national advisory board and a wider net: the Fall/Winter 1981 issue on revision included such respected scholars in rhetoric and composition as Nancy Sommers, Donald Murray, Ann E. Berthoff, and Linda Flower. Still, publication had been irregular (*JBW* had produced four volumes in the space of a decade), and the decision to devote each issue to a specific theme made the publication of unsolicited manuscripts on a variety of subjects unlikely if not impossible. In 1986, under the editorship of Lynn Quitman Troyka, this changed: *JBW* became a refereed journal with a large editorial board representing a variety of institutions nationally. The broadly pitched call for articles, first published in the Fall 1985 issue, shows how diverse and wide-ranging the field of BW was becoming:

> We invite authors to write about matters such as the social, psychological, and cultural implications of literacy; rhetoric, discourse theory; cognitive theory;

grammar; linguistics, including text analysis, error descriptions, and cohesion studies; English as a second language; and assessment and evaluation. We publish observational studies as well as theoretical discussions on relationships between basic writing and reading, or the study of literature, or speech, or listening; cross-disciplinary insights for basic writing from psychology, sociology, anthropology, journalism, biology, or art; the uses and misuse of technology for basic writing, and the like.

Fortuitously situated at mid-decade, that first issue of the repositioned *Journal of Basic Writing* represents a turning point of sorts. It was a particularly rich issue, framed by David Bartholomae's "Inventing the University"—with its famous observation that students must "appropriate (or be appropriated by) a specialized discourse" (9)—and Andrea Lunsford's forward-looking program for the field "Assignments for Basic Writers: Unresolved Issues and Needed Research." Also appearing in this issue, and too often overlooked (it is not in *The Bedford Bibliography for Teachers of Basic Writing*), was George H. Jensen's "The Reification of the Basic Writer." Taking his cue from Stephen Jay Gould's critique of intelligence testing, *The Mismeasure of Man*, Jensen argued that the definition of the basic writer, like the concept of "general intelligence," was shaped and reified with recourse to "political and social pigeonholes" (52). The chief villains of the piece were researchers (especially cognitivists) who oversimplified their characterizations of basic writers and assessments that provided a flat and tidy definition of basic writers as distinguished by a certain (low) level of cognition and writing ability. This type of research obscured "Shaughnessy's most consistent message," Jensen argued, "that basic writers are a diverse lot" (53). It may be that Jensen would have been more influential had he himself not used what he called "personality or cognitive style theory" (specifically the Myers-Briggs Type Indicator) to demonstrate (if not reify) "the diversity of basic writing classes" (62). Jensen implied that what instruments of measurement and cognitive research supposedly obscured could be demonstrated by an instrument of measurement developed by cognitive research; this might seem a coup, but it could also seem a contradiction. In any case, Jensen's argument sought to explode the ability of standardized assessments to sort basic writers effectively into anything like homogeneous groups and questioned and complicated the characterizations of basic writers made by a number of BW researchers, notably Andrea Lunsford ("Cognitive Development and the Basic Writer"), Sondra Perl ("The Composing Processes of Unskilled College Writers"), and Nancy Sommers ("Intentions and Revisions").

Interestingly, Lynn Quitman Troyka, the new editor of *JBW*, was spared Jensen's criticism though she herself was one of the relatively few to argue for the validity of mass assessments—something she did in the 1984 article "The Phenomenon of Impact: The CUNY Writing Assessment Test." Troyka had, however, stressed the diversity of basic writers in her 1982 article "Perspectives on Legacies and Literacy in the 1980's." In fact, the call for articles she fashioned as *JBW* editor included the caveat that "authors should describe clearly the student populations which they are discussing," since "[t]he term 'basic writer' is used with wide diversity today." It was a point she echoed in "Defining Basic Writing in Context" (1987), where she stressed that such diversity means we must "describe with examples our student populations when we write about basic writers" (13). Troyka came to conclusions similar to Jensen's regarding the difficulty of characterizing basic writers, though her study, based on a national sampling of actual writing done by basic writers, was much more influential. Troyka compellingly established the diversity, the astonishing range, that the term "basic writing" represented. It was as if the term, at least as it appeared in BW scholarship, had little meaning. What mattered was not *basic writing* but *basic writers*. That population, in all its particularity, is what demanded careful attention. And this attention, especially in pedagogical practices, needed to extend beyond just writing. Troyka stressed that "basic writers need to immerse themselves in language in all its forms" (13), including reading as well as writing.

Having reached a kind of adolescence, BW was rejecting as well as embracing influences. One was computer-assisted instruction (CAI), which had seemed to hold almost utopian promise in its early days: the labor-intensive work of teaching BW students (especially about matters of grammar) seemed susceptible to a benign form of automation. By the end of the decade, however, Stephen Bernhardt and Patricia Wojahn would note in their overview of "Computers and Writing Instruction" that, despite this start in CAI, especially for practice with grammar, "growth in computer use has largely been away from drill and practice toward uses as either heuristic devices or simply tools for writing." They approvingly cite an earlier overview, Mark S. Tucker's "Computers in the Schools" (1985), as being acute enough to register "the growing recognition that the machine is most appropriately used as a tool—as a word processor, a graphics process, a spreadsheet, or a database" (165–66).

A much greater disappointment was the growing realization that BW research was having relatively little impact on BW instruction. Nothing crystallized this more devastatingly than Joseph Trimmer's 1987 *JBW* article "Basic Skills, Basic Writing, Basic Research." It addressed the question of why, in spite of the efforts of BW researchers, sentence skills approaches still seemed to have hegemony (at least if one judged by textbooks available at the time). Building on research by Robert Connors ("Basic Writing Textbooks"), Trimmer surveyed 900 colleges and universities and interviewed editors at a score of publishing houses. Though it would be easy to blame the publishers for this sorry state of affairs, Trimmer's research told a different story, an appalling one of confusion, demoralization, and apathy. Trimmer asked how the surveyed institutions identified basic writers: "The 900 respondents reported 700 different ways to identify such students" (4). His results included the revelation that 70 percent of BW faculty were not professors but graduate students and adjuncts. And he found the editors of the publishing houses no less dismayed than he was by the failure of textbooks to keep pace with research: "These editors know what kind of books they should be selling, but they also know what kind of books sell" (6). Ultimately, Trimmer found BW faculty themselves the real obstacle to effective BW pedagogy, giving him another problem to puzzle through. Why should this be the case? "The simplest answer, of course, is that given the training, the incentives, and political status of these teachers, they see no reason to invest more of themselves than they already have in remedial English" (7).

The implication in Trimmer's article was that if BW teachers would attend to and act on good basic writing research, then all would be well. But the scholarship itself implied otherwise: BW research seemed not only open to question but also truly questionable, particularly in terms of its accuracy and applicability. Jensen and Troyka had suggested that characterizations of a generic "basic writer" were glib and reductive. This seemed particularly true of the work of the cognitivists: what initially seemed rooted in science ultimately seemed to lead to caricature. An early (and, in retrospect, prophetic) argument along these lines was "Cognition, Convention, and Certainty: What We Need to Know About Writing" by Patricia Bizzell (1982). She argued that Linda Flower and others who used theories of cognitive development radically simplified writers and writing, blurring individual differences and contextual complications for the sake of a clear (and fairly linear) account of the writing process. Bizzell called for balancing such a view with the ineluctable complexities of social interaction. Her own approach was effectively signaled by another article she published that same year: "College Composition: Initiation into the Academic Discourse Community."

Arguments against cognitivist characterizations of writers and writing began to intensify. By 1987, Janice N. Hays, coeditor of the 1983 anthology *The Writer's Mind: Writing as a Mode of Thinking*, felt so beset by attacks on cognitivist approaches that she published "Models of Intellectual Development and Writing: A Response to Myra Kogen et al.," a primer-like article addressing "prevalent misunderstandings about developmental models" (11). Among these "misunderstandings," Kogen's article with the seemingly innocent title "The Conventions of Expository Writing" was the explicit and immediate provocation. But Ann Berthoff's "Is Teaching Still Possible? Writing, Meaning, and Higher Order Reasoning" and Patricia Bizzell's "William Perry and Liberal Education" were also featured instances of opposition to developmental theories of writing.

This defense of cognitivism now seems a rearguard action, effectively trumped by Mike Rose's critique of such "developmental models," though they were models he himself had invoked and applied at the start of the decade. In "Narrowing the Mind and Page: Remedial Writers and Cognitive Reductionism" (1988), he enumerated three major problems with cognitive and developmental theories: (1) they "end up leveling rather than elaborating individual differences"; (2) they "encourage a drift away from careful, rigorous focus on student writing"; and (3) they "inadvertently reflect cultural stereotypes" (296–97).

Not one to skewer one approach without pointing to an alternative, Rose used the same article to direct attention to the "immediate social and linguistic conditions in which the student composes" (297). He had in fact elaborated what this meant in another important article published mid-decade: "The Language of Exclusion: Writing Instruction at the University." There he invoked Shaughnessy and her resistance to simplifications and stereotypes: "If we fully appreciate her message, we see how inadequate and limiting the remedial model is. Instead, we need to define our work as transitional or as initiatory, orienting, or socializing to what David Bartholomae and Patricia Bizzell call the academic discourse community" (358).

As Rose was issuing the call for socialization into the academic discourse community, the work that had the most significant impact on BW pedagogy since *Errors and Expectations* came out: David Bartholomae and Anthony Petrosky's *Facts, Artifacts and Counterfacts* (1986). The book, essentially the documentation of a successful "Basic Reading and Writing Course for the College Curriculum" (Bartholomae's descriptive subtitle published in the *Sourcebook for Basic Writing Teachers*), was influential for a number of reasons beyond the conjunction of reading with writing. The appeal of the program was in fact multifaceted: well-grounded in a specific institutional context (the University of Pittsburgh), it offered a fully realized curriculum, created collaboratively (with the collaborators describing its different aspects). Conceptually, it resolutely resisted "dumbing down" instruction for the sake of weaker students, advocating instead constructive "misreadings" and doing so by recourse to contemporary critical theory. Anecdotal yet scholarly, theoretical yet practical, general in its implications yet carefully situated and contextualized, it seemed to be just what the field needed.

The masterstroke was not to define the basic writer so much as to define what the basic writer must work on and work with. Cognitivists and others had tried to define the basic writer with recourse to schemes and abstractions. The charge laid against them, inevitably, was oversimplification, reductionism, reification, and caricature. They had neglected context. And *context*, in the Pittsburgh model, was key: BW students had to be situated in and socialized to the academic context, acclimated to "the academic discourse community." It would be the 1990s before the field would come to acknowledge just how problematic this goal was, a project of acculturation that would seem, from some perspectives, egregiously assimilationist. Caught in such a politically incorrect posture, the field would also be prepared, from some perspectives, to declare itself outmoded. What complicated that inclination to dismantle BW from the inside was the dismantling of it by outside forces, once again threatening to eradicate support structures

Historical Overview

and to limit access for weaker students—and doing so with motives Shaughnessy would have recognized as all too familiar.

THE 1990S

A book published in 1989 (on the eve of the nineties, as it were) and republished as a popular paperback in 1990 helped set the tone for a significant shift of attention. This book got personal about teaching and learning, about students and teachers. And its publication and reception were of such import as to make its appearance something almost everyone would notice. The book was Mike Rose's *Lives on the Boundary: The Struggles and Achievements of America's Underprepared.* When it was published in paperback, the subtitle became *A Moving Account of the Struggles and Achievements of America's Educational Underclass*; poignancy was, in fact, at the heart of its appeal. Already a force to be reckoned with, Rose made *Lives* about his own life to a considerable extent. A mix-up in test scores had placed him on the vocational track for a while in high school, and his account of this episode added special force to his ongoing argument against the easy labeling of remedial students—especially unexamined constructions of them as insufficiently developed or intelligent or literate and above all when so construed by high-stakes, single-shot assessments. His accounts of the students he knew as a caseworker were similarly multidimensional, offering a rich sense of their ethnic backgrounds, their economic and educational difficulties, their often untapped strengths.

Lives was the academic equivalent of a blockbuster. A few years after its publication, Mark Wiley was writing that it met with

> deservedly unequivocal praise. In fact, the book's overwhelmingly positive reception suggests that Rose managed to do what no one else has so far been able to accomplish: to get everybody to agree on something. In this case, it is the power and eloquence of *Lives* to validate and reaffirm the potential of America's underclass, those who have much to offer but who inevitably slip through the (I think rather large) cracks of the educational system and who in the process become the system's casualties. These are the students who are consigned to the lower tracks, who are

> labeled "remedial" and sometimes harshly judged as "uneducable."
>
> If it's possible to imagine a canon for composition, Rose's book, I suspect, would be a unanimous choice. (529)

Actually, Wiley said as much in responding to someone who might dissent from that unanimity. His "Building a Rose Garden: A Response to John Trimbur" (1993) points to an exception in the "unequivocal praise" *Lives* met with. Trimbur, in "Articulation Theory and the Problem of Determination: A Reading of *Lives on the Boundary*" (1993), had not disputed the enormous popularity of Rose's book but had worried about its cause: for Trimbur, it was too much the conventional success story, a kind of academic variant on Horatio Alger. But he concluded in the book's favor, reckoning that Rose had used the conventional frame to appeal to a wider audience with an important message.

Rose's *Lives* did, in any case, usher in the great decade of literacy narratives—autobiographical accounts of educational development and watershed moments in the acquisition of language and literacy. What's more, it helped to focus attention on both sides of the watershed for underprepared students: not just the confrontation with academic culture but also the home culture that sustained identity formation. In this it was complemented by "Arts of the Contact Zone" (1991), in which Mary Louise Pratt argued that different discourses grounded in different cultures should find a place for meeting and even mediation in the classroom. This was an invitation for teachers and students to negotiate racial and ethnic as well as cultural differences. Soon other work encouraging this type of negotiation began to appear. Keith Gilyard's *Voices of the Self: A Study of Language Competence* was published in 1991 and received an American Book Award in 1992. Gilyard looks at studies in Black English, bidialectalism, and code-switching in light of his own experience. Another influential literacy narrative was Victor Villanueva's *Bootstraps: From an American Academic of Color* (1993). At this time, an interest in the literacy stories of students began to infuse classroom practices as well (see Patthey-Chavez and Gergen; Lu, "Conflict").

The richness of these literacy narratives began to engender an anxiety of influence. Perhaps the most influential of the pioneering work, that done by Mina Shaughnessy—now almost canonical for many in basic writing—had overgeneralized and oversimplified the basic writer. In the early 1990s, Min-Zhan Lu launched the first major salvo in her campaign to realign the origins and direction of basic writing: "Redefining the Legacy of Mina Shaughnessy: A Critique of the Politics of Linguistic Innocence" (1991). In this essay, Lu maintained that by focusing so heavily on "error," Shaughnessy was isolating language from meaning and, at the same time, minimizing the significance of cultural and linguistic differences. Not long after, her extension of this argument, "Conflict and Struggle," appeared in the same issue of *College English* as Paul Hunter's "'Waiting for Aristotle'" (1992), his analysis of the 1980 issue of the *Journal of Basic Writing* published as a memorial to Shaughnessy—an issue, he argued, that defined her contribution so as to co-opt it for conservative ends. The response was an unprecedented six-author "Symposium on Basic Writing" (1993) in the next volume of *College English*. Four authors—including a co-worker of Shaughnessy's and an open admissions student who had gone on to become a professor—charged Lu and Hunter with decontextualizing and misrepresenting the historical and philosophical foundations of basic writing; Lu and Hunter responded to these charges.

The call for more careful historicizing of BW took an ironic turn not long thereafter with Bruce Horner's "Discoursing Basic Writing" (1996). Horner, a colleague and frequent coauthor of Lu's, argued that the representation of basic writing even and especially by its advocates had been decontextualized, cut off from the social realities that forged it; he called for a recuperative, alternative history. Meanwhile, finding Lu's critique of Shaughnessy a misrepresentation of BW's seminal figure, Jane Maher embarked on her biography of Shaughnessy, itself not only a recuperative act but also a countermove whose motivations she discussed in a *JBW* article ("Writing the Life"). More recently, Brian Ray, writing in 2008 and representing a new generation of BW scholars, reassessed the debate of the 1990s from a fresh perspective, arguing that when viewed through Donald Davidson's concept of linguistic charity (as articulated by Kevin Porter in "A Pedagogy of Charity: Donald Davidson and the Student-Negotiated Composition Classroom") the views of Shaughnessy and Lu are really not so far apart.

To return to the debate as it surfaced in the 1990s, about the same time that Shaughnessy's legacy was being critically reassessed, something else occurred that would lead to debates about the future of basic writing. In 1992 the fourth (and, to date, the last) National Conference on Basic Writing was held in College Park, Maryland. It featured David Bartholomae as the plenary speaker and focused on the theme "Critical Issues in Basic Writing: How Are We, Our Writing Programs, and Our Institutions Meeting or Failing to Meet the Needs of At-Risk Students?" The way Bartholomae chose to answer that question would have enormous impact on the field. At that point, early signs were that enriched perspectives could and would breed enriched pedagogy. In addition to the powerful personal narratives of scholars like Rose, Gilyard, and Villanueva that gave personal depth and cultural complexity to a field increasingly unhappy with pat labels and neat placements, there was the considerable success of Bartholomae's own program at the University of Pittsburgh, documented in *Facts, Artifacts and Counterfacts*. That 1986 book had been followed by Bartholomae's ascension to the leadership of the Conference on College Composition and Communication in 1988. The Pittsburgh program had been widely praised and adopted. In his plenary speech, Bartholomae recounted the success story:

> [T]his is a story I love to tell. It is convenient. It is easy to understand. Like basic writing, it (the story) and I are produced by the grand narrative of liberal sympathy and liberal reform. The story is inscribed in a master narrative of outreach, of equal rights, of empowerment, of new alliances and new understandings, of the transformation of the social text, the American university, the English department. I would like, in the remainder of my talk, to read against the grain of that narrative—to think about how and why and where it might profitably be questioned. I am not, let me say quickly, interested in critique for the sake of critique; I think we have begun to rest too comfortably on terms that should make us nervous, terms like "basic writing." Basic writing has begun to seem like something naturally, inevitably, transparently there in the curriculum, in the stories we tell ourselves about English in America. It was once a provisional, contested term, marking an uneasy accommodation between the institution and its desires and a student body that did not or would

Historical Overview

not fit. I think it should continue to mark an area of contest, of struggle, including a struggle against its stability or inevitability. ("Tidy House" 6)

Bartholomae was by no means alone in this struggle. When Bill Bernhardt and Peter Miller, who had succeeded Lynn Quitman Troyka as editors of the *Journal of Basic Writing*, approached Bartholomae about publishing his keynote, he suggested that they consider including other presentations as well. They did. The resulting Spring 1993 issue of *JBW* is a rich re-examination of basic writing as a field—but a highly critical one, not afraid to suggest that BW as an enterprise may be fundamentally misguided. With the help of hindsight, the issue seems a checklist of the misgivings and concerns about basic writing that would become increasingly grave over the next ten years, concerns seeming to support Bartholomae's suggestion that BW, as an institutionalized curricular construction, was suspect. Peter Dow Adams, outgoing co-chair of the Conference on Basic Writing, presented evidence that students who somehow escaped being tracked into BW classes actually fared fairly well in the mainstream. Tom Fox looked at the term "standards" as a kind of codeword used to justify exclusion. Jerrie Cobb Scott and William Jones examined the racism inherent in the deficit model of remediation, formed on the assumption that BW students are lacking rather than different and unassimilated. Jeanne Gunner addressed the sorry status of BW teachers, something Joseph Trimmer had already cited as keeping the field less productive and progressive than it might otherwise be. And Mary Jo Berger, a writing teacher turned college administrator, considered the chronic underfunding of BW instruction.

The one person to defend the status quo—and to resist Bartholomae's against-the-grain tack—was Karen Greenberg, then director of the National Testing Network in Writing (NTNW), who later became coeditor of the *Journal of Basic Writing* with Trudy Smoke. In her contribution to the Spring 1993 issue of *JBW*, Greenberg wrote:

> I believe in what I do. Therefore, I strongly disagree with many of the assertions made by David Bartholomae in his keynote speech at the Fourth Annual [sic] Conference on Basic Writing in Maryland. David characterized most basic writing courses as "obstacles rather than opportunities." He stated that most

basic writing programs "marginalize students" and "preserve them as different." He also accused basic writing teachers of "merely satisfying [their] liberal reflexes" by trying to make students "more complete versions of themselves" in courses that don't work. David was equally unimpressed with the assessment procedures used to place students into basic writing courses. He asked the conference participants, "Do you sort students into useful or thoughtful groups?" ("Politics" 65)

Greenberg answered yes to this question, but even she was careful to ground her defense of established practices for assessment and teaching in the details of her own context, the Developmental English Program she ran at Hunter College. As the only CUNY representative in the issue as well as the sole defender of current practices in BW assessment and instruction, Greenberg represented a legacy that others elsewhere were repudiating or at least calling into question.

Leading the charge was David Bartholomae, who, with Anthony Petrosky, had built a program at the University of Pittsburgh that purportedly moved the field well beyond Shaughnessy's early vision at City College. But even their legacy was subject to critique. In "On the Academic Margins," Deborah Mutnick wrote: "Despite the Pittsburgh program's theoretical advances, Bartholomae and Petrosky continued to elide the political basis for excluding social groups from cultural institutions like universities; their narrative of basic writing omits the race, class, and gender inequities that pervade higher education" (191).

Redressing inequities and exclusions had been a centerpiece of Shaughnessy's agenda in the early years, but then attention had turned to other questions, with answers sought in cognitive science and critical theory. With the fourth National Basic Writing Conference in 1992, however, the political dimension had returned with a vengeance. Bartholomae, explicitly reading against the grain of his own narrative and citing Mary Louise Pratt's recently published "Arts of the Contact Zone," was calling for "a curricular program designed not to hide differences . . . but to highlight them" ("Tidy House" 13). The highlighting of differences would in fact be reflected in some of the most important books of the decade, notably Mutnick's own *Writing in an Alien World: Basic Writing and the Struggle for Equality in Higher Edu-*

cation (1996) and Bruce Horner and Min-Zhan Lu's *Representing the "Other": Basic Writers and the Teaching of Writing* (1999).

The perceived need for a narrative of basic writing that acknowledged inequalities of race, class, and gender was also subsequently acknowledged by the Conference on Basic Writing (CBW). Though it had given up on national conferences as too expensive and logistically difficult, CBW decided to hold all-day workshops each year on the day before the Conference on College Composition and Communication (CCCC) began (Uehling). The second of these workshops, held in 1997, was devoted to "Race, Class, and Culture in the Basic Writing Classroom"; papers from it were published in another special issue of the *Journal of Basic Writing*, this time put together by new editors George Otte and Trudy Smoke. For all the weight these papers had and all the attention they deserved, one piece far outstripped the others in impact. It was Ira Shor's "Our Apartheid: Writing Instruction and Inequality." In figuring basic writing as "our apartheid," Shor claimed that the problem was structural: with students identified by suspect tracking mechanisms, BW represented a subcollegiate curricular level that would always see concentrations of students with socioeconomic disadvantages and cultural differences, always be tended by underpaid, overworked, and inadequately prepared teachers. Basic writing, according to Shor, did not need to be rethought or revised; it needed to be dismantled.

Shor's piece kindled fires of controversy. His characterization of basic writing as "our apartheid" and his call for its dismantling provoked heated discussion at a CBW post-workshop meeting, a meeting he did not attend; the discussion was picked up on e-mail lists like CBW-L and WPA-L thereafter. A special concern fueling the discussion was that others besides Shor (and with politics very different from his) were calling for the dismantling of BW programs. Public systems in Georgia and Florida had eliminated them from four-year colleges, and plans to do the same were moving forward in states from California to Massachusetts. CUNY, so thoroughly identified with advances made in the early days of open admissions, was itself in the process of dismantling BW, at least at the four-year schools. James Traub's *City on a Hill* (1994) cast City College, that seedbed of BW, as a once-proud institution devalued and dumbed-down by the admission of underprepared students. In the wake of this attack, New York's mayor, Rudolph Giuliani, encouraged CUNY's Board of Trustees to take a critical look at CUNY's admission and placement practices and appointed a special task force to review these policies. On January 25, 1999, the Board voted to phase out all "remediation" in its four-year colleges by January 2001. Such dramatic changes were by no means confined to New York. Across the country, policy makers well to the right of Shor on the political spectrum were demanding an end to remediation as a drain on resources and an institutionalized lowering of standards.

The editors of *JBW* received a number of responses to Shor and chose to publish two of them in the Fall 1997 issue, both making due note of this conservative trend. Karen Greenberg, who saw what was happening at CUNY, stressed that "there are reactionary political forces currently trying to achieve precisely this barring of access and precisely this reduction in size in colleges across the country" and claimed that Shor's proposal "would, in fact, justify the curtailment and the consequent reduction or elimination of basic skills programs" (94). Terence Collins, academic dean of the General College of the University of Minnesota, more tersely and colorfully remarked, "We who teach from the left are peculiarly fond of beating each other up while the right wing eats our lunch" (100). But he also said Shor's argument put him in mind of "Deborah Mutnick's warning [in the preface to *Writing in an Alien World*] to be careful in how we mount educational critique from the left, that in impolitic critique of Basic Writing we risk crawling into bed with the very elements of right wing elitism which access programs and many Basic Writing programs were founded to counteract" (99).

For the remainder of the decade, the *Journal of Basic Writing* would often include accounts of the dismantling of basic writing programs, sometimes on a statewide basis, like Gail Stygall's account of the "unraveling" of BW at the University of Washington. What these accounts showed was that such dismantling tended to disregard pedagogical considerations, whereas Shor's call for dismantling was in fact founded on concerns about pedagogy. Attacks on basic writing from the right took advantage of the vulnerability accompanying low-status programs for unwelcome students, whereas Shor's critique decried that lack of status and welcome.

Still, different as these points of attack from the left and the right were, they combined to make basic writing programs seem not only vulnerable but also almost indefensible. Even for champions of BW, defending the status quo was tough; however deserving the students were of attention, the attention granted them often seemed too arbitrary in its placements, too unsure of its methods and pedagogy. The key question—what would become of BW students once BW programs were gone—was almost imponderable. Hemmed about with contingencies, value-laden claims about what could be done or should be done for such students, the answer to that all-important question could seem too speculative until it was too late. Would basic writers survive without support (and stigmatizing placement), as some claimed? Should they have access to better instruction in their pre-college years, as others insisted? Such arguments among those interested in basic writing could go on endlessly, often while ignoring the obvious: the easiest, likeliest thing to do was not to test the efficacy of different placements or instructional structures but simply to slam the door, to cut off access.

To the extent that it was about access (or its evil opposite, exclusion), the debate around Shor's argument was by no means new. In fact, in an important sense, it had simply reversed the order of another recent debate: Edward White's 1995 defense of assessment and placement practices ("The Importance of Placement and Basic Studies") that Sharon Crowley critiqued in 1996. Like Crowley, who felt that tracking and placement procedures were fundamentally mechanisms of exclusion, Shor argued for radical restructuring of institutions—including the abolition or thorough reconfiguration of first-year composition. With basic writing, Shor was also able to point to significant experiments along these lines, notably Mary Soliday and Barbara Gleason's mainstreaming experiment at City College at CUNY and Rhonda Grego and Nancy Thompson's at the University of South Carolina. Yet these attempts at mainstreaming did not easily take root—the one at CUNY did not outlast its grant period—so the debate went on as a discussion of both politics and pedagogies.

What the arguments on both sides shared (and in a way that bodes much for the future and draws much from the recent past) was an ever deeper grounding in particulars. Like the highlighting of difference that made the personal political (and vice versa), the consideration of institutional change (hoped for or mourned) suggested that the politics of change sprang at least as much from local considerations as from larger political forces. Context was ever more important.

Ironically, too, at the same time that basic writing was being billed as "our apartheid," a major book arrived on the scene suggesting that, given enough time and support, students who had initially been placed in basic writing could succeed in the academy and beyond. This was *Time to Know Them: A Longitudinal Study of Writing and Learning at the College Level* published in 1997 by Marilyn S. Sternglass. As the title and subtitle suggest, Sternglass tracked a number of students at City College, most of them initially placed into basic writing, over an extended period (a full six years). Most were success stories, but more compelling than that heartening news was the depth of detail in Sternglass's account. How these students fared in a variety of courses over their entire academic careers was richly, thickly described, as was the impact of their personal and social circumstances on these careers. Unlike the largely autobiographical accounts of a Rose or a Gilyard or a Villanueva that were likely to be read (and perhaps too likely to be downplayed) as exceptional cases, *Time to Know Them* included the stories of students like those teachers met with all the time, often told in their own words. The book never became an academic bestseller like Rose's *Lives on the Boundary,* but it did garner gradually growing attention and admiration. In October 1998, Sternglass drew from it for her keynote address at the annual CUNY Association of Writing Supervisors Conference, and in Spring 1999 *JBW* published a version of that keynote as the lead article. In December 1998, *Time to Know Them* received the Mina P. Shaughnessy Award of the Modern Language Association at the organization's annual convention. In March 1999, it received the Outstanding Book Award at the annual convention of the Conference on College Composition and Communication. The careful, patient research the book represented was more powerful for many than the strongest polemic. Into discussions permeated by politics and invective, Sternglass injected the stories of students who struggled on while standards were supposedly ratcheted up and gates of access were beginning to swing shut. The lessons to be learned were the sort summed up in one of Emerson's aphorisms—"The years teach much that the days never know." The student experiences recounted in *Time to Know Them* cautioned against giving credence to easy generalizations and quick fixes to problems as complex as those faced by the field of basic writing as it prepared to move into the twenty-first century.

2000 AND BEYOND

The new millennium began with basic writing scholars taking stock of the field—looking back to the past and into the future. In her 2001 overview of BW pedagogy, "On the Academic Margins," Deborah Mutnick begins with a telling allusion to "Mark Twain's famous quip about his father: Shaughnessy seems to have learned a great deal since I carefully worded my critique in *Writing in an Alien World* of what I saw then as her essentialist depiction of the basic writer" (184). Mutnick goes on to say that Shaughnessy, dead for a quarter century, now seems to her to remain impressively relevant, still the figure to contend with.

The *Journal of Basic Writing* was also taking stock in another special issue published in 2000, the result of a fin-de-siècle invitation that editors Otte and Smoke made to luminaries in the field, one they summed up with the wryly punning question "W(h)ither Basic Writing?" The responses showed a wide range of opinion, perhaps even a widening of differences. Shor, for example, continued to argue for the abolition of basic writing—using accounts of students who could elude BW placement and yet forge ahead, guilty of the "Illegal Literacy" that gave his piece its title. Others in the issue argued against this position. Deborah Mutnick held that "to indict basic writing . . . obfuscates the real impediments to democratizing education" ("The Strategic Value of Basic Writing" 77). And Keith Gilyard wrote, "Shor thinks composition's future lies in discipline-based, field-based, critical social work. Critical? Field? Fine. But I'm not all the way on board with that vision for I'm not ready to give up an important interdisciplinary site, which I think courses in critical language awareness can be" ("Basic Writing" 37). Other ramifications of the debate—accounts of alternatives to BW as well as eliminations of it—continued to play out in this issue. Judith Rodby and Tom Fox described their mainstreaming work at Cal State Chico, while Terence Collins and Melissa Blum of the University of Minnesota General College mourned the loss of students to state-mandated cuts.

The issue included suggestions that there was more to mourn than program cutbacks. Lynn Quitman Troyka described "How We Have Failed the Basic Writing Enterprise" in an article criticizing the field's failure to grapple with certain tough problems, particularly those with political consequences. "Why," for example, "did we recoil from the public's demand that we show results?" (119). Troyka noted there were recent answers to some long-burning questions—she described Sternglass's *Time to Know Them* as "the most important BW research to date" (119)—but her indictment of the field's failures was sweeping and incisive. Similarly, William DeGenaro and Edward White decried BW researchers' "inability to communicate effectively, that is to say in a way that advances our knowledge of issues of developmental writing" ("Going Around in Circles" 27).

And yet, if the field had not communicated its answers effectively, then it had at least developed a central, critical question. The concluding section of DeGenaro and White's article begins, "To mainstream or not to mainstream. That is the question" (34). The most thorough answer to date is a book edited by Gerri McNenny and Sallyanne Fitzgerald (with a foreword by Marilyn Sternglass) and published in 2001—though it explicitly traces its genesis to that momentous fourth National Basic Writing Conference held in 1992 (1). The book is titled *Mainstreaming Basic Writers: Politics and Pedagogies of Access,* and the plurals in the title are telling. Regardless of whether a former sense of singular purpose for basic writing was really a kind of mythical hegemony (as some scholars like Bruce Horner aver), it is now a fragmented enterprise. Some chapters in *Mainstreaming Basic Writers* resist or question mainstreaming while others advocate it from a variety of sites and perspectives. One piece resisting mainstreaming is by Terence Collins of the University of Minnesota and Kim Lynch of Anoka-Ramsey Community College in Cambridge, Minnesota. Working in BW programs at their respective institutions (and focusing on that of the General College at Minnesota), they are unapologetically proud of BW's success at a specific site. Indeed, they argue that specificity makes all the difference: "'Mainstreaming' rhetoric too often (and too conveniently) implies that there is a single entity X (bad, essentializing, otherizing, exploitive basic writing) that ought to be transformed into entity Y (good, liberating, mainstreamed composition). Isn't it more complicated than that? And shouldn't we know better?" (83–84).

Sadly, the institution that Collins and Lynch were so proud of ceased to exist in 2005 when the General College was given departmental status within the University of Minnesota's College of Education and Human Development as the Department of Postsecondary Teaching and Learning (PSTL). Basic writing courses were transferred to the newly created Writing Studies Department in the College of Liberal Arts. The rationale given for this change by university administrators was that students in the General College were not succeeding at a high enough rate—as measured by time until graduation (University of Minnesota). In a sense, students who had previously received special support from the General College are now mainstreamed. Although the PSTL is attempting to keep something of the General College's legacy by crafting a curriculum of connected courses in interdisciplinary learning communities for first-year students, there have been losses for students placed in basic writing. It's harder to get into the University of Minnesota now.

By the fall of 2006, the *Journal of Basic Writing* was again assessing the state of BW in a special issue, this one in recognition of the publication of the journal's twenty-fifth volume. Leaders of the field were invited to contribute articles in a variety of areas including BW and public policy (Adler-Kassner and Harrington), the place of the increasing number of multilingual students in colleges and universities (Zamel and Spack), and—once again—how the field defines itself and thus relates to the larger institutional and political world (Gray-Rosendale).

Increasingly in the new century, that institutional and political world has been exerting pressure on basic writing and the students it serves. Like the University of Minnesota's General College, which was the victim of institutional pressures, colleges and universities across the U.S. are being pressured to eliminate basic writing. Legislatures in several states including California and Tennessee have passed laws eliminating or severely curtailing "remedial courses" in four-year schools. Pedagogically innovative BW programs have been created to meet these stipulations—for example, at the University of Tennessee at Martin (Huse et al.), Arizona State University (Glau, "*Stretch* at 10," "The 'Stretch' Program"), and San Francisco State University (Goen-Salter; Goen and Gillotte-Tropp). By offering some academic credit, such programs have begun to move BW instruction out of the anteroom that Shaughnessy described and ever closer to the college mainstream.

Regardless of where it is located or how it is structured, the success or failure of a mainstreaming initiative or BW program has to do with a host of factors: how students are defined (and define themselves), how programs are constituted, what theories drive the work, what practices are encouraged, what institutional support is provided (or withheld), and, as Mary Soliday's *The Politics of Remediation* (2002) has stressed, how the work is represented and understood by policy-makers as well as stakeholders. Soliday's book also stresses that it is never enough to examine the present moment, for what happens now is rooted in what went before. The unfolding, over time, of these issues of definition, of practice and theory, of the applications of scholarship and the structuring of professional support will be examined in more detail in the subsequent chapters.

2 Defining Basic Writing and Basic Writers

In the early 1960s, remedial work in college seemed to be fading away. In 1963, Albert Kitzhaber reported in *Themes, Theories, and Therapy* that the "number of colleges and universities offering remedial English courses has dropped sharply" and would drop further because of rising enrollments and raised standards (18). In "Basic Writing," Mina Shaughnessy acknowledged that "this type of course was waning," with the immediate qualification that, because of social changes in the 1960s, a new "remedial population" was on the way (178).

It was in fact this sense of a cultural shift and a new population granted access to college that caused Shaughnessy, in this same essay, to call the "'new' remedial English" "basic writing" (BW), thereby creating something else that could be called new: a field of teaching and scholarship constituted as such, conscious of itself and its mission and proud of work that had previously been hidden. Wanting to be seen as both new and necessary, basic writing has always needed to distinguish itself, to say what it is and whom it is for.

To an unusual extent, however, BW derives its conceptual existence by being distinguished from related kinds of instruction. First-year composition is the most obvious point of comparison and contrast: basic writing has to be more "basic" somehow, situated underneath or before what is nevertheless conceived as introductory. It is also, by its nature, associated with remediation, developmental education, "pre-college instruction," ESL (English as a Second Language), ELL (English Language Learning), and other related fields.

Still, over the years, first-year composition is the course to which basic writing has had the closest connection. It could be said that basic writing has recapitulated the fate of first-year composition. Starting out, as composition did, with a powerful and perhaps undue attention to error, BW broadened its purview to include a host of other instructional interests: matters of process, voice, genre, development, diversity, and so on. In so doing, it matured, no doubt, but it matured into something ever harder to distinguish (and to keep separate) from first-year composition, which had experienced its own markedly similar diversification of interests.

The other source of definition for basic writing, its student population, was always a troubled question. Leaders in the field were often critical of the assessments that defined their constituency. They were understandably loath to insist on hard and fast distinctions where none existed, at least none they found defensible. Finally, it turned out that the crucial distinction of basic writing, the difference and disadvantage it had in mirroring the development of first-year composition, is that, though first-year comp never had something like first-year comp to disappear into, BW did. When it seemed a budgetary or political liability, its opponents could argue it away because its advocates had brought it (and its students) ever closer to the point where their rightful place seemed to be first-year composition. The students either ought to find their way into mainstream composition courses, the logic went, or disappear altogether. Ultimately, they did both, in droves. (See chapter 5 for a fuller discussion of the status of basic writing at the beginning of the twenty-first century.)

But we are getting ahead of ourselves. In this chapter, we focus on matters of definition both for the field of basic writing and for the students it serves.

Early Definitions

Basic writing is distinguished first and foremost by its history. Attention to a new cadre of students, formerly excluded from higher education but then provisionally admitted, gave rise to the new field. Yet however new the students themselves might have been, the instruction given them was not created out of whole cloth but rewoven from existing strands. Mina Shaughnessy had to rename the field to save it from being stuck in the nether regions already denoted by terms like "remedial" or "bonehead" English ("Basic Writing" 178). This attempt at renaming and re-creation was never wholly successful. The stigmata of remediation, structurally integrated into BW from the start, persisted as issues of funding, staffing, and status. The struggle to achieve selfhood and respectability as a field included redefining the curriculum for the sake of the students, improving their access and progress. But it never managed to redefine the way basic writing itself was marginalized. Relegated to the margins of the institution, BW ultimately came to represent, at least to some, a locus of instruction that could save its students from marginalization only by disappearing, allowing students to flow unobstructed into the "mainstream." Mainstreaming is by no means the end of the story for basic writing; however, it is a way of underscoring that BW itself was never fully accepted into the academy and so gives us good reason to attend not only to how BW defines itself but also to how it gets defined.

Basic Writing as a Fix-It Station

Regarding basic writing, academia responded to profound change as if it were a temporary disruption of the presumably enduring status quo. Just as colleges and universities responded to growing enrollments with temporary positions that became permanent features of the landscape, BW became a kind of halfway house addressing problems that presumably would or should be solved by better college preparation—though it would take a social revolution to redress the disadvantages of students who wind up in basic writing. This was a predicament sounded prophetically by Mina Shaughnessy. In the conclusion to *Errors and Expectations,* she had strong words (by no means for the first time) for "an educational system that has failed in countless ways and for countless reasons to educate all its youth. Now that we have begun openly to admit to this failure, we can hope for reforms which over the next decade may close the shocking gaps in training between the poor and the affluent, the minority and the majority" (291). Yet the next decade—in fact, the next quarter century—did not see the closing of these gaps. The Reagan years instead saw the coinage of the term "permanent underclass"; with that came a sense that the so-called "underprepared," like the poor, would always be with us. In that light, what Shaughnessy went on to say seems still more important:

> Colleges must be prepared to make more than a graceless and begrudging accommodation to this unpreparedness, opening their doors with one hand and then leading students into an endless corridor of remedial anterooms with the other. We already begin to see that the remedial model, which isolates the student and the skill from real college contexts, imposes

> a "fix-it station" tempo and mentality upon both teachers and students. (293)

The warning notwithstanding, this is precisely what became of BW: it was institutionalized as the "fix-it station."

Basic Writing as a Back Formation of First-Year Composition

One explanation for the persistence and subordination of basic writing in the college curriculum is that something similar had happened before. First-year composition, situated after basic writing in the college course sequence, had gone before, chronologically speaking, and in so doing had defined the situation. BW was basically a back formation of first-year composition, itself brought into being to address a literacy crisis, one hemmed about with assessments and the search for quick fixes.

As John Brereton has noted, the pressure on college enrollments was just as intense in the early days of freshman composition as during the dawn of open admissions: college enrollments nearly doubled from 1890–1910, the decades that saw the birth and solidification of first-year composition as a college requirement (7). Most agree that the focus and upshot of this earlier literacy crisis was concentrated at Harvard, partly because of the institution's stature and influence. And it was rooted in the vision of Harvard's president at the time, Charles W. Eliot. Edna Hays, in her 1936 book on college entrance requirements, quotes from his annual report of 1873:

> The need for some requisition which should secure on the part of the young men preparing for college proper attention to their own language has long been felt. Bad spelling, incorrectness as well as inelegance of expression in writing, ignorance of the simplest rules of punctuation, and almost entire want of familiarity with English literature, are far from rare among young men of eighteen otherwise well prepared to pursue their college studies. (17–18)

Social transformations in the wake of the Civil War had brought a new sort of student (and above all, many more students) to the doorsteps of colleges and universities, including Harvard. And Eliot's pronouncement on their fitness for college study would have its echoes in what was said about open admissions students a century later. Similarly, Shaughnessy's belief (or at least hope) that educational reform would eradicate what basic writing was created to address is mirrored in Eliot's conviction that better pre-college preparation would eliminate the need for Harvard's composition courses. These courses were, after all, conceived less as college instruction than as remediation to make students fit for college work. Mary Trachsel writes, "Eliot proposed that such fundamental literacy instruction was actually the responsibility of the preparatory schools and fully intended the college freshman composition course he instituted in 1874 to be nothing more than a temporary bridge between preparatory schools and college"; nevertheless, "freshman composition soon became ensconced as a permanent fixture of Harvard's curriculum" (42). The moral of the story is that structures set up as accommodations for new or changed student constituencies do not wither away but instead become self-perpetuating. By 1894, as James Berlin reported in *Rhetoric and Reality,* the composition course that was supposed to become superfluous became entrenched as the one university requirement at Harvard (20). Within another decade, hundreds of other colleges and universities had made it so as well.

What could be wrong with that? Well, as Wallace Douglas noted in his now-classic account, that may not be quite the right question to ask: "The interesting questions are those that ask why and how rhetoric in its truncated and debased modern form has been able to survive, and indeed flourish, as the study of written composition, or as practice in the production of written compositions and communications" (99). The answers lie in what happened at Harvard, starting with a president who complained that students came to that institution unable to spell and punctuate correctly or to avoid other telltale signs of being dubious inductees into the club of the educated elite. Thus, wrote Douglas, "the purposes of composition, as it came to be conceived in the latter days of rhetoric" narrowed down to "the acquisition of certain linguistic forms of relatively narrow currency, which today would be said to represent good or appropriate English, but which in more candid times could be described, simply and without apology, as signs of social rank" (110). It was the foredoomed fate of a "brush-up" course to perform a narrower function than opening up the full range of rhetorical possibilities; if this didn't dumb down what instruction in English might be, it certainly constrained the possibilities. And it's surely significant that, from Eliot's first salvo to the entrenched composition requirement's eventual focus, the instructional emphasis was on making students' writing presentable. The preoccupation of composition (and later basic writing) with matters of form and surface (often preceded by the word "mere" in indictments of this preoccupation) are rooted in this emphasis.

In the 1920s Yale, like Harvard before it, found the need to institute a form of basic writing, designated unapologetically as the "Awkward Squad." Using archival records, Kelly Ritter examined the way this "course" was conducted between 1920 and 1960. The young men designated by their English instructors as belonging to the Squad, which was not listed in the official catalog, "had no support beyond the tutors who drilled them weekly in spelling and grammar, until such time as they were deemed fit to return to the mainstream" (Ritter 21).

A more serious consequence of Harvard's fashioning of first-year composition related to institutionalization rather than pedagogy. The implications of the institutional positioning of composition were diagnosed by Albert Kitzhaber in his 1963 doctoral dissertation and were summarized some thirty years later by Donald Stewart, who described Harvard's impact on subsequent English instruction:

> (1) reducing writing instruction to a concern for superficial mechanical correctness, (2) greatly increasing an unproductive and debilitating fixation on grammar instruction, (3) dissociating student writing . . . from any meaningful social context, and (4) contributing significantly to the division between composition and literature people in English departments, a division which saw writing instruction increasingly become the responsibility of intellectually inferior members of English department staffs. (455)

Whatever, exactly, the causal connection between that last effect and the others, it is ultimately the division between composition and literature faculty that mattered most. Writing instruction would forever be the grunt work, the job of the downstairs staff in the "upstairs/downstairs" relationship between literature and composition in English departments (a relationship given theoretical articulation in the first chapter of Robert Scholes's *Textual Power*). Writing instructors (and later BW instructors) would do battle against the other exercises in reduction—that writing correctly was all that mattered, for instance, or that their instruction was only about form and not content. They could even emerge victorious in some of these battles, but they would always be a tier down, the degraded gradation. The division of labor was one in which the kind of work mattered more than the degree (though Robert Connors, in "The Rhetoric of Mechanical Correctness," has documented the egregious overwork of composition instructors, particularly in the early days). This enduring scheme of things forever consigned composition to the lower level.

Thus when basic writing had to find its place, that place was pre-defined. As Ira Shor puts it, "In education, BW is less than freshman comp, below comp"; institutional logic would inevitably relegate it to the status of "a gate below the gate" ("Our Apartheid" 95, 94). With such a structure as first-year composition in place, hierarchically as well as historically situated, only one kind of slot could be waiting for BW. If the students it was to serve were to be given access, their entry point would necessarily be placed beneath the established, official point of entry. But structures are not scripts. Within a pre-determined structure, basic writing would find room for self-definition, and the early moves would prove critical.

A Sense of Mission and Purpose

Gatekeepers can let in as well as close out, and there is no question which role the early leaders of basic writing embraced. Even before open admissions, in the days when Mina Shaughnessy was administering "pre-Bac" and SEEK instruction, she was devoted to those who in former times would not have come to college. She was, in her own metaphorical terms, an "anteroom" staffer, a part-timer turned administrator (but, significantly, not a member of the professoriate), and the programs she oversaw and inspired were never granted full integration and collegiate status. But they were defined, and more especially self-defined, by a sense of purpose and even mission. *Errors and Expectations* opens with an account of this exercise in definition, one that started not with structures and precedents (for these were felt to be lacking) but with the students:

> . . . those who had been left so far behind the others in their formal education that they appeared to have little chance of catching up, students whose difficulties with the written language seemed of a different

> order from those of the other groups, as if they had come, you might say, from a different country, or at least through different schools, where even very modest standards of high school literacy had not been met. (2)

So different were these students that developing appropriate instruction for them meant proceeding inductively, especially since "there were no studies nor guides, nor even suitable textbooks to turn to" (Shaughnessy, *Errors* 3). Initially, teachers of these new students felt themselves at a loss, and Shaughnessy memorably includes herself among them. By the time of the publication of *Errors and Expectations,* however, she could write that things had changed: "The teachers who five years ago questioned the educability of these students now know of their capabilities and have themselves undergone many shifts in attitude and methodology since their first encounters with the new students" (3–4). Still, this had not given the field definition, except as a frontier (Shaughnessy's famous, favorite metaphor for BW—she also used it in her bibliographic essay "Basic Writing"):

> Despite such advances, the territory I am calling basic writing (and that others might call remedial or developmental writing) is still very much of a frontier, unmapped, except for a scattering of impressionistic articles and a few blazed trails that individual teachers propose through their texts. And like the settlers of other frontiers, the teachers who by choice or assignment are heading to this pedagogical West are certain to be carrying many things they will not be needing, that will clog their journey as they get further on. So too they will discover the need of other things they do not have and will need to fabricate by mother wit out of whatever is at hand. (*Errors* 4)

The need to jettison unwanted baggage is at least as striking as the acknowledged need for new approaches. Most striking of all is how loosely and vaguely the field is described, especially in terms of teaching practices. Much more is said about basic writers than about basic writing. With her introduction to *Errors and Expectations,* Shaughnessy may be said to have blazed the most important trail of all with this reluctance to prescribe and define. Not just here but hereafter, the definition of basic writing by its practitioners would focus more on whom it was for than what it was. Shaughnessy's introduction painted pedagogy only with the most general strokes, but she was ready to get quite specific about the students, talking about how they talked and felt as well as how they wrote, describing them in concrete as well as figurative terms—above all as urban and "other":

> Natives, for the most part, of New York, graduates of the same public school system as the other students, they were nonetheless strangers in academia, unacquainted with the rules and rituals of college life, unprepared for the sorts of tasks their teachers were about to assign them. Most of them had grown up in one of New York's ethnic or racial enclaves. Many had spoken other languages or dialects at home and never successfully reconciled the worlds of home and school, a fact which by now had worked its way deep into their feelings about school and about themselves as students.
>
> They were in college now for one reason: that their lives might be better than their parents', that the lives of their children might be better than theirs so far had been. (2–3)

Struggling and straddled between cultures, racially and/or linguistically different, these products of a system that made education generally but not equally available were effectively hailed as the raison d'être of BW. Their motivations—above all, the quest for upward mobility—were as evident as their disadvantages. The students were in a sense more readable than the writing they generated, calling out for action that was much clearer in purpose than in procedures. Teaching them at all was obviously a step toward social justice. Just how to teach them was less clear.

Though Shaughnessy had not defined BW as a full field of pedagogical approaches, she did define the way it would define itself: begin with the students, define their needs, and then address those needs. Again and again, the sequence would play out in a cycle of diagnosis and prescription. What would not change, what would endure, was the sense of mission and purpose Shaughnessy derived from the students BW was to serve.

Adjustments and Revisions

Ironically, the resolve to start with the students was always at least as much a problem as a solution. For Shaughnessy, starting with them had meant starting with the errors in their writing; the definition inevitably focused on output rather than intake (on writing rather than reading as a literacy-shaping factor), and attention to matters of form diverted attention from matters of content (concentrating on how writers wrote in terms of error control rather than thought and expression).

Cognitivist Definitions

Perhaps because social causes for BW placement seemed such a "given," the search was on for something like scientific grounds for defining basic writers. For a time, schemas of cognitive development shaped and dominated the discussion. It didn't matter if the focus was on literacy (as in Frank J. D'Angelo's "Literacy and Cognition: A Developmental Perspective" [1983]), on the composing process (as in Mike Rose's "Rigid Rules, Inflexible Plans, and the Stifling of Language: A Cognitivist's Analysis of Writer's Block" [1980]), on assessment (as in Lee Odell's "Measuring Changes in Intellectual Processes as One Dimension of Growth in Writing" [1977]), or even error (as in Thomas Farrell's notorious "IQ and Standard English" [1983]). Like some booklength collections that came out in the decade after Shaughnessy's death—collections like *Cognitive Processes in Writing* (Gregg and Steinberg [1979]) and *The Writer's Mind: Writing as a Mode of Thinking* (Hays et al. [1983])—these pieces testify to a fascination with developmental models in basic writing and composition scholarship. And they all get prominent mention in Andrea Lunsford's 1986 "Basic Writing Update" of Mina Shaughnessy's bibliographic essay on BW. There Lunsford, herself the author of such pieces as "Cognitive Development and the Basic Writer" (1979), even noted that Shaughnessy's sense that "error is a way of learning" represented the application of "the insight of philosophers such as Michael Polanyi and Gilbert Ryle" (208)—themselves developmental theorists of a kind.

It may have been the very multifacetedness of developmental theory (or theories) that spelled the end for the dominance of cognitivist definitions. George H. Jensen's "The Reification of the Basic Writer" would take one "personality or cognitive style theory" (specifically the

Myers-Briggs Type Indicator) to demonstrate that other theories (or theorists) were not doing justice to the "the diversity of basic writing classes" (62). In "Narrowing the Mind and Page: Remedial Writers and Cognitive Reductionism" (1988), Mike Rose would mount a critique of such "developmental models"—models he himself had used previously. And Lunsford, in another bibliographic piece (coauthored with Patricia Sullivan) just a few years after her update of Shaughnessy's "Basic Writing," would concede that no developmental theory could adequately define basic writers, who were "too protean to be captured by any single psychological model" (22).

A greater blind spot for cognitivists was not what they failed to capture but what they turned away from. All the attention to global descriptions of writers' minds and stages obscured the social mission of basic writing for the sake of generalized stages and generic schema. As Maureen Hourigan noted retrospectively in 1994, "Those who sought to investigate the cognitive processes that writers employ when faced with a writing task generally ignored the influence of class on students' composing processes . . ." (27). Even early critiques of cognitivist approaches registered this inattention to social context—as did, for instance, Patricia Bizzell's "College Composition: Initiation into the Academic Discourse Community" and "Cognition, Convention and Certainty: What We Need to Know About Writing" (both published in 1982). The irony is that the fascination with cognitivism was rooted in that core goal of basic writing—defining the basic writer. Yet pursuit of that goal caused researchers to stray far from focusing on the social conditions that for so many, from Shaughnessy on, did so much to define the basic writer.

Contextual Definitions

Gradually, attention circled back to students as individuals and their writing as primary evidence; there was a return to seeing things in context, not as patterns of behavior but as specific moves made in a classroom—and made for the sake of making moves in a larger social context. The watershed document in this refocusing of attention was Lynn Quitman Troyka's "Defining Basic Writing in Context" (1987). It approvingly cited George Jensen's critique of what Mike Rose would call "cognitive reductionism" and called for a richer, rounder treatment of the basic writer, one giving attention to reading as well as writing. What gave the piece special valence was its position as the specially commissioned lead-off in Theresa Enos's collection *A Sourcebook for Basic Writing Teachers*. In fact, all of the pieces in the first part of the *Sourcebook*, titled "Contexts for Basic Writing Teachers," spoke to Troyka's recommendation to heighten attention to reading and larger issues of literacy.

But this recommendation was also the root of new problems and tensions. "Defining Basic Writing in Context" represented the "gathering of data from a national sample of students to answer the questions such as, 'Nationally, what is basic writing?' and, 'Nationally, what typifies the writing of basic writers?'" (3). Troyka found the results to be rich, provocative, and complex: "But the message is clear. Basic writers are a diverse group" (12). Troyka made rigorous attention to evidence-on-the-page the necessary basis for developing definitions and answers to her initial questions. But what followed from this seems rather unexpected:

> What implications for research and teaching might be derived from the realities of our democratic society as well as the study I report here? I would like to suggest two broad concerns. First, the matter of definition. Writing is not writing only. Too long have most discussions of writing ignored reading. Too infrequently in our journals do we see essays that speak of reading as a complement to writing. (12)

Strange as it may seem to see this redirection of attention from writing to reading, it seems stranger still to see what emerged as the other of the "broad concerns." The emphasis on difference and diversity seemed to be leading not only to an acknowledgement but also perhaps even to a celebration of range, variety, and multiplicity. But that is not how the piece concluded:

> My second concern is the matter of identity. Basic writing has begun to lose its identity. The bandwagon effect seems to be taking over. The term *basic writing* is applied loosely to various populations of students, thus diminishing the energies we must spend on those students central to our undertaking. (13)

The question is not the scholarly or pedagogical propriety of Troyka's conclusions—both are inferable from the study and both are potentially salutary—but they are so far from being foregone conclusions as to give pause. Close attention to writing results in a call for more attention to reading. A demonstration of diversity calls for a kind of purification of the sampled population, a narrower and more efficient refocusing. The former conclusion is justified by being "derived from the realities of our democratic society as well as from the study," whereas the latter speaks to the core "purpose in this paper": "to offer data that will help us to resist generalizing from small samples of basic writers" (13). There is at least the appearance of contradiction here, which prompts the question of why it surfaces, especially from a leader of the field so thoughtful and influential as Troyka—someone who, at this point in time, had already put in some years as the editor of the *Journal of Basic Writing* (*JBW*). The answer does not lie in inevitable breakdowns in discursive logic but in the pressures bred into the field from its inception.

For basic writing, definition was never enough. For all the concern leaders of the field would develop about medical metaphors—Troyka herself here describes the word *remedial* as "negatively medical" (4)— BW was a field in which definition was always in large part diagnosis, and diagnosis led, quickly and inexorably, to prescribed treatment. The whole point of the field was always, after all, to do something for a population of students. Knowing and saying what that was (or should be) was always the first order of business. Here, in Troyka's piece, a more mature development of the field, diagnosis and prescription were accompanied by a reluctance (or at least a conflicted readiness) to do just that. The whole point of "Defining Basic Writing in Context" is that effective, rigorous, well-grounded definition is difficult, and that, without it, prescriptions for basic writers are dubious: "We need, for example, to avoid thinking that the writing processes of a few basic writers apply to all, that all basic writers must edit when we decide they should rather than when they want to, that all basic writers suffer from too many 'shoulds' or too much anxiety" (13). Nevertheless, Troyka departed from her own evidence—and significantly invoked the social mission of BW with a reference to "the realities of our democratic society"—in delivering her own very generalized diagnosis and prescription: that basic writers need more reading, more attention to language and literacy (and not just to writing narrowly construed). This is not so much an inconsistency as a response to the field's categorical imperative and top priority: Act as if you not only know the students but also as if you know what they need—and say what that is. Troyka had responded in a way that chimed nicely with a movement already afoot: the basic reading and writing program developed at the University of Pittsburgh.

Prescribing Without Defining

The cognitivists had shown how work in BW could get bogged down in definition. They earnestly confronted the question of what defined the basic writer, but unwieldy explanatory models of intellectual development brought to bear on a diverse student population produced results that were ultimately inconclusive and unsatisfactory. The masterstroke made by David Bartholomae and Anthony Petrosky at the University of Pittsburgh was to refuse to get bogged down in defining basic writers: they would jump right to what those students needed. Diagnosis and prescription would and could be virtually one and the same. The students, after all, were a preconstituted group—already defined as basic writers by being so assessed and tracked (as they were at so many institutions, if rarely by the same means). The issue was to show what worked for these students. This they did in *Facts, Artifacts and Counterfacts: A Basic Reading and Writing Course for the College Curriculum* (1986). The book was a compendium of teaching practices authored by a host of teachers working in the Pittsburgh program. Clearly, the book seemed to say, there are more important things to be done than defining the basic writer. Why get bogged down in definition?

Why, indeed? Bartholomae, who led off the second part of Enos's basic writing *Sourcebook* just as Troyka had led off the first, effectively shifted the burden of definition from diagnosis to prescription. Defining basic writers was almost a waste of time, or so he suggested in his specially commissioned piece, "Writing on the Margins": "As a profession, we have defined basic writing (as a form or style of writing) by looking at the writing that emerges in basic writing courses. . . . We know who basic writers are, in other words, because they are the students in classes we label 'Basic Writing'" (67). The question was less who basic writing students were (since the answer was essentially tautological) than what sort of teaching was most appropriate for them; the real goal of definition ought to be the description of effective teaching practices. Definition *was* prescription. And it was not accomplished with sweeping generalizations but with a particularized laying-out of the full curriculum, authored collaboratively. It's not hard to see why the approach achieved a popularity that endures to this day. Here was a book teachers could use as well as embrace. Rich and multifaceted as the curriculum was in assignment sequences, treatment of error, and so on, its overarching goal could be put quite simply: the idea was to initiate students into academic discourse.

Initiation as a Goal

The need to initiate basic writers into the ways of academic discourse seems—or seemed—indisputable. Why it came to be controversial—not only fiercely debated but also disavowed to some extent by its initial proponents—has something to do with the way in which Bartholomae and Petrosky skipped over the question of definition and went right to treatment/prescription. The outlines of this leap can be seen in the brief preface Theresa Enos gave to her *Sourcebook*. There she included the replies from three of the book's contributors to her request that they give "definitions of the term *basic writing* to include in this preface" (v). Karen Greenberg focused instead on *basic writers:* "Basic writers are people who simply have not had enough experience writing in a variety of roles and registers for a variety of concerned readers" (v). Patricia Bizzell's response was similar, if more elaborate, conditional, and cautionary: "If basic writers need academic cultural literacy in order to achieve full participation in the academic community, then a way must be found to give students access to this knowledge while at the same time encouraging some critical distance on it" (vi). Robert Connors was the only one of the three to focus on *basic writing,* as Enos had requested, defining it as "that kind of student writing which disturbs, threatens, or causes despair in traditional English faculty members" (vi). All the respondents had rather more to say, but this is enough to raise the key question: Is the real point to help BW students or to make sure they will not offend the faculty who read and evaluate their work? The question seems unfair, but it is not without a point. Basic writing was brought into being for a purpose, and that purpose, put frankly, was at least as much to shield faculty from the rawness and inexperience of a new wave of open admissions students as it was to support those students in their quest for access to college instruction. Shaughnessy and her recruits, drawn from outside the professoriate, were charged with handling what professors could not handle, taking at least the roughest of the rough edges off the type of student writing that "causes despair in traditional faculty members." The goal had always been initiation, but the very word acknowledges how unaccommodating and one-sided this demand for change would be. The students must change to fit the institution, not the other way around.

The scholar who acknowledged this most clearly, and who also seemed most troubled by it, was Patricia Bizzell. She was, arguably, the first and most important proponent of initiation after Mina Shaughnessy. Bizzell took up the cause of basic writers even as she took up arms against E. D. Hirsch's call for "cultural literacy" in his book so-named—a book that acknowledged Shaughnessy as an influence (10). In fact, Bizzell's arguments about the necessity of some form of initiation (which included "What Happens When Basic Writers Come to College?" and "College Composition: Initiation into the Academic Discourse Community") were always more qualified than her arguments against a single form of "cultural literacy" (as in "Arguing about Literacy"). Characteristically, her contribution written specifically for the *Sourcebook*, "Literacy in Culture and Cognition," argued against monolithic notions of cultural or social literacy and instead for more modest and nuanced ideas of literacy, the sort of "literacy that confers a reasonable degree of education and economic success and political participation" (135).

The way to nurture this type of literacy may have been described by Bartholomae and Petrosky. But perhaps that way took basic writing too far—or not far enough. Richer in described teaching practices than Bizzell's work, their approach may have been less wary in its justifications. Bartholomae was the member of the pair who would achieve more prominence. His "Inventing the University," the outline of the prescribed immersion in academic discourse detailed in *Facts,* is clear about his debt to Bizzell (which, he says in an endnote, "should be evident everywhere in this essay"). But he seems a good deal more emphatic than Bizzell about students' need to learn the rules and the ropes—and a good deal less emphatic about their need to develop "critical distance" from imposed demands on discourse and behavior. Just how nuanced his view is seen to be may depend on how much guarded irony he is granted when he says (in statements so often cited they became litanies) that the basic writing student "must know what we know, talk like we talk" ("Writing Assignments" 300) and "must learn to speak our language" ("Inventing" 135).

What did that mean, exactly? It meant many things, of course, but most of all it meant learning the conventions, from the conventions of standard English to those of sophisticated academic discourse. Why conventions matter so much was something Bartholomae took from Shaughnessy. The problem of definition was forever surfacing in terms like "nonstandard" or "nonacademic," terms that implied not the definition of something but rather its lack—"the absence of whatever is present in literate discourse," as Bartholomae put it in his essay in Enos's BW *Sourcebook* ("Writing on the Margins" 67). This is part of his extended gloss on a snippet from Shaughnessy's *Errors and Expectations,* which is worth quoting here:

> The term BW *student* is an abstraction that can easily get in the way of teaching. Not all BW students have the same problems; not all students with the same problems have them for the same reasons. There are styles to being wrong. This is, perversely, where the individuality of inexperienced writers tends to show up, rather than in the genuine semantic, syntactic and conceptual options that are available to the experienced writer. (40)

Here Shaughnessy effectively outlines the problem of definition that would haunt the BW teachers and scholars who followed her. The key to understanding basic writers lies not in what they are but in what they have not yet become. They are too unconventional in a strict and significant sense, significant because this unconventionality makes their writing all the more idiosyncratic and difficult to define. Yet these students are not innocent of language in its written form, nor are they somehow "preacademic."

This is a point Bartholomae stresses as he explains why Shaughnessy's insight effectively preordained the failure of the cognitivists' whole attempt at defining the basic writer (as an abstraction, a type). In consequence, he says (to the entire field) that

> we are stuck, and we are stuck because we have begun to imagine the problem as an abstract problem and because we have chosen to define the problem . . . within the language and methods of developmental psychology. Basic writers, we are asked to imagine, work with a style that is preacademic. They are

> caught at some earlier step in cognitive development (at the level of concrete rather than formal operations, for example), or they belong to a culture that is pretextual (an oral culture, like those that preceded the development of alphabetic writing) and that hinders the cognitive development required for literate participation in a textual culture. ("Writing on the Margins" 69)

Fundamentally, the problem with such definitions was that they located "the basic writer outside the conceptual structures that his more literate counterparts work within" (69). This was untenable, Bartholomae argued, and it was also dangerous. It engendered failures of sympathy and imagination in those who most needed to be sympathetic and imaginative as they worked with basic writers: "We define them in terms of their separateness. We do not see ourselves in what they do" (69).

Bartholomae's move, implicit in his title "Writing on the Margins," was in some sense not a huge step; he argued that basic writers should not be seen as outsiders but should rather be seen as located on the margins of academic culture: "These marginal students (and I will call them basic writers, but out of default, since I argue that this is a slippery label) are where they are because of the ways in which they read and write" (67). These were literate students, in other words; they only needed to become more so. In some ways, this conception of basic writers seemed reasonable, even obvious. Yet there were huge consequences to this position (or positioning), not all of them positive. It is true that the pedagogy Bartholomae advocated was in many ways empowering to both students and teachers. If all students really needed was schooling in conventions they were not utterly unacquainted with in the first place, then teachers presumably had the necessary directions, and students didn't have an enormous distance to travel. But what they were traveling toward was an odd sort of El Dorado. The academic status quo was embraced as a desideratum that basic writers disrupted by virtue of their incomplete initiation. Not completely outside, they were not completely inside either, and this raised questions about increasingly fuzzy distinctions that seemed mere matters of degree. Other questions inevitably followed. Was more complete initiation really assimilation? Was full insider status predicated on becoming entirely conventionalized? Was something short of that, something that preserved otherness and difference, somehow a sign of failure or incompleteness? Was academic discourse really so homogenous and hegemonic that it made sense to speak of being inside "it"?

Problems with Initiation as a Goal

The significance of questions about the implications of "initiating" basic writers into academic discourse can be seen in what Bartholomae was saying only a few years later precisely because of his success in having redefined the terms of engagement. By the time he gave the keynote at the fourth National Basic Writing Conference in 1992, that success had become a problem: "In the name of sympathy and empowerment," said the later, self-chastening Bartholomae, "we have once again produced the 'other' who is the incomplete version of ourselves, confirming existing patterns of power and authority, reproducing the hierarchies we had meant to question and overthrow . . ." ("Tidy House" 18). But now, Bartholomae confessed, that sympathy has been recast as condescension and a form of estrangement, that empowerment as something more sinister—something like conversion or even colonization. (For a more extended account of Bartholomae's remarks at the 1992 Basic Writing Conference, see chapter 1.)

The change in stance was no doubt influenced by countless factors. One factor was the work of Min-Zhan Lu. From a point very much on the left of the political spectrum, Lu launched a critique of Shaughnessy and specifically of her supposedly essentialist view of language. Her first salvo was "Redefining the Legacy of Mina Shaughnessy: A Critique of the Politics of Linguistic Innocence," published in 1991 and drawn from a dissertation supervised by David Bartholomae. At the heart of Lu's critique was her sense of Shaughnessy's inattention (even obliviousness) to "the potential dissonance between academic discourses and [basic writers'] home discourses" (27). This was something Lu could speak on with personal authority (see her "From Silence to Words: Writing as Struggle").

Lu was by no means the only one to speak out on these issues. Literacy narratives of the time (e.g., Mike Rose's *Lives on the Boundary*, Keith Gilyard's *Voices of the Self: A Study of Language Competence*, and Victor Villanueva's *Bootstraps: From an American Academic of Color*) drew attention to tensions between academic and home culture. (For a fuller discussion of these narratives, see chapter 1.) Such accounts further complicated attempts to define the basic writer. Diversity among basic writers had earlier presented a considerable challenge. But now, with the trope of the divided self recurring in literacy narratives and scholarship, the diversity without met the diversity within. Individuals were themselves multiple—in their roles, their voices, their cultural contexts.

Bartholomae had once chastised the field for a lack of sympathy for basic writers: "We do not see ourselves in what they do" ("Writing on the Margins" 69). Now he found that view trumped by full-blown identification with them—not only more or less vicariously in Rose but also especially in the compelling, self-divided accounts of Lu and Gilyard. In the latter accounts, particularly, assimilation was not an interest or an option; difference (and resistance on behalf of it) came to be valued rather than targeted for elimination or sanded down by convention. Bartholomae's keynote at the 1992 BW conference showed he had been paying attention. He effectively declared that he had gone too far in advocating a kind of homogenization for the sake of integrating or initiating the basic writer into the world of academic discourse; now, invoking Mary Louise Pratt and her idea of "the contact zone," he was advocating something quite different, a "curricular program designed not to hide differences . . . but to highlight them, to make them not only the subject of the writing curriculum but the source of its goals and values (at least one of the versions of writing one can learn at the university)" ("Tidy House" 13).

The importance of Bartholomae's changed direction to the quest for definition in basic writing cannot be overestimated. Here the person who had done most to minimize the enterprise of defining the basic writer—rejecting conceptual and developmental distinctions, insisting that the basic writer already came endowed with a fair share of literacy and academic conventions—now backed away from this minimal definition of the "marginal" student as if that were extreme overstatement. Basically, the basic writer no longer had definition in scholarly terms. True, there were, in addition to literacy narratives, case studies like those provided in Deborah Mutnick's *Writing in an Alien World*, but these defied generalization except as cautionary tales detailing the dangers of generalizing. Even Shaughnessy had been wary of abstract definitions of what a basic writer was, but she and Bartholomae had clearly pointed to a state or status the basic writer should attain. Now uncritically making that initiation into the world of academic discourse the objective was untenable, retrograde, and politically incorrect. If the basic writer was chiefly defined by something not yet attained, and that something was a set of conventions at least as much in need of critique as inculcation, then the definition was more question than answer, more problem than solution. Who was the basic writer? That was now a trap masquerading as a question.

This perception—that trying to define the basic writer was fraught with dangers—was a recurrent issue at the 1992 BW conference (and the special Spring 1993 issue of *JBW* devoted to it). There was a profound and pervasive sense that supposing students needed to move beyond one state to another (and a better) unfairly demeaned the one and privileged the other. Jerrie Cobb Scott indicted "the recycling of deficit pedagogy in basic writing and other programs targeted for marginalized students" (47). William Jones, who shared Scott's conviction that "basic writing is fundamentally framed in terms of deficit," emphatically called that framing racist since "*basic writer*, the term itself, was used with notable frequency, as euphemism and code for minority students" (73–74). Tom Fox argued that a focus on "writing standards" obscured "the powerful forces of racism, sexism, elitism, heterosexism that continue to operate *despite* the students' mastery of standards" (42–43). He called for redefined, more broadly construed standards that acknowledge "the social forces that really do prevent access" and "remind us of the blurred and perhaps ultimately unhelpful boundaries between 'basic' and 'regular' writers" (44). Taken together, these positions constituted a profound reversal for a field founded on defining (and thus aiding) a special kind of student. The very project of defining seemed wrong in everything from motives to outcomes, at least for some of the field's leaders.

A Point of Crisis

This shift of position was less radical or sudden than it might seem. Even the earlier, unreconstructed Bartholomae had questioned the boundaries used in defining BW, insisting that they were slippery rather than hard and fast. Still, the business of defining basic writing and especially the basic writer had reached a crisis point. If (with some adjustments for social injustice) the difference between basic writers and other college students was only a matter of degree, how great was that degree? This was an important if unsettling question. With other marks of distinction called into question, what was left to define the basic writer but assessment and consequent tracking? These had always been suspect, never more so than at the 1992 conference on basic writing. It was there (and in the Spring 1993 issue of *JBW* devoted to it) that Peter Dow Adams made one of the earliest and most compelling arguments for mainstreaming. After reviewing the scholarship and documenting practice in basic writing, he concluded that everything that had been learned about appropriate and effective teaching in recent years had "gradually but consistently pushed the pedagogy of the basic writing classroom in one direction: toward that of the freshman composition classroom" ("Basic Writing" 24). But this was by no means the clincher. It seemed that at his home institution (Essex Community College in Maryland), many students with BW placement instead wound up in freshman composition—mainly because there was little to prevent them from registering for it save the designated placement. And those who managed to elude basic writing fared quite well. In fact, Adams found, his "data would seem to indicate that students' chances of succeeding in the writing program are actually reduced by taking basic writing courses in which they are placed" (33).

It may appear, at least on the evidence presented thus far, that the definition of basic writers or even basic writing was a moot question. But other contributors to the 1993 special issue of *JBW* dissented. One of them was Karen Greenberg, the lone representative of the City University of New York (CUNY), effectively BW's birthplace. She was careful to stress that she was speaking of local testing and teaching practices when she said, "I believe that CUNY's current policy of testing entering students' skills and requiring them to take appropriate developmental courses embodies a 'right-to-succeed' philosophy" ("Politics" 70). CUNY's testing and placement procedures at that time did, in fact, contrast markedly with those Adams described for his institution. Developed by teachers, CUNY's testing was by writing sample, holistically scored on a six-point scale by faculty at each of the different colleges. Adams's institution, by contrast, was using a commercially developed multiple-choice grammar test, and apparently teachers were halfhearted about enforcing the placements determined by it. But there was another, perhaps more significant reason why students were finding it so easy to circumvent their assigned placements at Essex Community College. Adams allowed that his institution—indeed, his whole state system—was under "extreme financial strain. Vacancies are remaining vacant, broken equipment is remaining broken, and faculty are learning the meaning of furloughs. And then, this summer, talk has begun of actually eliminating programs" (25–26). As it turns out, this retrenchment was one of the reasons for Adams's study, undertaken in hopes of demonstrating that basic writing instruction was important, since it suddenly seemed so vulnerable.

The Vulnerability of Basic Writing

Basic writing's vulnerability had always been an issue—indeed, a critical part of its definition. The remaining two pieces in the special Spring 1993 issue of *JBW* addressed an ongoing vulnerability that had become entrenched since the 1970s. They were Jeanne Gunner's "The Status of Basic Writing Teachers: Do We Need a 'Maryland Resolution?'" and Mary Jo Berger's "Funding and Support for Basic Writing: Why Is There So Little?" Significantly, both cast their cases as extensions of composition's plight within the university. Gunner's title invoked the Wyoming Resolution (see Robertson et al.), an ultimately unsuccessful attempt to improve conditions for teachers of writing in post-secondary institutions. Gunner referred to the Wyoming Resolution in order to highlight the still worse plight of BW teachers:

> The concerns of teachers of basic writing as a distinct professional group have not been part of the professional discussion; clearly, we have failed to make an impact on the profession at large. Our failure, I argue, is due to the fact that we have yet to constitute ourselves as a professional group. Instead, we have been content with our identity as composition's version of the Peace Corps, volunteer teachers going into the educational hinterlands to do good in the face of appalling conditions, assuaging the larger profession's social guilt, and expected to find our labor its own reward. (61)

Berger, in explaining the chronic underfunding of basic writing, similarly cast BW teachers and BW itself as under-recognized. She explained that she was drawing on a piece titled "The Spare Room," in which Ernest Boyer and Arthur Levine explain that faculty tend to the major and students to the electives, but general education (including composition) goes begging—is, hence, the "spare room." Berger elaborated on the figure: "In my mind, basic writing, with other developmental studies, does not live IN the spare room but rather is hidden from almost everyone's view—including most of those who teach general education courses—on the top shelf of the infrequently opened spare room closet" (82–83).

This lack of recognition, this near-invisibility—part of the ongoing structural reality that marginalized students are served by marginalized faculty and programs—seems especially significant in light of the retreat from defining the student constituency that basic writing serves. In a sense, basic writing had reached a juncture where it was no longer capable of clearly articulating its own raison d'être. Suffering from what Gunner called "lack of status that stems from our being narrowly associated with the classroom and curriculum" ("Status" 61), BW teachers were not only overworked and underpaid, but they were also engaged in work that was increasingly difficult to define outside of local contexts and assessments. Hard at work, they were also hard-pressed to give clear definition to the work they were doing or for whom. To add insult to injury, many of the scholars who had complicated the matter of definition were deserting the field. Gunner observes the irony that although basic writing had begun to achieve some status because of the growth of scholarship in the field, "researchers and theoreticians who began as basic writing professionals have allied themselves with more status-bearing professional groups, leaving basic writing behind" ("Status" 61). Ultimately, Gunner herself moved on and up, becoming editor of *College English*, the official journal of the College Section of the National Council of Teachers of English (NCTE).

The Crisis as Reflected in the Journal of Basic Writing

The first issue of the *Journal of Basic Writing* (*JBW*) to come out under the editorship of Karen Greenberg and Trudy Smoke (Spring 1995) testified to the crisis in basic writing. It was the shortest issue since *JBW* had become a national journal, yet it had the longest editors' column. There, the editors registered what had been happening to the field—and how discomfiting they found it:

> We have listened carefully (and uncomfortably) to our colleagues' critiques of basic writing. . . . Some have characterized basic writing programs as tracking systems which serve to preserve the idea of nontraditional students as being "different." Several scholars

> have asserted that basic writing courses "ghettoize" students, prevent them from joining the mainstream of college-level courses, and often serve as obstacles rather than opportunities. Others have challenged our profession to provide evidence that basic writing courses work.
>
> We have begun questioning whether our definitions are still accurate, whether our placement procedures are still valid, whether our strategies do, in fact, still work. (2)

The editors' response to such challenges was not, as it had been for Greenberg at the 1992 National Basic Writing Conference, to level a series of counterclaims. Instead, the editors opted for an open-ended question: Should the journal be renamed? Some who responded to the question (actually made before the publication of this issue, which contains the results) felt the matter wasn't worth pursuing. These included Thomas Farrell and Mike Rose, both of whom were cited in the editors' column and neither of whom felt that an established identity and readership should be fiddled with. Those who did respond at length basically affirmed the importance of the journal, whatever its title. For instance, Joseph Harris (who succeeded Bartholomae as composition director at the University of Pittsburgh) wrote of "Negotiating the Contact Zone" in an article so titled. Like Bartholomae in "The Tidy House," he drew on Mary Louise Pratt's idea of the contact zone as a means of making BW a site of cultural negotiation, not assimilation. In "Basic Writing in Context: Rethinking Academic Literacy," Lee Odell drew on Peter Dow Adams's critique of tracking as well as Bartholomae's critique of BW in general to argue for an expanded notion of what academic literacy is—something Patricia Bizzell had been urging for years. In "Language and Authority: Shifting the Privilege," J. Milton Clark and Carol Peterson Haviland argued for using texts in a variety of languages to tap into the growing linguistic diversity appearing in writing classrooms.

With the next issue of *JBW*, the name remained unchanged, but a still greater sense of change and urgency had emerged, signaled with the first words of the editors' column:

> As we edit our second issue of *JBW*, we are aware of the serious challenges facing our profession, our stu-

> dents, and our colleges. Several hundred participants attended our basic writing panel at the 1995 Conference on College Composition and Communication last spring. Most spoke with eloquent anguish about the dissolution of their programs and the loss of resources for basic writing courses across the nation. They, and we, are troubled by the devaluing of literacy and education as government and public priorities. We believe that basic skills courses democratize higher education by providing students with academic access and support. Thus, the role of *JBW* as a voice for our profession has become more critical. (1)

The sense of basic writing as embattled but defensible permeated the issue. Significantly, a majority of the articles related to the perceived need to redesign curricula or assessments. These built to a kind of climax at the end of the issue, with Thomas Hilgers revealing that nearly half of all colleges and universities tracking students into BW used multiple-choice tests to place them, and Edward M. White affirming that assessment and placement, done right, could have demonstrable benefits for basic writers ("The Importance of Placement"). White was the big gun in the issue, a nationally recognized expert in writing assessment and also an important figure on both the Council of Writing Program Administrators and the Executive Committee of the Conference on College Composition and Communication. He mustered data that, he argued, showed students with BW placement experienced improved access and retention.

Another big gun fired back. The subsequent issue carried Sharon Crowley's "Response to Edward M. White's 'The Importance of Placement and Basic Studies.'" She reminded those who needed reminding that she had long been calling for "abolishing the universal requirement in introductory composition," believing that "Freshman English is a repressive institution." Tracing its roots to the nineteenth century and Harvard, she argued that "the universal requirement began life as an instrument of exclusion" (89). Thus far, she could be confident that those who knew her work from elsewhere would find these arguments familiar. But she did not stop there. "In the current mean-spirited political climate," she wrote, "I doubt whether we serve 'new students' well by using mass examinations to segregate them into classrooms that can be readily identified as remedial or special" (90).

CLIMATE CHANGE FOR BASIC WRITING

It is scarcely an exaggeration to say that everything hinges on that change in context Crowley crystallized as "the current mean-spirited political climate." Basic writing had come in for harsh critique before: its assessments questioned, its placements called ghettoization. But White's defenses of good instances of both—from his perspective, demonstrations that they were providing the identification and support that aided students in making academic progress—were really not questioned by Crowley. This was not a failure of understanding on her part. For Crowley, the more general problem with placements and assessments was that these supposedly necessary forms of shelter and support for students prior to their confrontation with freshman English were unnecessary and wrong because freshman English was unnecessary and wrong, though she was also clear that this institutionalized rite of passage was unlikely to go away soon. The real and immediate problem for Crowley was the change in political climate. She goes on to cite representatives of the National Association of Scholars declaiming against the prevalence of remediation and its presumed cost. Her suggestion was strategic: BW could be targeting the very students it was supposed to protect, labeling them as remedial while calls to cut remediation (and thus to eliminate BW students) became more strident in the public arena.

Responding to Calls to Eliminate Basic Writing

There were several possible ways to respond to Crowley's "Response." One was to go on disputing the right way to do BW. Programs and assessments could be defined and redefined, attacked or defended. In fact, this was already happening: as an instance, Crowley's "Response" was preceded in the Spring 1996 issue of *JBW* by Kay Harley and Sally I. Cannon's "Failure: The Student's or the Assessment's?" The problem with discussions of what was right or wrong about basic writing was that they were always unavoidably local. Even White, with his national reach and reputation, had focused his argument on two large but hardly all-inclusive studies, one done by the California State University and the other by the New Jersey Basic Skills Council.

Alternatively, there was the option of accepting Crowley's premise that the fundamental problem was that basic writing, like required composition, needed to be eliminated, not reformed or redefined (much less defended as-is). But BW did not have the established durability of required composition, a century-old requisite that had managed to become remarkably entrenched in the college curriculum.

There was a third option. With political forces mobilizing against basic writing and other forms of remediation, it might well be time to make a case for BW in the court of public opinion, to rise above the disagreements within the field in an effort to defend the field itself. As Crowley had suggested (still more powerfully than Bartholomae had in the 1980s), arguments over how to define basic writing were effectively a waste of time: it was already defined. Its definition resided in the tracking, the assessment, and the placement of BW students. For so many who argued for BW as a place for initiation into college, this was the given. Basic writers had been found wanting, and so the question was how to remedy their deficiencies, even if terms like "remedial" and "deficient" were under erasure. Crowley had put her finger on a cruel paradox: the very mechanisms instituted to ensure adequate support for "new students" were painting those students and the programs that served them as targets. The cuts had begun, spurred by recessionary economies and calls for higher standards. Basic writing had always been hard to define and justify pedagogically, harder still to refine and reform. But nothing could be easier than to eliminate it.

Countering the cuts that had already begun might have been impossible. Logically, it meant battling it out in the political arena, trading sound bites and oversimplifications. Even if BW practitioners could do this (and some, like Harvey Wiener, urged that they should ["The Attack on Basic Writing"]), they were overworked and simply hadn't the time. Instead, within the BW community, there was a growing acceptance of the idea that BW students represented only differences of degree while institutionalized placements were so many lines drawn in the sand. Yet, if BW students weren't all that different, then a clear case could not be made for special support. Experiments with mainstreaming basic writers were undertaken and represented a kind of blending of BW into regular composition. The programs that garnered the most attention were Rhonda Grego and Nancy Thompson's at the University of South Carolina and Mary Soliday and Barbara Gleason's at CUNY's City College. By the end of the 1990s, mainstreaming of basic writers could be fairly called a movement (well represented, together with arguments against it, in *Mainstreaming Basic Writers: Politics and Pedagogies of Access* [McNenny]).

"Our Apartheid"

Still more attention—in fact, outright notoriety—went to the option of abolition. The person who brought that to the fore in the mid-1990s was Ira Shor. Repeatedly citing Crowley (and the history of Harvard's institution of the composition requirement), he shared her dim view of freshman English but was far more emphatic about the need to eliminate basic writing: "Our Apartheid," he called it, and said that "BW is less than freshman comp, below comp, often non-credit bearing, so its rise . . . into an empire of segregated remediation fits an age when the status quo urgently needed to divide and conquer and depress young people aroused for social change and for economic success" (95).

Fighting words, to be sure—and they would provoke angry responses—yet there was more truth than perhaps even Shor realized in that phrase "divide and conquer." Not because of any conscious or malign design—on the contrary, because of the need for individual institutions to exercise some degree of self-determination—basic writing was everywhere different. Joseph Trimmer, a decade earlier, had surveyed nearly a thousand different institutions offering BW programs and found that scarcely any shared the same definition of a basic writer. Yet, however defined, every basic writer at every institution with a BW program was an identifiable target for the remediation-removers. Frequently (as was the case at CUNY, the cradle of open admissions), the same means used to identify basic writing placement was used to determine, or rather deny, college access altogether.

Shor's characterization of basic writing as "Our Apartheid" and his call for its dismantling led to heated discussions at the convention where it was presented (in a workshop sponsored by the Conference on Basic Writing at the 1996 Conference on College Composition and Communication) and on the listservs thereafter. The responses to Shor published in *JBW* voiced the concern that forces of conservative reaction like the editorialists for the National Association of Scholars cited by Crowley were also calling for the dismantling of BW programs. Karen Greenberg, for example, argued that "if Shor's vision came to pass," it would mean the triumph of "reactionary political forces." She further asserted: "No one should make the mistake of believing that the current atmosphere of draconian cutbacks would not operate in this way if opponents of basic skills courses are successful in their goal" ("A Response" 94). Terence Collins similarly argued that Shor's position was a strategic mistake: "Shor's piece is a thrilling synthesis of disparate perspectives on how students get sorted and ground up in a factory model of higher ed, but in its strained assertions about Basic Writing practice it will likely serve simply to distract us from direct action against more pressing forces of exclusionism" ("A Response" 100).

Context-Contingent Definitions

Significantly, the responses to Shor's critique of basic writing relied on the strategy of getting ever more specific about how basic writers and basic writing get defined. Collins took virtually every objection that Shor raised against basic writing and showed how, whatever might be the case elsewhere, the objections couldn't be leveled against BW as practiced at the General College of the University of Minnesota. He concluded that Shor's was a "too-homogenized sense of how we all have created Basic Writing from our multiple perspectives in our multiple sites" (100). This was also effectively the thesis of Greenberg's response to Shor, which began, "One of the problems in thinking about basic writing is that this term means nothing apart from its context." Shor, she insisted, was guilty of "oversimplifying the term and demonizing it. In reality, basic writing differs at every school; at each college, administrators, teachers, and students all participate in the process of constructing basic writing and basic writers" (90). History, as always, would have the last word. Basic writing was phased out at Greenberg's institution, CUNY's Hunter College, in 2001, and the University of Minnesota's General College was disbanded in 2005. (See chapter 1 for a fuller discussion of these developments.)

In the 1990s, there was a growing trend to resist general definitions of basic writing. Given the theoretical climate within the academy at the time, this resistance seemed strategic, even wise. But in the face of what Crowley had called "the current mean-spirited political climate" (90), this strategy militated against the development of a united front in defense of BW. And BW needed defending. Whole statewide efforts coalesced to assume the proportions of a national anti-remediation movement, something captured in the introduction to the 1998 report "College Remediation: What It Is, What It Costs, What's at

Stake" (prepared by Ronald Phipps, senior associate of the Institute for Higher Education Policy, and sponsored by the Ford Foundation):

> Over the past several years, attempts have been made to limit remedial education in states such as Arkansas, California, Louisiana, Oklahoma, Tennessee, and Virginia. More recently, in states like New York and Massachusetts, efforts are underway to reduce the amount of remedial courses offered in postsecondary education. Legislators in Texas and other states are troubled that tax dollars are being used in colleges to teach high school courses, and some states like Florida have shifted virtually all remediation efforts to the community college level. The legislatures in New Jersey, Montana, Florida, and other states have considered proposals that would force public school systems to pay for any remedial work that one of their graduates must take in college. (1)

"Basic Writing at a Political Crossroads"

Confronting a steamrolling effort to reduce or remove remediation from colleges and universities, BW scholars proliferated definitions rather than consolidating them—often with the full consciousness of the threat to BW. Published the same year as the "College Remediation" report cited in the previous paragraph was an important article by Susan Marie Harrington and Linda Adler-Kassner, "'The Dilemma That Still Counts': Basic Writing at a Political Crossroads" (1998). The authors said at the outset, "Our internal debates about the nature of basic writing are exciting, but political exigencies challenge us to formulate a clear statement of purpose. Without forgetting the diversity of students currently enrolled in basic writing classes, we should be able to define basic writing in keeping with current theory and in awareness of the political climate" (8). But Harrington and Adler-Kassner's review of two decades of scholarship did not allow a clear definition to emerge:

> Given what we see in the diversity of basic writing scholarship in the last twenty years, we are faced with an important question: where do we go? We began

> this project with an attempt to define basic writers in a rich yet satisfying manner. Perhaps unsurprisingly, our reading and analysis has not allowed us to frame a simple definition that will settle the heated disputes now raging in hallways and legislatures. (16)

Instead, what Harrington and Adler-Kassner urged was further attention to what seemed to them important but neglected areas of BW scholarship. They gave most attention to the area they knew would be most unpopular, the study of error. Acknowledging that "error analysis is not a trendy subject in research these days," they asserted that it needed much more attention than it was getting: "While most writers and readers would agree that there are other dimensions of writing that are more important, such as focus, purpose, or rhetorical context, it is error that stigmatizes in a way that weaknesses in those other dimensions do not" (17). For whatever reason, Harrington and Adler-Kassner's call to refocus attention went largely unheeded, effectively underscoring their own contention that "the move away from an oversimplified view of correctness has led to a reduction of interest in language use" (17).

Interest in language use did experience an uptick of a kind those authors had not called for—one that played into the ongoing trend to complicate and blur distinctions. The next special issue of *JBW* (Spring 2000) featured a number of prominent scholars pronouncing on the state of BW at the invitation of the editors, George Otte and Trudy Smoke. In this issue the hope was repeatedly expressed that academia might learn from BW (rather than the other way around)—and not least of all with respect to language use. In "Basic Writing and the Issue of Correctness, or, What to Do with 'Mixed' Forms of Academic Discourse," Patricia Bizzell asserted that "to prepare students now for success in school, it may no longer be necessary to inculcate traditional academic discourse. Rather, what is needed is more help for students in experimenting with discourse forms that mix the academic and non-academic . . ." (5). "For instance," Min-Zhan Lu and Bruce Horner argued in the same issue of *JBW*, "if academic language represents the language of those who teach in the academy and the language of those whose writers we regularly assign our students to read, then the popularity of Gloria Anzaldúa's writing in college readers suggests that the new voice endorsed by the academy is increasingly more diverse and hybrid" ("Expectations" 45). In a sense, Susan Miller only made explicit the implication of such claims when she urged that change should extend beyond language use to institutional structures, stressing that "the righteousness of both old and new forms of academic superiority needs testing, not just commitment to either self annihilation or to holding the earliest BW forts. We should hope for more than shifted discourses in stable sites" ("A Future" 62).

But even shifted discourses could be too much to hope for. The agency ascribed to BW could be quite remarkable, even utopian; Lu and Horner opined that it had already taught academia much, and that was the one thing that should not change: "We can expect, and demand, that our colleagues and institutions learn to expect and depend on basic writing to continue to do so, to the benefit of all" ("Expectations" 50). But this was only the best possible construction that could be put on events at the turn of the century. The same issue of *JBW* had Terence Collins and Melissa Blum mourning the students they had lost to cuts, Shor continuing to argue for the abolition of BW, Keith Gilyard and Deborah Mutnick (in separate articles) countering that argument, and William DeGenaro and Edward White bemoaning the lack of "professional consensus on matters in Basic Writing, since the researchers in the field do not seem to listen much to each other or to build on each others' findings" (23). Most emphatic of all was Lynn Quitman Troyka, whose title "How We Have Failed the Basic Writing Enterprise" left no doubt that, to her at least, failure was a fait accompli, not just a threatened outcome.

Capitulating on Definition

Troyka held that the fundamental failure was that "we didn't tend to public relations" ("How We Have Failed" 114). But that "we" seemed to assume more unity than actually existed, particularly if the dissensus among the luminaries in the Spring 2000 issue of *JBW* was any indication. When BW scholars did make a bid for a common definition and a common cause, they were likely to be treated with indifference if not scorn by others in the field. Harrington and Adler-Kassner's unheeded call for a refocusing of attention on error in "The Dilemma That Still Counts" is one case in point. Another more striking case is "A Method for Describing Basic Writers and Their Writing: Lessons from a Pilot Study" (2000) by Deborah Rossen-Knill and Kim Lynch.

Explicitly an attempt to define basic writers across different institutions, the study involved multifaceted (and rather complicated) surveys and diagnostics. It included a proviso about sensitivity to context: "Importantly, while we have found our method—our particular mix of tools—extremely useful, we do not suggest adopting it without consideration of the contexts in which it will be used" (97). Such sensitivity notwithstanding, the authors met with profound resistance: "Not surprisingly, as we sought to learn about basic writers as a group, we confronted the greatest objection to our work" (115). As evidence, they cited one (anonymous) respondent who claimed what they were attempting "is almost impossible, and I think, possibly pernicious," saying they risked seeming "to pathologize 'basic' writers." The authors apparently took such comments to heart: "We understand and, to a certain extent, agree that it could be dangerous business to classify or pigeonhole basic writers" (115).

That resistance to classification, for all sorts of reasons, might be said to be the real point of consensus as the 1990s came to an end. Like other fields, basic writing (at least as a scholarly enterprise) had always moved forward by agonistic debate, oppositional exchange honing general claims to ever finer distinctions. In the case of BW, general characterizations of the basic writer had been challenged and disputed until they were virtually nonexistent. Reversing this tendency would have required more than just an against-the-grain adjustment. Michael Apple, in a concluding section of his *Cultural Politics and Education* tellingly titled "It Ain't All Local," argued that reversing this tendency would have meant making a most difficult move, especially for scholars driven by a sense of social justice: "studying the Right"—and, yes, even learning from it. According to Apple, "The rightists have recognized how important it is to build social movements that connect the local with the global. They have been more than a little successful in reorganizing common sense by engaging in a truly widespread education project in all spheres of society—in the economy, in politics, and in the media and cultural apparatus" (114). Apple gave a good sense of what an effective public relations campaign for BW would have entailed—and what it would have been up against.

In a less general way, so did others. A number of contributors to *JBW* around the turn of the century—notably Gail Stygall, Steve Lamos, Mary Kay Crouch and Gerri McNenny—analyzed the social forces and state mandates that were behind the reconfiguration and/or disappearance of BW programs. Other works moved from local cases to more general and extended analyses as did Tom Fox's *Defending Access: A Critique of Standards in Higher Education*. Such analyses could not be expected to be disinterested, but that meant that they were fundamentally and unavoidably scholars' reactive responses to powerful political trends. In this David-and-Goliath struggle, the scholars were not only beaten in terms of seizing the initiative and capitalizing on public-relations resources but also even in terms of rhetoric, at least according to Stanford Goto. Arguing that policy makers employ discourse that is hierarchical, linear, progressive, programmatic, and quantitative—in a sense everything that academic discourse is not—Goto argued that BW advocates almost inevitably respond with mismatched rhetoric that is fated to have no impact on policy (or at least on policy makers). Goto took Fox as an example:

> In a sense he is preaching to the converted, rallying supporters of accessible education. In doing so, he employs professional language and theoretical constructs that are familiar to composition instructors, particularly those who embrace critical multiculturalism. If we composition educators were to present Fox's argument or any other discipline-based argument to policy advocates, we would need to find ways of penetrating the vertical, quantitative discourse. (8)

A very real question is whether anyone truly expected basic writing to match the rhetoric or impetus of the anti-remediation forces. Those forces had sent a clear, short message to the BW administrator, if not the BW teacher/scholar: blend or die. Small wonder that mainstreaming was the hot topic in the latter half of the 1990s. Fox himself exemplified this trend. His contribution to the Spring 2002 special issue of *JBW*, coauthored with Judith Rodby, was an account of mainstreaming at Cal State Chico. It is true that this mainstreaming project was done in the right ways, and for the right reasons, but it is no less true that it was done in a state that left BW administrators no choice but to blend into the mainstream, whatever their convictions and arguments about expanded access.

Yet striking the apocalyptic note of doom for basic writing is no more accurate or appropriate than succumbing to utopian suggestions that it should transform the academy instead of being subsumed by it or excised from it. The sites for basic writing have been reconfigured and relocated in many cases, but BW has by no means disappeared. Basic writers have begun to make their presence felt outside of BW programs, notably in a growing number of accounts of such writers in writing-across-the-curriculum work (see Sternglass, *Time*; Zamel; Zamel and Spack; Cohen; and Fishman and McCarthy). What is more to the point, their reduced presence at four-year institutions has been counterbalanced by a corresponding increased presence at two-year institutions as state systems like those in Florida, Texas, California, Massachusetts, and New York have relegated students with BW placement to community colleges. When William Lalicker surveyed the configuration of BW programs in 1999, he found he had to develop a fairly extensive typology for the variety of shapes these took; in his results, he listed, in addition to the more traditional or standard configuration (which he called the "baseline"), no fewer than five alternative models—of which mainstreaming was but one. Regardless of whether these models all served the same sort of student (however defined), the real issue was *how* they served the student. Similarly, after noting how often "the discourse of student need" is unexamined or co-opted, Mary Soliday, in *The Politics of Remediation*, concluded by shifting her "focus from institutional access to writers' access to mainstream cultures" (145), countering the initiation model with an alternative: "translation pedagogy" (146–85). She exemplified this by her own teaching (at City College, where BW has been phased out, at least as a visible program) and by accounts of her own students "contesting the status of academic writing from within an institution" (150).

However basic writing and the students it serves are defined, it continues, becoming ever more varied in its contexts and methods. Bartholomae had once made serving basic writers the first order of business because their definition (at least in terms of assessments and placements) was a given. Now, early in the twenty-first century, the premise is quite the opposite but with the same sort of result; the definition of basic writing is so much a matter of contestation (and, for strategic reasons, so often a subterranean or surreptitious sort of definition) that the first order of business again becomes serving the student. Because what was once generally accepted now seems so much in doubt or dispute, definition must matter less than method, placement less than pedagogy. What is basic writing? Who is the basic writer? No longer questions with any clear answers, they have been supplanted as the key questions by what may be a better one: What exactly is it that BW does? That is the focus of the following chapter, "Practices and Pedagogies."

3 Practices and Pedagogies

Basic writing began as an effort to give access to college writing to students who had not had access before, and early efforts grew out of the existing field of composition. The first BW teachers were, for the most part, people whose experience was in teaching college writing. Serving as both a threshold to as well as a proving ground for first-year composition, basic writing always had rich ways of mirroring aspects of the so-called mainstream. So it's important to see that such instruction began as something more like a branching tributary than an utterly new and distinct stream.

From the start, Mina Shaughnessy saw the task of "re-purposing" existing writing instruction as the fundamental charge for basic writing. She said as much in her introduction to the second issue of the *Journal of Basic Writing* (*JBW*), the new journal created for the new field, a themed issue called simply "Courses":

> Indeed, what begins to appear to be the major "innovative" task in basic writing is to determine (1) what of the available knowledge about the teaching of writing can be put to use in basic writing and (2) how that knowledge and the methods it has generated can be adapted to the needs of basic writing students. (2–3)

This issue of *JBW* was built around extended course descriptions submitted by those teaching in the new trenches. Their courses (see Desy, Campbell and Miller, Ponsot, Mills, Petrie, and Pierog) were indeed constructed around full visions, not just particular methods; they covered everything from reasoning soundly to accessing feelings as well as thoughts. Shaughnessy found the most impressive thing about the course descriptions was their "diversity of purpose and method" (3). Looking at these descriptions over the stretch of decades is instructive, raising the question of how much writing instruction has really changed—or, for that matter, how much it should.

In many cases, early leaders of BW rooted their research in the classroom, advocating the "scholarship of teaching" before that became a buzz phrase designed to reanimate pedagogy in a host of fields. In the inaugural issue of the *Journal of Basic Writing*, for instance, that is how Mina Shaughnessy cast the work of her coeditors, "who after several years of talking together about their experiences in the classroom decided to prepare short papers for their meetings so that their ideas might be more carefully explored. This first issue of the *Journal of Basic Writing* grows out of that exchange . . ." (3).

In *The Making of Knowledge in Composition* (1987), Stephen North points to Shaughnessy as the prime example of what he calls Practitioners, those identified primarily as teachers rather than researchers or theorists. North calls the body of knowledge generated by Practitioners "lore," something distinct from research and scholarship, even when it appears as research or scholarship (22–24). Lore, according to North, is "the accumulated body of traditions, practices, and beliefs in terms of which Practitioners understand how writing is done, learned and taught" (22). A miscellaneous catch-all of "what works" rather than a unified codification, lore is important to Patricia Harkin for that very reason. In "The Postdisciplinary Politics of Lore" (1991), she shows how Shaughnessy, untrammeled by adherence to a particular method or theory, could bring sociological, psychological, and cognitive explanations to bear on the same passage of student writing. For Harkin, "lore," especially as exemplified by Shaughnessy, can bridge disparate fields and suspend apparent oppositions, developing experiential explanations of instructional issues that would elude work constrained by a rigorous theory or method.

Harkin demonstrates this by countering John Rouse's charge (in "The Politics of Composition" [1979]) that Shaughnessy misunderstood and misapplied the rules for linguistic socialization with the consequence that she was not only wrong in her thinking but also oppressive in her practice. Harkin's analysis shows Rouse to be at least as afflicted by inconsistencies and extra-theoretical imperatives as he finds Shaughnessy to be. Ultimately, Harkin sees Rouse's presumed rigor (which he thinks places his work on a different plane than Shaughnessy's) as an instance of the academic fallacy Stanley Fish calls "theory hope," the supposedly false belief that there is anything to justify practice besides contingent, context-bound preferences (Fish 355; Harkin 132–33).

These days, we needn't accept Fish's dismissal of theory to see it as scarcely less contingent than practice. Both seem operable more as fashions or trends than immutable rules or guidelines. Yet practice has had an oddly enduring impact in basic writing, confirming North's remarks on the durability of "lore," from which, he says, "nothing can ever be dropped" (24). Granted, perspectives on practice keep shifting—from an emphasis on sentence skills to one on cognitive development to one on discourse communities, from the preoccupation with the BW student as nontraditional or "other" to an insistence on that student's integration into the mainstream or an acceptance of the hybrid nature of academic communities. But the practices themselves seem to persist beneath the changed perspectives.

In this chapter, we review BW practices and pedagogies over the years by focusing on three pivotal points of concern: *error, assessment,* and *teaching.*

Error

What gave basic writing a focus at the outset was a strong sense of what BW students did—or did not do—as writers. And what primarily distinguished them from their peers was the preponderance of errors in their writing. Addressing those errors became the first order of business. That is why, with the proviso that basic writing was always about much more, the story of its practices has to begin with approaches to error.

The archives of the *Journal of Basic Writing* attest to this early focus on error. The first issue, published in 1975, bore the one-word theme "Error," and the third, from 1977, dealt with "Uses of Grammar." As Shaughnessy recounted in the Preface to *Errors and Expectations,* the crystallizing moment for her was when she sat alone in her office at City College and began to read the first set of papers from the students enrolled in the SEEK Program, her oft-quoted encounter with "writing [that] was so stunningly unskilled that I could not begin to define the task nor even sort out the difficulties" (vii). Of course, the work she was prefacing was compelling evidence that she had defined (and risen to) the task—and had defined it primarily in terms of an engagement with error. No one would ever again develop such a gift for "observing [students' errors] fruitfully" as Shaughnessy put it in introducing the first issue of *JBW*. But even such prodigious gifts of observation as Shaughnessy's do not necessarily translate into practice. Problems persist because they are not solved. Ultimately, *Errors and Expectations* gave hope, not solutions.

The explanatory power of that work notwithstanding, it has remarkably little to say about what to *do* about error—not understand or appreciate, not reason through, but *do*. For example, the book has one sustained exercise: fifteen pages devoted to what has come to be known as the "double-s rule," a rule for avoiding subject-verb agreement problems. Basically, the idea is that, since nouns form the plural by adding an *s* and present-tense verbs in the third person show singularity the same way, adding an *s* to both (or to neither) is likely to be a problem. But the rule is naturally not without exceptions, so that "using the -s-form of the verb" is, for Shaughnessy, not one rule but many (given here as they are in her book but without the intervening discussion, duly numbered and uppercased just as they appear—as if the imperative form were not enough):

1. DO *NOT* USE THE -*S*-FORM WHEN A SUBJECT IS PLURAL.
2. DO NOT USE THE -*S*-FORM WHEN A SUBJECT IS *I* OR *YOU*.
3. DO NOT USE THE -*S*-FORM WHEN YOU ARE WRITING IN THE SIMPLE PAST TENSE.
4. DO NOT USE THE -*S*-FORM OF ANY VERB THAT FOLLOWS AN AUXILIARY VERB.
5. DO NOT USE THE -*S*-FORM OF THE VERB WITH THE INFINITIVE. (146–50)

These exceptions (significantly, all "shalt nots") have their own exceptions. For instance, the one about the simple past tense notes the exception that "*was* is the only -s-verb in the past tense" (148). So what begins as a simple lesson for subject-verb agreement ultimately entails grammar lessons in number, person, and tense as well as in a variety of verbal forms (including irregular as well as infinitive and auxiliary forms).

Teaching Complication 1: The Need for Complexity

Typically, Shaughnessy is aware of the complexities she is opening up. She even resolves to make them a selling point, a difference in the way the basic writer must be taught:

> This lesson, lengthy and involved as it must seem to anyone who has taught this inflection the conventional way—with a definition of *person* and *present tense* and a few exercises—is nonetheless but an introduction to the -s-form. No attempt has been made to introduce the subjunctive, which raises special problems not only because it requires a plural verb with a singular subject (if he *were* . . .) but because it uses be as a finite form (I move that he *be* . . .), as BEV does, though with a different meaning (*I move that he be . . .* recommends something that has not happened, whereas *He be sick* speaks of a condition that is constant or continuing). The use of relatively simple subjects is an even more important limitation of the lesson, requiring a subsequent lesson on the location of complex subjects (inverted subjects in questions and in *there is, are* patterns; noun clauses and infinitive-phrase subjects; subjects separated from verbs by long modifiers, etc.) and on the conventions for counting subjects (compound subjects, *either-or* subjects, *each-everyone-everybody* subjects, units of measure subjects, collective noun subjects, and several others). (*Errors* 152–53)

The complexities for the teacher (to say nothing of the students) may overwhelm, but Shaughnessy does not want to oversimplify. Lying back of her discussion of subject-verb agreement (as the abbreviation BEV—for Black English Vernacular—announces) is some sophisticated work in sociolinguistics, which had achieved significant advances well before Shaughnessy's landmark work on error. For instance, the decade prior to the publication of *Errors and Expectations* had seen the publication of half a dozen major works from the Center for Applied Linguistics collectively titled the "Urban Language Series" under the general editorship of Roger Shuy and featuring works by William Labov and Walter Wolfram as well as Shuy himself. The chief revelation, apparent in titles like *The Social Stratification of English in New York City* (Labov [1966]) and *A Sociolinguistic Description of Detroit Negro Speech* (Wolfram [1969]), was that English was subject to wide variations attributable to racial and social differences. These variations were not, moreover, something to be homogenized out of existence. Recognition of language difference throughout the series was accompanied by the principled position that, as Ralph Fasold and Roger Shuy's preface to *Teaching Standard English in the Inner City* (1970) puts it, "the teacher's job is not to eradicate playground English—or any other kind. Instead, teachers should help children to make the switch comfortably from one setting to another" (xi).

Teaching Complication 2: The Need for Tolerance

The call for tolerance had been codified in 1974 as "Students' Right to Their Own Language," a position statement of the National Council of Teachers of English (NCTE). This statement, which provided teachers with "suggestions for ways of dealing with linguistic variety" and urged that students be exposed to "the variety of dialects that comprise our multiregional, multiethnic, and multicultural society, so that they too will understand the nature of American English and come to respect all its dialects," inspired controversy from the first. But it remains a position statement of the NCTE to this day (see the organization's current website).

Although the position statement was controversial, it had a good deal of research on its side, which was marshaled in a special issue of *College Composition and Communication* (25.3 [1974]) in an annotated bibliography of 129 entries. In "Grammar, Grammars, and the Teaching of Grammar," an overview of this research as well as that of the subsequent decade, Patrick Hartwell would go so far as to say that such research

> makes the question of socially non-standard dialects, always implicit in discussions of formal grammar, into a non-issue. Native speakers of English, regardless of dialect, show tacit mastery of the conventions of Standard English, and that mastery seems to transfer into abstract orthographic knowledge through interaction with print. Developing writers show the same patterning of errors, regardless of dialect. Studies of reading and of writing suggest that surface features

of spoken dialect are simply irrelevant to mastering print literacy. (123)

In some ways the logical outcome of the NCTE position statement, Hartwell's oft-cited overview explicitly allows for a laissez-faire approach to error.

Teaching Complication 3: The Need (Still) for Correctness

But if a council proposes, then the teaching force disposes, and teachers remained uptight about error. In actual practice, most teachers neither stopped championing standard English nor did they, in the language of the position statement, cease to characterize "nonstandard dialects as corrupt, inferior, or distorted forms of standard English." Some of the blame for teachers' continued focus on error has been laid at Shaughnessy's door. Errors, by definition, mean things are wrong, not just different, and she had highlighted the term in a work written to show basic writing teachers the way. This was to a certain extent an essential strategy for her time and place. As Robert Lyons observed in his 1980 memorial essay, Shaughnessy was in no position to ignore errors: "It was clear from several essays on Open Admissions and from several letters to the *Times* that examples of unskilled writing by non-traditional students were considered a powerful weapon by those opposed to the broadening of higher education" ("Mina Shaughnessy and the Teaching of Writing" 5). Shaughnessy used *Errors and Expectations* to show that examples of student work were not arguments against educating their authors; they represented instead wholly explicable linguistic challenges and teaching opportunities, above all in the errors they presented.

What's more, throughout that work she had attempted to redefine the term "errors" even as she used it to stake out her primary focus; for instance, in the chapter on "Common Errors," Shaughnessy held that errors "are the result not of carelessness or irrationality but of *thinking*" (105). This avowal that errors were not so much mistakes as salutary missteps critical to the learning process put her well to the left of center, even and especially as someone upholding the standard. But her position was also a demanding one, in some ways more demanding than the call for tolerance. As Marcia Farr and Harvey Daniels noted in *Language Diversity and Writing Instruction* (1986), "While most writing teachers would undoubtedly endorse Shaughnessy's sympathetic view of their students' predicament, they also feel a strong professional obligation to attend closely to student errors" (44). Shaughnessy's way was enormously burdensome—not just sympathetic but empathetic, and accompanied by all the apparatus of traditional grammar instruction. Fortunately (at least for a time, for it would ultimately prove no less complex or demanding), another avenue was open to BW teachers: error analysis.

Imported from English as a Second Language (ESL) instruction, error analysis had its most influential formulation in Barry Kroll and John Schafer's "Error-Analysis and the Teaching of Composition," first printed in 1978 in *College Composition and Communication* and reprinted in 1987 in *A Sourcebook for Basic Writing Teachers* (Enos). Error analysts were less interested in analyzing errors per se than in analyzing why they occurred. Kroll and Schafer, both with experience as ESL teachers, emphasized the importance of analyzing the processes of which the error was only the end result. They stressed two processes in particular: interference from another language and intermediate steps in language learning (so-called "interlanguage"). In her own way, Shaughnessy had stressed both as well while work in applied linguistics, endorsed by professional organizations like the NCTE, had acknowledged the importance of recognizing systemic language differences within English. In other words, making the connection between a phenomenon like "interlanguage" in bilingualism and the same phenomenon in bidialecticalism was no great stretch.

Teaching Complication 4: The Need for Process Analysis

Even more important, quite possibly, was the explicit connection error analysis had to other important movements in writing instruction. The fact that it was process-oriented made it that much more timely and palatable. The process movement, advanced by research like Janet Emig's *The Composing Processes of Twelfth Graders* (1971) and textbooks like Susan Miller's *Writing: Process and Product* (1976), had settled in as the new orthodoxy. Writing teachers who wanted to be au courant knew the general themes if not the details of the process approach. When Kroll and Schafer wrote that the work on error they were drawing from ESL represented the culmination of a "general movement from approaches emphasizing the *product* (the error itself) to approaches focusing on the underlying *process* (why the error was made)" (243), they were using language that basic writing teachers would understand and appreciate, even relish, for its "process" orientation.

Scarcely less significant was their identification with another movement: cognitivism. "Error-analysts are cognitivists . . ." wrote Kroll and Schafer; this meant they understand that "errors help the teacher identify the cognitive strategies that the learner is using to process information" ("Error-Analysis" 244). Very much in the spirit of Shaughnessy's dictum that "errors are the result . . . of *thinking*," the invocation of cognitivism gave the patina of high-powered theorizing to error analysis in an article that invoked Freud as well as Shaughnessy.

What error analysis lacked was clear application. Just how would this approach to student error play out in the classroom? Kroll and Schafer were by no means indifferent to this concern, but they had not mapped out a workable method. What they had been clear about was that an instance of a single error could be worth sustained study—study focused more on the why than the what. Multiplied across multiple assignments and many students, error analysis seemed a formidable undertaking, especially so for classroom teachers.

Teaching Complication 5: The Need for Interpretation

What makes the difficulty of error analysis particularly clear was highlighted in an article titled simply "The Study of Error." That title might bespeak something much more general, but David Bartholomae's 1980 article focused on a single essay by a single student. He showed how, in having the student read the piece aloud and then answer questions, the instructor can uncover at least seven categories of reasons errors happen—complete with clues to how serious or systematic such errors are. These range from errors open to overt correction (mistakes the student acknowledges and corrects) to those caused by overcorrection (mistakes the student makes by misapplying "rules," for instance, writing "childrens" because of a misapplication of the rule for forming plurals). Is a particular error a problem with verb forms, syntax, or knowledge of conventions? Bartholomae's article effectively demonstrated that this question couldn't be answered simply by looking at the error. In fact, the error couldn't even be defined until there was some sense of intention and context. A sustained interview with the student was in order, its centerpiece the student's reading of his or her own writing.

Andrea Lunsford's 1986 "Basic Writing Update" (of Shaughnessy's 1976 bibliographic essay "Basic Writing") singled out this "thoughtful and provocative" article by Bartholomae as the most significant work since Shaughnessy's on analyzing student error. But her citations made it clear that "The Study of Error" had not mapped an easy path to follow:

> Starting with the theory that "allows us to see errors as evidence of choice or strategy among a range of possible choices or strategies" (p. 257) and a definition of error analysis as "the double perspective of text and reconstructed text [which] seeks to explain the difference between the two on the basis of whatever can be inferred about the meaning of the text and the process of creating it," Bartholomae argues that studying students' oral reconstructions of their own texts will provide "a diagnostic tool, . . . a means of instruction, . . . [and a way to] chart stages of growth in basic writers" (p. 267). (213–14)

Unquestionably, Bartholomae's honing of error analysis had given BW an important method. But it was fraught with cautions about what real knowledge of errors and their origins required. Its "double perspective of text and reconstructed text" ("The Study of Error" 267) meant there could be no easy assumptions based on surface evidence. There had to be careful reconstructions of student intentions (often ultimately unknowable), tracings of the multiple paths that might lead to a single mistake. Small wonder, then, that Lunsford concluded the section of her "Basic Writing Update" devoted to error by saying, "In practice, meanwhile, my sense is that many, many basic writing classes depend primarily on grammar workbooks for their class structure and 'lessons'" (215).

A colleague of Bartholomae at the University of Pittsburgh, Glynda Hull, wrote what is arguably the best account of the pedagogical application of error analysis (and particularly the rich investigative approach to it) in her contribution to *Facts, Artifacts and Counterfacts* (Bartholomae and Petrosky, eds.). She made the method palatable not by simplifying it but by making it an inviting experiment. Her piece, aptly called "Acts of Wonderment," began with the challenge to find the pattern in a series of mistakes made in basic addition problems. Moving from examining mathematics mistakes to mapping language errors, Hull made the latter seem fascinating but also doable detective work. It was indeed work, often collaborative work with students involving interviews and talk-aloud protocols. Hull's accomplishment was to make all this effort seem worthwhile despite its complexity.

"Computer-Adjusted Errors and Expectations" (Otte [1991]) ratcheted up the complexity with computerized error analysis, generating information on patterns of error (error frequency and error distribution by type) that teachers would never have time to map in such detail. Results across a single class showed a significant range in kinds and proportions of error. Computerized error analysis demonstrated more than ever that errors varied from one student to the next; why errors happened seemed to depend on a unique configuration of apparently incalculable variables in individualized writing processes, literacy backgrounds, and language behaviors.

If teachers were intimidated by the complexities invoked by such methods, then publishers were all but completely confounded. How could they possibly develop textbooks that took this seemingly infinite variety into account? In pedagogy-focused research, errors were looking ever less susceptible to mechanical approaches. Error analysis, evolving into a method that gave special attention to social contexts and cognitive processes, was a means of dealing with error that defied any kind of packaged approach. It required personalized and detailed detection, something a fill-in-the-blanks workbook could never accomplish.

Teaching Complication 6: The Need for Negotiation

Finding effective and practical approaches to dealing with error even defied those who would circumvent the textbooks. Bruce Horner's "Rethinking the 'Sociality' of Error: Teaching Editing as Negotiation," confronts the problem that students do not see errors as their teachers do, so they "correct" what isn't an instance of error while leaving actual errors uncorrected. But the problem defined by Horner remains a general one. As Susanmarie Harrington and Linda Adler-Kassner point out, "Horner outlines a pedagogy for teaching error as negotiation between readers and writers, but does not look at the work of individual writers as he does so. While we know something about which errors occur, we know very little about what students do as they revise to correct error" ("The Dilemma That Still Counts" 19). Horner's work is not dismissed out of hand, of course, and the real problem may lie elsewhere; the acts of negotiation he outlines, like the feats of interpretation delineated in Bartholomae's "Study of Error," seem to demand such time and effort that the prospect is too challenging for BW instructors, with their heavy teaching loads, to take on.

Writing in 1998, Harrington and Adler-Kassner describe the focus on error as fading from teaching practice, effectively stymied by the complexities it has turned up. Because "errors are far and away the most likely dimension of writing that will mark basic writers" (particularly but not exclusively in placement and exit assessments), they call for increasingly sophisticated forms of research, from "cognitively-based work" to "culturally-based work," yet that sophistication comes with a cost, even a loss:

> As attention has shifted from a close focus on correctness to more rhetorical views of error, research attention has shifted away from error analysis towards generic conventions and other rhetorical matters. And while we fully support a move away from mindless correctness to a rhetorical integration of language and form, we contend that the move away from an oversimplified view of correctness has led to a reduction of interest in language use. ("The Dilemma" 17)

The redirection of attention is also, in the absence of an easy fix, a turning away from the problem of error.

Teaching Complication 7: The Need for (and Lack of) Consensus

The problem that error represents for basic writing and basic writers remains. Though Harrington and Adler-Kassner are right to applaud the move away from oversimplification, they are just as right to see its downside: a discomfiting, even paralyzing, complexity that suppresses interest in the problem even as it overwhelms practice. Since errors were the identifying stigmata of basic writers, they figured importantly in assessments, and how they were viewed helped define assessments as well. Their causes and cures, rooted in writing and thinking processes as well as in matters of social context, also led basic writing instructors to issues ranging from cognitive development to social identity. Even technology came in, as a possible fix, or at least the medium for one. In all of these ways of addressing the problem, however, things quickly became much more complicated than they first appeared. No simple or single method or model emerged to guide practice; no consensus settled on the field to define procedure. On the contrary, competing and complicating discoveries in each of these subfields made teaching practice harder to negotiate, the challenges more formidable, and the research more intricate and elaborate. All the while, the field and the student at its center became more vulnerable. For better or worse, lore proved the first as well as the last resort for many basic writing instructors. For so many of them who were part-timers or neophytes, grad students pressed into service or adjuncts hired at the last minute, there wasn't time to get trained in more enlightened approaches to error or to delve into the thickets of research. But there was always the grammar workbook, the durable stand-by, the living fossil of BW instruction.

Assessment

One area in which lore has had an especially powerful effect on teaching practice is in the assessment of student writing. An early snapshot of the state of affairs in writing assessment, particularly as it related to basic writing, is the lead-off piece in the issue of *JBW* with the theme "Evaluation" (Spring/Summer 1978). Rexford Brown, then director of publications for the National Assessment of Educational Progress, began by noting that writing evaluation generally varies enormously if not chaotically: "We are all very careful to respect each other's right to a private grading system, even if it is arbitrary, wrong-headed, nasty, or capricious" ("What We Know Now" 1). The need to respect one another's values presumably explains the popularity of holistic scoring (the judgment that need not pronounce on anything specifically) with organizations like the Educational Testing Service (ETS), but Brown stressed that holistic assessment is "incapable of establishing proficiency in any concrete sense" and is "a very unsatisfactory system for the evaluation of growth" (2). Problematic as they are, holistically scored tests (using actual samples of student writing) represent "a luxury only the rich could afford anyway"; multiple-choice tests are "cheaper and easier to score," but have "glaring weaknesses" (3). Almost the only good thing Brown could say for either kind of test was that "the proliferation of such tests over the years has softened the profession up just a bit more to the idea of measurement and the possibility that there are some shared units of quality upon which to build more accurate and useful systems of evaluation" (4). He then went on to sketch a utopian "ideal instrument" combining student writing and objective items, the scoring of which would rely on computerized textual analysis, cross-checked against holistic and criterion-based systems, all based on more careful definitions and stronger consensus than heretofore achieved.

The reality for BW assessment was that multiple-choice, machine-read tests would continue to proliferate, while more well-meaning and/or well-off programs would engage in holistic scoring. Because holistic scores, in Brown's opinion, are "entirely relativist and value-free," they could tell teachers little about how to proceed with instruction, particularly in individual cases. He found multiple-choice tests rather more informative but even more insidious for that very reason: ". . . since the approach of many such tests is to emphasize difference between standard and nonstandard usages, writing courses all too often become, unintentionally, cultural programming laboratories" (4).

Teaching to the Test

The common assumption, as Brown had suggested, is that assessments functioned as constraints on teaching, shaping expectations and even curricula. In 1991, though much had changed, Brown would say that he found "an enormous amount of teaching to the test" ("Schooling and Thoughtfulness" 6). But firsthand accounts of the effect of assessment on teaching are rare. One example, from the 1978 "Evaluation" issue of *JBW*, was Rosemary Hake's "With No Apology: Teaching to the Test." It quickly became clear that Hake was no test-led sheep. Her article was really a detailed account of the thinking that went into the design of the writing test in use at Chicago State, a test developed carefully and collaboratively, tapping the best available research. Ultimately, as she confronted "the humanistic antipathy generated by competency testing," she concluded that "we can only ask two questions":

> If there are valuable writing performances which cannot be defined and therefore measured, should we not still insist upon identifying and measuring those that can be and finding better ways to teach them? As we isolate performances which resist precise statement and measurement, may we not, even so, find better ways to state, measure, and teach them? (55)

These did seem to be the right questions, and answering them seemed the right thing to do—even, as Hake concluded, an appropriate focus of what "universities are supposed to do" (55).

Primarily under the auspices of the Instructional Resource Center (IRC) founded by Mina Shaughnessy, the City University of New York (CUNY) had already attempted to address these questions by encouraging faculty involvement in the assessment of writing. Marie Jean Lederman's "Evolution of an Instructional Resource Center: The CUNY Experience" (1985) describes the IRC's role in the "development, implementation, and monitoring" of the CUNY Writing Assessment Test (WAT) (45). After the initial implementation of the WAT, a 1981–1982 review of the exam "involved more than one hundred faculty members from the university and from other colleges" and led to refinements in the scoring scale (45). Faculty involvement was the hallmark, in fact, with the IRC acting as the conduit for faculty-led audits of test scoring, surveys of student and faculty attitudes, and faculty-authored monographs and bibliographies. All this activity created a sense of CUNY leadership in assessment (Lederman notes citations of IRC monographs in *College English* and *College Composition and Communication*), but it was actually more important in creating a sense of faculty ownership of assessment.

An exception to this benign view of CUNY's faculty-developed writing assessment—one that addressed the student's point of view—was Judith Fishman's "Do You Agree or Disagree: The Epistemology of the CUNY Writing Assessment Test." This piece, which appeared in *WPA: Writing Program Administration*, was a scathing criticism of the WAT, especially the bald choices it invited students to make with its "agree or disagree" prompt. Recounting the complaints of students discomfited by the apparent demand to choose a stance on things like the role of religious faith in people's lives, Fishman argued for writing situations that gave more flexibility and also more context. She cited success, for instance, with a prompt that had students imagine the imminent end of the world and write about what mattered most to them.

Harvey Wiener, the editor of *WPA*, invited Lynn Quitman Troyka to respond, and she did in the same issue with "The Phenomenon of Impact: The CUNY Writing Assessment Test." She countered the anecdotes of students' negative experiences with the "big picture": the WAT was proving a reliable instrument, both in terms of inter-reader reliability and tracked placements. She also averred that the end-of-the-world scenario seemed hardly less discomfiting to students than the "agree or disagree" prompt. Above all, she noted that the WAT was an evolving instrument, that a large task force of faculty led by Troyka had refined the scale and design, and that there would no doubt be further improvements.

CUNY's work in assessment had inspired not only its own faculty but had also led to two grants to the IRC from the Fund for the Improvement of Postsecondary Education (FIPSE), one to establish the National Testing Network in Writing (NTNW) and the other to establish the College Assessment Program Evaluation (CAPE). Both grants were designed to extend work in assessment (including training and support) to other institutions.

This level of funding and activity could not be maintained indefinitely, and it wasn't. After six years as the director of the IRC, Marie Jean Lederman left for a deanship at one of the CUNY colleges. The review and refinement of the WAT done under Lynn Quitman Troyka in the early 1980s was the last such ever done. Troyka (and Shaughnessy before her) had insisted that ongoing re-evaluation of the WAT was essential, but it hadn't happened. Before the 1990s were over, CAPE and NTNW were defunct organizations; the IRC and the WAT were no more.

The demise of the WAT did not, however, signal the end of institutionally imposed testing at CUNY. In the fall of 1999, the University's Board of Trustees, under pressure from New York City mayor Rudolph Giuliani, voted to require "nationally standardized" tests in reading, writing, and mathematics (Arenson). The WAT was replaced by the ACT writing test, an exam in which students were given sixty minutes to respond to a tightly controlled prompt in letter form. The sample prompt given by the Borough of Manhattan Community College on its website was typical of this test: "The Parks Board has received a donation to improve the appearance of the city. It is considering two options: (1) planting more flowers in the parks and expanding recreational areas or (2) planting more flowers and trees along city streets. Write a letter to the Parks Board explaining which option you favor and why" (BMCC). ACT writing exams were assessed at borough-wide centers by specially trained CUNY faculty members who were paid for this work.

Many CUNY faculty members were unhappy with the ACT exam. They questioned whether this nationally normed exam developed by a testing company in Iowa provided a better measure of the readiness of students in New York City for "college-level writing" than the faculty-developed WAT, which it replaced. Eventually this dissatisfaction led to the formation of a CUNY-wide writing task force that worked to develop a more appropriate exam. The resulting test asks students to write, not a letter, but an essay in which they respond to a brief reading passage. While some issues are not yet resolved, the plan as this book goes to press is for the new exam to replace the ACT in October 2010. At this point a variety of indicators may be used to determine a student's readiness to enter first-year composition—and thus to attain entry into a four-year CUNY college—passing scores on the CUNY placement tests in reading, writing, and mathematics, SAT scores, or scores on the New York State Regents exams.

Teacher Resistance to Institutionally Imposed Testing

While many in politics and the press were demanding "standardized" tests of writing competence, faculty were increasingly questioning the validity of such tests. In the 1980s, a voice like Judith Fishman's, railing against the CUNY Writing Assessment Test (WAT), could be cast as out of tune with a larger chorus of support. In the 1990s, a full chorus of faculty voices was raised against such assessments. An early critic was Pat Belanoff, once a CUNY professor who went on to teach at SUNY Stony Brook; in 1990, Belanoff, in speaking to an organization of ESL teachers (wrestling with the explosive growth of that subpopulation of students), predicted that the WAT would be gone by 2000 (and it was—replaced by other, nationally recognized tests). Her argument, especially as it bore on ESL students, was an especially dramatic instance of what would be heard over and over again: students were simply too different and diverse to be effectively evaluated by standardized assessments, particularly when their touted reliability and validity seemed (or so Belanoff held) largely a fiction ("The Myths of Assessment"). Throughout the 1980s and 1990s, Belanoff had worked to develop and implement portfolio assessment as an alternative to standardized testing of writing (see, for example, Belanoff and Elbow; Belanoff and Dickson).

Case studies supplemented and substantiated Belanoff's charges against standardized assessment. In "Failure: The Student's or the Assessment's?" (1996), Kay Harley and Sally Cannon gave an account of one such failure, the case of a nontraditional, African American student whose differences were rendered strikes against her by assessment practices not designed to reckon with them. Barbara Gleason was still more emphatic, not least of all in her title "When the Writing Test Fails: Assessing Assessment at an Urban College" (1997). Gleason used three case studies of students' experiences to suggest the inefficacy and unfairness of the "CUNY Writing Assessment Test [which] has commanded national attention and served as a model for testing at many other colleges and universities" (309). Consistently, such case studies represented institutionalized assessment as an external imposition, a preemptive strike on the teacher's own ability to make evaluations and decide curriculum. The general idea was that teachers and their students were being steamrollered by a vast testing apparatus. As Deborah Mutnick would say in *Writing in an Alien World: Basic Writing and the Struggle for Equality in Higher Education* (1996), "The disempowerment of Basic Writing teachers has the same socioeconomic roots as the alienation and despair of many Basic Writing students" (29).

All these studies placed assessment in a context of complicating circumstances, showing that cookie-cutter assessments could never do justice—and would frequently do injustice—to the complexity of students' lives. These students' disempowered teachers, bristling at the unresponsiveness of mass assessments, were understandably giving vent to their frustration. Ultimately, such accounts underscored the need for a new agnosticism about assessment. If tests did so little good, and could do so much harm, then who needed them? Kurt Spellmeyer put the point compellingly in "Testing as Surveillance" (1996):

> Who benefits from the testing boom? Ideally, the answer is everyone—the students, the teachers, the institutions, the big-hearted funding agencies. But who really benefits? In New Jersey, where I live and teach, fourteen years of high school proficiency exams and college-level basic-skills entry tests have failed to produce any change in the performance of the state's students. But if assessment has done nothing to improve the performance of our students, it has helped to create a substantial new bureaucracy. . . . While standardized testing has many possible uses—and while some of them might be consistent with a democratic culture—college-level testing in my state has primarily served to intimidate the masses of adjunct

instructors who get "stuck" with the job of remediation. (177)

In the middle of the decade, the Conference on College Composition and Communication issued a Position Statement on Assessment (1995). One member of the drafting committee, Thomas Hilgers, summed up its potential impact by noting (in "Basic Writing Curricula and Good Assessment Practices") how far current practices were from those recommended by the Position Statement:

> Tens of thousands of college-bound students are "placed" into writing classes on the basis of an assessment of something other than writing. Even those schools that use direct measures of writing typically employ 30- to 40-minute samples of impromptu writing. The Position Statement indicts most of these current practices. It must make us rethink our placement practices. It has already been a force for change at my school, the University of Hawai'i, where incoming students draft and revise two essays during five hours. The CCCC Statement has made us consider the inclusion of writing samples created under different circumstances and for different audiences. . . . (72)

Hilgers underscored how the Position Statement confronted those doing assessments with stipulations few programs could meet—particularly in urging programs not to rely on a single assessment instrument or a single administration.

Spurred by teacher discontent with existing assessments and by the 1995 CCCC Position Statement, there was a new interest in alternatives and changes in strategy. By the end of the 1990s, assessment expert Kathleen Blake Yancey stressed that questions about assessment were wide open. Methods shouldn't be considered till there was a thorough analysis of context and purpose, a reading of what she called "the rhetorical situation" of assessment ("Outcomes Assessment and Basic Writing").

A dramatic shift had taken place in the space of a dozen years. In 1986, Richard Lloyd-Jones introduced his bibliographic essay on writing assessments by saying, "The assessment of writing abilities is essentially a managerial task. It represents an effort to record quantitatively the quality of writing or writing skills of a group of people so that administrators can make policies about educational programs" (155). But the disputations and experiments of the 1990s brought assessment much more closely into alignment with specific curricula and teaching goals. Alternative assessments such as portfolios had almost become commonplace.

By the time the next CCCC Position Statement on Assessment was approved in 2006, it was clear that, at least in the minds of the leaders of the field, assessment was far more than a mere managerial task. This statement highlights the complexity of good assessment practices and emphasizes the need for assessments to be tailored for specific student populations and educational purposes. If the purpose was to place students in the appropriate writing course, then the assessment of a writing sample should be done by trained instructors, never a computer program, and many factors should be considered: "Decision-makers should carefully weigh the educational costs and benefits of timed tests, portfolios, directed self-placement, etc. In the minds of those assessed, each of these methods implicitly establishes its value over that of the others, so the first cost is likely to be what students come to believe about writing" (Conference on College Composition and Communication, "Writing Assessment: A Position Statement"). But at the same time that leaders of CCCC were articulating these lofty goals, wholesale assessment was occurring in the United States in ways that were far from the best practices set out in the Position Statement.

State-Mandated Testing

The focus of screening and placement during the 1990s had shifted from basic writing programs to high school exit examinations, with more than half of the states following a program of mandated assessments set out by the National Governors Association (Otte, "High Schools as Crucibles of College Prep" 109). In the most extensive study of this state-mandated testing, *The Testing Trap* (2002), George Hillocks concludes that the consequences are, for the most part, counterproductive, especially given the way test preparation cuts into learning time "to prepare students for tests that do more harm than good" (207). The overall impact of these assessments remains a question. According to Gary Orfield and Johanna Wald, "High-stakes tests attached to grade promotion and high school graduation lead to increased dropout rates, particularly for minority students" (39).

That determination, made in 2000, seems supported by more recent developments.

In 2002, then president George W. Bush signed into law the federal No Child Left Behind Act, which requires states to administer regular standards-based tests in order to qualify for federal education funding. The effects of this widespread testing, however, continue to cause concern, particularly among those who work with BW students. A study released in August 2004 by the Center on Education Policy acknowledges that "few states can really say how many students do not receive diplomas because they failed an exit exam" but sees

> new evidence of negative impacts of exit exams, such as dampening some students' motivation to try harder, encouraging some students to pursue a general educational development (GED) certificate instead of a regular diploma, and creating incentives for educators to hold back students in non-tested grades. Some of the research suggests that these effects are significantly greater for certain groups of students, such as minorities, English language learners, and poor students. (*State High School Exit Exams* 10)

Even those students who manage to graduate from high school are still often at a disadvantage. In her 2004 article "Teaching and Learning in Texas: Accountability Testing, Language, Race, and Place," Susan Naomi Bernstein describes the effects of the Texas system of standardized testing on the students who were later placed in her basic writing course at an open admissions college in Houston. Students who in their earlier educations had been drilled in writing to pass the required tests were ill-prepared for "the intellectual inquiry demanded in college reading and writing courses" (9).

Not all the effects of this testing boom have been negative. The power of high school exit exams has spawned collaborations between colleges and high schools in such states as New York and California (Otte, "High Schools as Crucibles"; Crouch and McNenny, "Looking Back, Looking Forward"). That many students still arrive in college needing BW instruction has helped Royer and Gilles's work with directed self-placement at Grand Valley State University in Michigan to find adoptions elsewhere ("Basic Writing and Directed Self-Placement"). And mainstreaming experiments have produced any number of carefully tailored assessments, a fact nicely summed up in the title of Sallyanne Fitzgerald's concluding summary in McNenny's *Mainstreaming Basic Writers*, "The Context Determines Our Choice." Redesigning assessments (particularly as tailored, locally designed alternatives) will no doubt go on among teachers and program administrators but not as a panacea, not even a local one. Too many critical assessments and decisions are now visited on students before they leave high school. Of those who go on to college, too many still need basic writing instruction without believing they do.

TEACHING

Given all the things Shaughnessy knew a basic writing teacher had to consider, the teaching program she laid out in detail focused on something fairly limited (and presumably more manageable): the basic writer's writing. Initially stunned by the prevalence of error in her students' writing and knowing that others would be no less so, she understandably chose to focus on error first and foremost. This was nevertheless a process-oriented stance. Looking for patterns, uncovering the logic of error, she found herself focusing on processes of writing and of thought itself. The focus on error has been considered earlier in this chapter but not the attention, in Shaughnessy's approach, that it gave to process. An especially impressive example is the opening of Chapter 3 of *Errors and Expectations*, the chapter on syntax. Shaughnessy begins with a detailed description of "a practiced writer" composing a sentence, working rapidly through "almost an infinite number of ways of saying what he has to say," constrained but also directed by the choices made, moving "with increasing predictability in the directions that idiom, syntax, and semantics leave open" (44). The passage as a whole conveys a rich sense of possibilities but also difficulties since the practiced writer does struggle—though the struggling is "for aptness and meaning, not merely correctness" (44). Then Shaughnessy turns to the basic writing student for whom the process is in some ways more complicated for being more impoverished in its possibilities and choices:

> BW students at the beginning of their apprenticeship seldom enjoy this kind of ease with formal written sentences. For them, as for the foreign-language student, the question is rarely "How can I make this

> sentence better?" but "How can I make this sentence right?" Their concern is with the syntax of competence, not of style, for they lack a sure sense of what the written code will allow. Much of this uneasiness, for the native speaker at least, can be blamed on the writing process itself, which, because it involves different coordinations from those of speech, creates a code-consciousness that can inhibit the writer from doing what he is in fact able to do in the more spontaneous situation of talk. (44–45)

These are, of course, only the preliminaries before Shaughnessy gets to the particulars, but even here—not least of all in the nod to second-language acquisition and the footnote to indicate that the phrase "syntax of competence" does not mean what "competence" means in Chomskyan linguistics—there is a rich attention to process.

The Importance of Process

Attention to process came to be central in the next stages of mapping out a teaching program for basic writing. The seminal work here was done by Sondra Perl, more or less contemporaneously with Shaughnessy's own work on *Errors and Expectations*. In a study done in 1975–1976 and inspired to some extent by Janet Emig's work with twelfth graders, Perl discovered that BW students did indeed have complex writing processes. She also confirmed, from another perspective, that errors were the great problem, in part by confirming Shaughnessy's sense that concern over error was as debilitating as error itself. Perl showed through "composing aloud" protocols that BW students tended to disrupt the composing process with editing concerns, often resulting in additional errors and hypercorrections. Even if the goal was error control, error had to be put in its place. But doing that could be extraordinarily difficult, Perl noted, and for an important reason that teachers of BW students may not have adequately taken into account:

> These unskilled college writers are not beginners in a *tabula rasa* sense, and teachers err in assuming they are. The results of this study suggest that teachers may first need to identify which characteristic components of each student's process facilitate writing and

which inhibit it before further teaching takes place. If they do not, teachers of unskilled writers may continue to place themselves in a defeating position: imposing another method of writing instruction upon the students' already internalized processes without first helping students to extricate themselves from the knots and tangles in those processes. ("Composing Processes of Unskilled College Writers" 436)

The idea that what BW students bring with them may be as much of a challenge as what they have to learn was extraordinarily important. But it would take some time before this concept was fully explored, partly because it concerned so much more than the students' internalized writing processes; it was ultimately a matter of their identities. For the time being, as the 1970s became the 1980s, the consensus was that basic writers' approaches to writing were really the first order of diagnostic business. Perl's work, valuable as it was, provided a general diagnosis only in a limited sense; in fact, what made her work so valuable was that she was wary of easy generalizations. Even her general recommendations warned against oversimplified, step-by-step approaches to the writing process. In "A Look at Basic Writers in the Process of Composing" (1980), for example, she highlighted four aspects of the writing process (essentially invention, flow, voice, and audience) but stressed that her model's features were not sequential: "As features, rather than steps or stages, the four are interwoven or alternating strands of the overall process itself" (31).

Cognitive Schemes and Their Limitations

Perl's concept of "interwoven or alternating strands" of complex, individualized writing processes was difficult for teachers to put into practice. Instead, many of them wanted maps. Writing teacher Linda Flower's partnership with cognitive psychologist John Hayes gave them what they wanted. Flower and Hayes's early work together, notably "The Cognition of Discovery" (1980) and "A Cognitive Process Theory of Writing" (1981), yoked a particular strand of developmental psychology to models of the writing process. Part of a larger research project, which merits treatment as such in chapter 4, this work offered the outlines of teaching programs as well. Ultimately, however, research on cognitive theory and the writing process failed to produce effective teaching methods for the very reasons these mapping projects were so attractive initially: they were generic, schematic, and transplantable from one context to the next—but not sufficiently attuned to individual differences.

Initially, though, cognitive development seemed to have a fair amount of explanatory power—a suggestive but not exhaustive way of explaining difficulties BW students had with abstract thinking, the consideration of audience, and other supposed requisites of academic discourse. A focus on cognitive development freed basic writing instruction from fixating too closely on error while still retaining an attention to language. It was, in fact, derived primarily from two thinkers who were attentive to language formulation: Jean Piaget (especially in *Language and Thought of a Child*) and Lev Vygotsky (in *Thought and Language*). Both, importantly, focused on childhood development, though Vygotsky was more attentive to context (and also, for that reason, less schematic and easy to apply). Whole BW programs—e.g., Anna Berg and Gerald Coleman's at Passaic County Community College, Andrea Lunsford's at Ohio State, and Robert Fuller's at the University of Nebraska—would use testing to track and Piagetian schema to structure BW instruction. Much about this cognitive approach to instruction was salutary. For example, work with challenging concepts and readings was sanctioned by the special place that concept formation occupied in Piaget's framework. But, ultimately, the problems with cognitivism, all traceable to root premises, made the framework unattractive to teachers as well as researchers.

These problems were effectively summed up at the outset by Shaughnessy's caveat in her "Basic Writing" bibliography about the need "to determine how accurately the developmental model Piaget describes for children fits the experience of the young adult learning to write for college" (166). As teachers and researchers began to react against deficit definitions of BW students that focused on inadequacies rather than potential, the cognitive model came to seem an extreme example of deficit definition. Researchers using cognitive approaches tended to focus not merely on students' tendency to make mistakes but on their inability to think, at least at the college level—as when Andrea Lunsford observed in "Cognitive Development and the Basic Writer" (1979) that "basic writing students are most often characterized by the inability to analyze and synthesize" (40). This was compounded by an infantilization of the BW student, as if this young adult were somehow unable to proceed beyond thought structures characteristic of children between the ages of six and eleven. Finally, pedagogy itself was a problem. Piaget held that intelligence came from the progressive growth of embedded structures for thinking and that cognitive development was a maturation process rather than a teaching project. Developing a cognitive approach to teaching basic writing meant superimpositions and graftings much more than it meant applications and derivations of cognitive theory.

One more major problem with cognitivism and early representations of the writing process was the insensitivity of such models to context. Absent even when its importance was acknowledged, context could not be manifested in generalized schemes. Flower and Hayes, for instance, would often represent the writing process as a flow chart. The process could be represented as recursive—"flow" arrows need not suggest unilateral direction—but the whole thing was abstracted from any specific setting. Such abstraction effectively excluded rhetorical imperatives like purpose and audience except in the form of abstract exhortations.

Attention to processes of thought and writing had given BW instruction the outlines of a teaching program, but it was one with many (perhaps too many) blanks to fill in. And there were other causes for concern. From a present-day perspective, emphasis on cognitive processes had resulted in an approach to BW instruction that, however provisional, was also politically incorrect. BW students were defined as students whose writing processes were impoverished and entangled, whose thought processes were substandard and immature. There had to be better ways to define the teaching project. And there were, of course, but none seemed to have the capacity to galvanize and structure a full program the way cognitivism or process approaches had done, at least for a time.

A Grab Bag of Instructional Strategies

In the early days of basic writing, most teaching ventures and proposals discussed in journals and at conferences focused on specific strategies, collectively amounting to a kind of grab bag. Telling examples can be found in the issue of *JBW* with the theme "Applications: Theory into Practice" (1978). It contained pieces by Andrea Lunsford on Aristotelian rhetoric, Thomas Farrell on Walter Ong's orality/literacy distinction, Louise Yelin on Marxist literary theory, and Marilyn Schauer Samuels on Norman Holland's psychology of reading.

Lunsford and Samuels turned out to be advocating different kinds of role-playing. Farrell recommended a whole set of techniques, including journal writing, summarizing, novel reading, sentence combining, and "oral-imitation" (a kind of role-playing). Yelin concluded that "as we teach our students the codes and structures of Standard English and acquaint them with the values and practices of academic life, we must also offer them . . . a way of understanding that inscribed within each act of signification, within each social process and practice, is a whole structure of social relations" (29).

It is not hard to imagine that many BW teachers welcomed all these specific suggestions. The attention to role-playing in particular seemed encouraging. The invitation, for both the teacher and the student, was not only to focus on grammar but also to psych out the whole rhetorical situation. So there were alternatives to "skills" approaches (or, as in the case of Yelin's Marxist analysis, critically conscious takes on such approaches). Above all, there was plenty to suggest that basic writing instruction could be seen not only in terms of traditional approaches to teaching writing but also in terms of communicative competencies and forms of comprehension (orality, literacy). Not that traditional approaches were neglected. The "Strategies" section of the *Sourcebook for Basic Writing Teachers* (Enos [1987]), a section that runs to nearly 350 pages, includes treatments of vocabulary, grammar, the writing process, classical rhetoric, invention, personal as well as expository prose, revision, correction, collaboration (including peer critiquing), and the use of computers.

This list of "strategies" from the *Sourcebook* looks like a fairly exhaustive inventory of what writing instruction concerned itself with in the 1980s. In fact, with the demise of cognitive approaches, the question for the next stage was what remained to make BW instruction special. If its students were not cognitively immature, then were they at least distinctive in some way? What was there about BW instruction that distinguished it from writing instruction in general? It was a fair question answered in one way when *The Random House Guide to Basic Writing*, coauthored by Sandra Schor and Judith Fishman and published in 1978, was reissued in 1981 as *The Random House Guide to Writing*. In fact, Laura Gray-Rosendale notes that in the 1980s "the question 'Who is the Basic Writer?' had shifted within certain circles to 'Who isn't the Basic Writer?'" (*Rethinking* 9).

For some teachers, understandably, this was a problem. The most important statement to that effect was Lynn Quitman Troyka's "Defining Basic Writing in Context" (1987), which featured the results of a national sampling of the writing of BW students. The samples revealed such heterogeneity as to raise concerns, at least for Troyka. Given such concerns, it may seem odd that Troyka would seek not to tighten the definition but to broaden it; however, it is not uncommon for those contesting the definition of BW instruction or the BW student to find the definition too narrow as well as too broad. In Troyka's case, the focus on writing, however heterogeneous, was at the expense of a broader and more salutary focus on literacy, specifically on reading.

Facts, Artifacts and Counterfacts: *A Redefined Teaching Project*

The book that would reshape basic writing to answer Troyka's call for a broader focus on literacy was *Facts, Artifacts and Counterfacts: Theory and Method for a Reading and Writing Course* (Bartholomae and Petrosky [1986]). The teaching program had its roots much earlier than its publication date suggests in David Bartholomae's "Teaching Basic Writing: An Alternative to Basic Skills," one of several BW programs featured in the special issue of *JBW* devoted to "Programs" (1979). At that time at the University of Pittsburgh, Basic Reading *and* Writing was a special six-hour, bottom-rung course developed for students with the lowest level of placement ("Teaching Basic Writing" 99–100). Even here, reading was not the only and perhaps not the chief issue. The key point was implied in Bartholomae's 1979 subtitle: this was an alternative to a skills approach. Cognitive approaches had also offered an alternative, but their appeal was complicated by the need for appropriate testing and tracking, shared (even mandated) curriculum design, and a need to spend serious time getting acquainted with some sectors of psychological research. That approach might (and did) appeal to program administrators, but it was beyond the scope of the typical teacher. Bartholomae spoke of more familiar things, things dear to an English teacher's heart: not only the importance of reading but also academic conventions, acts of interpretation, modes of discourse (rather than modes of thought), and the rituals of college life.

Bartholomae got to this broadened approach eventually and with considerable help from his colleagues. Back in 1979, he was better at saying what his "alternative to basic skills" *was not* than at saying what it *was*. In explaining why the Pittsburgh program eschewed a "study skills approach," he wrote,

> Our goal was to offer reading as a basic intellectual activity, a way of collecting and shaping information. As such, we were offering reading as an activity similar, if not identical, to writing. The skills we were seeking to develop were not skills intrinsic to "encoding" or "decoding:" that is, they were not basic or constituent skills, like word attack skills, vocabulary skills or the ability to recognize paragraph patterns.
>
> We wanted to design a pedagogy to replace those that define reading as the accurate reception of information fixed in a text, and fixed at the level of the sentence or paragraph, since that representation of reading reflects our students' mistaken sense of what it means to read. ("Teaching Basic Writing" 101)

But what did it mean to "offer reading as a basic intellectual activity"? That is less than clear, and Bartholomae didn't help matters by explaining where answers were sought: "We reviewed the recent work in psycholinguistics and reading, work which defines comprehension in terms of the processing of syntax, where general fluency and comprehension can be developed through activities like sentence-combining" (102).

As an "alternative to basic skills," Bartholomae's 1979 article seems a baby step, whereas *Facts, Artifacts and Counterfacts*, published just seven years later, was a mighty leap. Some of this is due to the passage of time, and some of it, admittedly, is a matter of packaging. But the chief reason the program came to seem such an advance may have most to do with where Bartholomae and his cohorts went looking for answers to the question of how to define reading and writing as intellectual activities. The title for their book is derived from George Steiner's *After Babel*, specifically where he resists the idea that discourse is chiefly about information transfer and affirms its capacity for the "counterfactuality" of interpretive freedom. Steiner is only the first in an array of literary theorists whose names are dropped in Bartholomae and Petrosky's introductory essay as they invoke various fields of study: these include Jonathan Culler (deconstruction), Stanley Fish (reader-response theory), Hans-Georg Gadamer (hermeneutics), Frank Kermode (narratology), and Edward Said (cultural studies). Heretofore, English teachers or graduate students in English had more often than not consulted work in the social sciences for insights into their own teaching. Now what they were seeing in *Facts, Artifacts and Counterfacts* was the affirmation that their own discipline—English—could offer useful and exciting ways of approaching their work with BW students.

Basically, Bartholomae and Petrosky were saying that the real reason why basic writing students, presented with a reading, would so often fail (or claim to fail) to "get it" was that this is what reading meant for these students: a mere (but also impossible) matter of "getting it," an exercise in total comprehension. The problem was that, especially from the student's perspective, reading was viewed as a flat matter of right or wrong, success or failure. The solution, according to Bartholomae and Petrosky, was not to aid and abet the quest for complete comprehension. That was impossible because, as literary theorists showed from a dazzling array of angles, reading was a constructive, meaning-making, *interpretive* act. This was the thing to get at, and the best way to drive home the constructive nature of reading was to make responding to reading a matter of writing. This gave the act of writing a purpose and focus and gave the act of reading a visibility and accountability. The conjunction of reading and writing was undergirded by the conviction that "students can learn to transform materials, structures and situations that seem fixed or inevitable, and that in doing so they can move from the margins of the university to establish a place for themselves on the inside" (Bartholomae and Petrosky 41).

In laying out this vision, Bartholomae and Petrosky expressed concern that they were making students more the objects than the agents of transformation: "we seem to be saying that they cannot imagine what they say as anything else but a version of the words of their teachers. There is a distinction to be made here, however, one that defines the relation of the student and the institution as a dialectical relationship, that makes reading and writing simultaneously an imitative act and an individual performance" (40). What the students are offered, in other words, is "a way of seeing themselves at work within the institutional structures that make that work possible" (40).

There was much more to this book subtitled *Theory and Method for a Reading and Writing Course*, but these general outlines and statements help to explain why Peter Dow Adams, in reviewing it for the newsletter of the Conference on Basic Writing in 1988, declared it "a revolutionary book that proposes major breaks with past approaches and deserves to have a significant effect on how all of us teach basic writing in the future" (3). *Facts, Artifacts and Counterfacts* enfranchised teachers trained as scholars in literary/critical methods to bring those methods to bear on their teaching. It not only made a place for context in its pedagogy (and a central place at that) but made the role of context explicitly dynamic. It did not "dumb down" either the learning or the learners; on the contrary, BW students were challenged with difficult texts and assignments. And all this could be had just from the introductory essay. What followed were detailed assignment sequences as well as essays on pedagogy, student authority, error, revision, and the interrelations of reading and writing.

Facts, Artifacts and Counterfacts seemed almost ideal as a teaching program to many, but there were some nagging questions. One problem was that everything about the course really made as much sense for traditional students as for basic writing students. In fact, the textbook that Bartholomae and Petrosky developed out of this program, *Ways of Reading* (which has gone through many subsequent editions), was—and is—used primarily in first-year composition, not in basic writing. As assignment sequences and even specific assignments were appropriated for "regular" writing courses, it was fair to ask in what ways this program was specifically about and for BW students.

Back in 1979, Bartholomae had been frank enough to say that much of what passed for definition actually came from the vagaries of assessment: "It's hard to know how to describe the students who take our basic writing courses beyond saying that they are the students who take our courses" ("Teaching" 106). To show he wasn't being flip, he gave specifics about placement at his school (mostly a reliance on SAT verbal scores) and then elaborated:

> Those of us working with basic writing programs ought to be concerned about our general inability to talk about basic writing beyond our own institutions, at least as basic writing is a phenomenon rather than a source. We know that we give tests and teach courses and we know that this is done at other schools, but we know little else since there is no generally accepted index for identifying basic writing. (106)

Ultimately, this line of thinking would take him to the things he said in his keynote at the 1992 National Conference on Basic Writing, in which he questioned the whole BW enterprise (this address was subsequently published as "The Tidy House: Basic Writing in the American Curriculum").

Another strand of thinking in Bartholomae's discussions of pedagogy provided a strong answer to the question of what was distinctive about basic writing. Even if Bartholomae saw his BW students as accidents of assessment, they had been judged and found wanting—not by him but by his institution. The avowed goal of *Facts* was to allow such students to "move from the margins of the university to establish a place for themselves on the inside" (Bartholomae and Petrosky 41). Either the institution had to accommodate them, or they had to accommodate to the institution. As this idea was expressed in the introductory essay to *Facts*, "The student has to appropriate or be appropriated by a specialized discourse, and he has to do this as though he were easily and comfortably one with his audience, as though he were a member of the academy. And, of course, he is not" (8). In this explanation of why a change must take place, that added bit makes it very clear what (or rather who) must change. The teaching program outlined in *Facts, Artifacts and Counterfacts* is not just about teaching students but about initiating them, even assimilating them, into an unfamiliar world.

Initiation isn't automatically negative—a rite of passage doesn't have to be an act of conversion—but there were those who raised objections, most notably Peter Elbow, who argued against Bartholomae's position in a series of debates at conferences and in journal articles. In Elbow's view, there was nothing so very homogeneous and coherent as the academy or academic discourse to be initiated into; he felt that the argument for initiation was really an argument for the suppression of the personal, the individual. In their published form, Elbow's views are best represented by their earlier (and more moderate) expression in "Reflections on Academic Discourse" (1991) and a more adamant take in "Being a Writer vs. Being an Academic: A Conflict in Goals" (published in 1995 in *College Composition and Communication* along with Bartholomae's "Writing with Teachers: A Conversation with Peter Elbow").

But this issue of initiation was much more than a dispute between two views or two respected compositionists. It marked a point in the road where some turned off for reasons that looked and felt as much like a generational shift as a matter of diverging viewpoints. Though Elbow was older than Bartholomae, his views were shared and amplified by a new crop of teachers and scholars coming to the fore as the eighties became the nineties, people who had special reasons to be wary of initiation and assimilation. Composition scholars such as Victor Villanueva, Keith Gilyard, and Min-Zhan Lu would argue for multiculturalism and against the tendency of the dominant culture's institutions to strip away racial and ethnic loyalties—and the linguistic and cultural resources that came with them (for a more detailed discussion of these sources, see chapters 1 and 2). In "Redefining the Legacy of Mina Shaughnessy: A Critique of the Politics of Linguistic Innocence" (1991), Lu took Shaughnessy to task for cutting off students from the ways "they might resist various pressures academic discourse exercises on their existing points of view" (35). Though the "essentialist view of language" critiqued in this article is Shaughnessy's, the assimilationist tendencies Lu ascribed to it had, by the 1990s, reached well beyond her, all the way to Lu's thesis advisor, David Bartholomae.

The Politics of Identity

In a field where questions of identification were always paramount, the politics of identity was bound to emerge as a focus. If the texts of BW students had been a challenge to parse, that challenge paled before the task of duly acknowledging their identities. This was so complex an undertaking that a new form came to the fore, both as scholarship and classroom practice: the literacy narrative. The one sure thing when grappling with the complexity of identity was that labels and assessments and placements couldn't begin to do it justice, which is to say that the focus—in the form of a harsh spotlight—was very much on the institution, the source of such reductive labels and simplifications.

Not everyone in BW could shed such light from the perspective of a Villanueva or a Gilyard or a Lu, of course, but their works were preceded by a still more important precedent. In 1989, Mike Rose published *Lives on the Boundary*, an autobiographical account in which he describes how, through a mix-up in test scores and a suspect demographic profile (an Italian-American from South L.A.), he had been slotted into the dead-end voc-ed track in high school, escaping it largely by luck (the good sort countering the bad luck that landed him there in the first place). The perspective struck many as a revelation—crystallizing both the consequential complexities of getting stuck with the remedial label and the stark injustice of it.

Autobiography could do justice to both the complexities and the injustice. Writing from the perspective of a student but also describing the struggles and successes of the basic writers he worked with at UCLA, Rose had shown what students themselves could do. The personal narrative could become a powerful teaching tool. It had to be reconfigured a bit, made to focus on encounters with literacy and language. But those adjustments had their built-in justifications, and they brought an added advantage: the BW student, speaking from and about her situation, was acknowledging her situatedness. She was doing this not only for herself but also for her teacher, offering a bracing corrective to the tendency to underthink and overgeneralize where each student was coming from. Framing all this was a sense that education had been insufficiently democratic, its advantages as unevenly distributed as wealth. Just as theorists from I. A. Richards to Stanley Fish had inspired a sense of the complexity of discursive constructions, whether of texts read or texts written, another set of theorists helped to galvanize and direct the political dimension of the emergent teaching program. First and foremost among them were John Dewey and Paulo Freire, both emphasizing (albeit in different ways and from different contexts) the importance of experience-based democratic approaches.

This was not, of course, a sudden displacement of an earlier assimilationist agenda by a newly politicized pedagogy. Rose had long advocated a Deweyan vision. And Freire, in particular, had been building in influence throughout the 1980s, not only in the work of Patricia Bizzell (who recounted Freire's pervasive influence on her work in *Academic Discourse and Critical Consciousness*) and Ann Berthoff (who wrote the foreword to Freire's *Literacy: Reading the Word and the World*) but also in practice-centered work like *Freire for the Classroom: A Sourcebook for Liberatory Teaching*, edited by Ira Shor. In the 1990s, Freirean pedagogy came to the fore as a means of challenging ways of teaching that had begun to seem, for a new generation of teachers, too settled and accommodationist. A wonderful expression of this new resolve to let the students speak for themselves and begin to change their world is to be found in the preface to *An Unquiet Pedagogy: Transforming Practice in the English Classroom* (1991) by Eleanor Kutz and Hephzibah Roskelly. Just a page or two after the brief foreword by

Freire, Kutz and Roskelly explain that their book is "about how teachers can build on the language and knowledge and social experience that their students bring to their classrooms" as they give voice to the beliefs that animate their project:

> We recognize that connections between words and actions, between teaching and learning, are not apolitical. Although we may have avoided direct political statement in the book, the call for change is nonetheless clear. We believe that attitudes that cause cultural difference to be seen as deficiency must change. We believe institutional structures that assign—and consign—people to levels of ability based on prejudicial evaluation must be altered. Institutional change begins with individuals in conversation—learning from one another, mutually reinforcing, challenging, and reshaping thought and action. It's talk that nurtures change, talk that moves outside to change the listener or the classroom or the society and inside to change the mind. (xii)

There's more than a hint here of the delicate balance that must be struck: between advocating political change and propounding a political program, between having a sense of direction and being so directive as to seem preemptory. It was a challenge Freire himself saw as a political necessity, as he noted in his "Letter to North American Teachers":

> The teacher who is critical of the current power in society needs to lessen the distance between the speeches he or she makes to describe political options and what she/he does in the classroom. In other words, to realize alternatives or choices, in the day-to-day classroom, the progressive teacher attempts to build coherence and consistency as a virtue. It is contradictory to proclaim progressive politics and then to practice authoritarianism or opportunism in the classroom. A progressive position requires democratic practice where authority never becomes authoritarianism, and where authority is never so reduced that it

> disappears in a climate of irresponsibility and license.
> (Shor, *Freire* 212)

This idea that the writing classroom needs to be decentered (but not anarchic), revolving less and less around the teacher's authority, has its necessary complement; there must be ways of investing authority in the students, authorizing and valuing what they have to say. Increasingly in the 1990s, critical pedagogy was seen as a way of decentering authority in the classroom and democratizing education (see Shor, *Empowering*).

One way of enacting critical pedagogy in some classrooms relied on asking students to write literacy narratives. The use of personal narratives, even those that focused on literacy specifically, was hardly new, as instanced, for example, by Margaret Byrd Boegeman in "Lives and Literacy: Autobiography in Freshman Composition" (1980). What was new was making the students' literacy narratives do much of the work formerly done by the teacher—exploding stereotypes (as in Vincent Piro's "Renaming Ourselves" and Mary Soliday's "Translating the Self and Difference through Literacy Narratives"), exploring connections between orality and literacy (Akua Duku Anokye's "Oral Connections to Literacy: The Narrative"), acknowledging difficulty (Min-Zhan Lu's "From Silence to Words: Writing as Struggle"), even exploring and/or resisting connections to published writing (Stuart Greene's "Composing Oneself through the Narratives of Others" and J. Blake Scott's "The Literacy Narrative as Production Pedagogy"). Whatever purpose, precisely, the literacy narrative was asked to serve, it consistently had one ineluctable effect: focusing attention on individual difference.

Issues of identity and self (and the ways in which they are socially constructed) were coming to the fore in teaching even as the writing subject (as a theoretical as well as pedagogical concern) was highlighted in books like Susan Miller's *Rescuing the Subject: A Critical Introduction to Rhetoric and the Writer* (1989) and Lester Faigley's *Fragments of Rationality: Postmodernity and the Subject of Composition* (1994). It was almost as if a diversity within was confronting a diversity without, a fragmented self confronting a heterogeneous classroom or educational institution or society. The challenges, both for the BW student and the BW teacher, were formidable. Managing this diversity became the subject of pedagogical inquiries and narratives, with success stories (*The Discovery of Competence: Teaching and Learning with Diverse*

Student Writers [1993] by Eleanor Kutz, Suzy Q. Groden, and Vivian Zamel) as well as stories of struggle (*A Kind of Passport: A Basic Writing Adjunct Program and the Challenge of Student Diversity* [1993] by Anne DiPardo).

Literacy as a Social Practice

In her influential chair's address at the 2004 Conference on College Composition and Communication titled "Made Not Only in Words: Composition in a New Key," Kathleen Blake Yancey emphasized just how diverse the entire field of composition had become by the beginning of the twenty-first century. Writing was experiencing what she described as "a tectonic change" (298) as new technologies became widely available and widely used. Nearly all of this new writing, as Yancey pointed out, was self-sponsored, done willingly outside of school and without the intervention of teachers. Basic writers as well, once considered to be on the wrong side of "the digital divide," were participating in various types of digital composing from instant messaging and email to blogging and social networking. How have basic writing programs and instructors responded to these momentous changes? It's impossible to know just how many BW classrooms have been transformed. But the pages of the *Journal of Basic Writing* soon began to describe pedagogy that reflected changes that were happening outside the classroom.

In an article titled "Redefining Literacy as Social Practice" in the Fall 2006 issue of *JBW*, which celebrated the journal's twenty-fifth volume, Shannon Carter articulated a pedagogical approach that works against what Brian V. Street has termed the "autonomous model of literacy" on which standards testing is based. According to Street, an ideological model of literacy, in contrast to an autonomous model, "posits . . . that literacy is a social practice, not simply a technical and neutral skill; that it is always embedded in socially constructed epistemological principles" (Street 2, qtd. in Carter 97). In this article and in her book on the same subject (*The Way Literacy Lives: Rhetorical Dexterity and Basic Writing Instruction*), Carter documents an approach, developed for teaching basic writing at her home institution, Texas A&M University at Commerce. In a carefully sequenced series of assignments, basic writers are helped to develop "rhetorical dexterity" as they "read, understand, manipulate, and negotiate the cultural and linguistic codes of a new community of practice [academic discourse] based on a relatively accurate assessment of another, more familiar one" ("Redefining" 94) such as a specific workplace or recreational pursuit. Rather than equipping students with a set of easily transportable "literate strategies," this pedagogical approach, according to Carter, helps students to "redefine literacy for themselves in more productive ways" (119). As they work toward achieving rhetorical dexterity, students begin to develop a meta-awareness of how what they know about one discourse community in which they are highly competent can help them to achieve competence in a new academic discourse community.

Hannah Ashley, like Carter, emphasizes the multiple and shifting discourses that surround us. In "The Art of Queering Voices: A Fugue" (2007), Ashley writes: "Part of the work that we accomplish in our writing courses should focus on the general principle of discourse as unprincipled. An always unstable, contingent performance, reflecting and affecting relations of power" (8). Using the lenses of Bakhtinian and queer theory to highlight the importance of reported speech in academic writing, Ashley shows how writers can use these voices "in earnest, or queered: performing a voice in part, or out of context, or juxtaposed alongside other voices, in order to poke fun at it, pervert it, break down the reverence for it" (13). Her teaching goal, as expressed in this article and an earlier one, coauthored with Katy Lynn ("Ventriloquism"), is to help students see how these different voices interact with one another and gain more control in using them to achieve their own ends as writers—in other words, to work toward rhetorical dexterity.

Other articles published in the *Journal of Basic Writing* since 2000 explore ways of encouraging alternate discourses and rhetorical dexterity in basic writing classrooms. For example, in "Represent, Representin', Representation: The Efficacy of Hybrid Texts in the Writing Classroom," Donald McCrary draws upon his own recent teaching. In working with basic writers in Brooklyn, he assigns readings that include hybrid discourse using Black English or other languages. He then gives students the option of employing hybrid discourse in their own writing. His goal is "to awaken students to their multiple literacies, as they dismantle the barriers—linguistic, cultural, psychological—erected by standard English supremacy" (89).

Jeffrey Maxson ("'Government of da Peeps, for da Peeps, and by da Peeps': Revisiting the Contact Zone") asks students to understand language use by playing with it in assignments where they use parody and translation to rewrite passages of academic prose in less formal idioms. And Chris Leary ("'When We Remix . . . We Remake!!!': Reflections on Collaborative Ethnography, The New Digital Ethic, and Test Prep") describes a project in which he and his BW students read texts on composition theory and, working collaboratively, "remixed" these other writers' texts to "enter the conversations that those texts are a part of" (91). At the same time, since students were faced with the need to pass the ACT writing exam at the end of the course, they used playful techniques, sometimes involving remix, to prepare for the test. As Leary concludes: "In this environment, even test prep can be unmoored and resituated. Just as we do with texts, images, and materials, we can keep recontextualizing test prep until we like what it means and what it does" (102). Drawing creatively on new technology that is now widely available, teachers across the U.S. are incorporating digital technology and new media in their BW classrooms (see, for example, "Technologies for Transcending a Focus on Error: Blogs and Democratic Aspirations in First-Year Composition" by Cheryl C. Smith and "New Worlds of Errors and Expectations: Basic Writers and Digital Assumptions" by Marisa A. Klages and J. Elizabeth Clark).

The indisputable fact is that basic writing, as a pedagogical challenge, has never been more complex—or more exciting. While wrestling with the problems of social injustice and the complexities of social construction, it has all the old problems to deal with as well—error, assessment, tracking, and institutional marginalization. But it also has many opportunities afforded by new approaches and new technologies. The downside is that teachers and students may feel overwhelmed by all that is being asked of them. The conservatory function of lore and the inertia of institutions pretty much ensures that literacy narratives, liberatory pedagogy, and the recognition of multiple literacies and hybrid discourses will not supplant grammar instruction or externally imposed assessments but will instead be added to the instructional mix, often in the same program. Whether the teaching focus is on Shaughnessy's reading of error or Perl's attention to process, Lunsford's gauging of development or Bartholomae's acquisition of academic literacy, Ashley's emphasis on queering voices or Carter's call for rhetorical dexterity, the logical consequence of any of these approaches is to emphasize a pedagogical approach that is intensely individualized, unique for each student. If a difference has emerged in recent years, it is that the pull toward individualization has reached a kind of tipping point, one that threatens to undo the underlying rationale for basic writing: the notion that BW students need a special form or level of support. If these students are all so different, then what form would or could that special support take? And if they are all so unique, then what makes them different from (and thus necessitates their separation from) the "regular" or "mainstream" student?

Experiments in Mainstreaming

As originally conceived, mainstreaming was predicated on providing a special kind of support even as it merged students into the mainstream. For Mary Soliday and Barbara Gleason of CUNY's City College, this special support was "enrichment" meant to benefit mainstream students as well as those with BW placement. For Rhonda Grego and Nancy Thompson of the University of South Carolina, it was the provision of "studio" sections for weaker students running concurrently with regular writing classes. For Gregory Glau and the students of the "Stretch Program" at Arizona State University, support took the form of more time to complete the work of the regular English curriculum. In each instance, however, the students continued to be defined as special cases; "mainstreaming" wasn't meaningful unless it worked for students demonstrably outside the mainstream. In consequence, mainstreaming programs had the effect of reifying BW students and BW instruction even as they suggested that all students could and should be merged into the mainstream.

To some extent, the title Grego and Thompson gave to the article describing their project was all too apt. Experiments in mainstreaming were at least as much about "Repositioning Remediation" as eliminating it. This realization was confirmed in the titles of later articles about successful mainstreaming experiments at SUNY New Paltz ("Re-Modeling Basic Writing" by Rachel Rigolino and Penny Freel) and at the University of Tennessee at Martin ("It's Not Remedial: Re-envisioning Pre-First-Year College Writing" by Heidi Huse, Jenna Wright, Anna Clark, and Tim Hacker). But as John Paul Tassoni and Cynthia Lewiecki-Wilson point out in "Not Just Anywhere, Anywhen: Mapping Change through Studio Work," whenever remediation is "repositioned," it involves "incursion into an institutional landscape that . . . [is] not transparent, unclaimed, or uncontested. . . .

[T]hus remaking an institutional landscape involves issues of power and colonization" (68).

Yet seen from another angle, these "experiments" in mainstreaming were extremely important for the whole field of composition. For one thing, the mainstreaming experiments recognized that in approaches to academic literacy not only the students but also the institution would have to adapt. And, as the term "mainstreaming" signified, the students could be made to feel a part of the institution, if only provisionally and by grace of special support. Whether BW students had been so thoroughly segregated as to justify Shor's use of the term "apartheid," there is no question that their placement in special BW courses and programs had separated them from the flow of college life. But in mainstreaming experiments, the idea that such students were not yet ready to engage in college instruction was held in abeyance if not eliminated entirely.

The Fragmentation of the Teaching Enterprise

Mary Soliday devoted the fourth of five chapters in her important book *The Politics of Remediation* ("Representing Remediation: The Politics of Agency, 1985–2000") to the causes and consequences of the move against remedial programs and remedial students in the late 1990s. Tracing much of the impetus for these attacks on remediation to significant cutbacks in state and federal funding for public higher education in the 1980s and to (often related) increases in tuition, Soliday notes that coping with such losses of revenue meant shifting "the burden to students, so that a substantial part of the costs for higher education was privatized" (114). Though another means of coping was to "downsize or abolish remediation and equal opportunity programs" (115), this shifting of costs to the students was also highly significant since not all students could bear that shifted burden. At baccalaureate-granting colleges and universities, percentages of students from wealthier families increased, while those from poorer families decreased. Consequently, both remedial programs and students likely to be placed in them shifted downward to community colleges. Soliday has a one-word term for the result—stratification:

> Stratification is the strategic management tool that institutions use to respond to crises in growth. Strategies include privatizing the costs of education, tightening admissions, and downsizing selected

> tiers. Remediation's shifting attachment to various segments plays one powerful role in this complex process. The downward movement of remedial education reflects a parallel movement of students by class, ethnic, and racial background. (115)

The movement of basic writing out of four-year schools and into community colleges is a trend that has intensified in recent years (see Lavin and Hyllegard, Greene and McAlexander). One consequence of this downward movement is to make it less likely that those still teaching "remedial writing" have access to the research or even the "lore" that could support such teaching. In a paper originally given at the Conference on Replacing Remediation in Higher Education (held at Stanford University in 1998), then revised and published in web-accessible form in 2000, W. Norton Grubb notes that "educators in two- and four-year colleges have virtually no contact with one another; even though there are journals and associations to which the two groups might contribute, like *College Composition and Communication*, in practice these are dominated by four-year colleges" (5). Relegating basic writing instruction to community colleges exacerbates the problems that have always affected it; community colleges tend to have higher faculty workloads, less demand for and reliance on scholarship, and more part-time instructors—all things that mean less recourse to the knowledge base about BW teaching methods and programs. Noting as much, Grubb does not say that "skills-oriented remediation" necessarily dominates, but he does say that "the appearance of more student- and meaning-centered teaching seems random and idiosyncratic, because the odyssey . . . is usually one that instructors make on their own, through trial and error, with at best a little help from their friends. In most community colleges, there are few institutional resources to help instructors make this transition . . ." (11).

At the beginning of the twenty-first century, teaching basic writing seems more context-bound and more various than ever before. As Laura Gray-Rosendale wrote in 2006, "During the last seven years the notion of the basic writer's identity as in situ—or context dependent—has emerged more fully than I ever could have anticipated" (9). Latter-day BW instruction is not one thing but many and serves different student constituencies. Depending on where a BW program is located, it may be primarily for African-Americans (as in Keith Gilyard and Elaine Richardson's "Students' Right to Possibility: Basic Writing and

African American Rhetoric" [2001]) or for Latinos (as in Raul Ybarra's "Cultural Dissonance in Basic Writing Courses" [2001]) or for Native Americans (as in Laura Gray-Rosendale, Loyola K. Bird, and Judith F. Bullock's "Rethinking the Basic Writing Frontier: Native American Students' Challenge to Our Histories" [2003]), primarily a construction of class (as in Carolyn Boiarsky's "Working Class Students in the Academy" [2003]) or largely an urban phenomenon (as in Patrick Bruch's "Moving to the City: Redefining Literacy in the Post-Civil Rights Era" [2003]). It may also involve an institutional adjustment (as in Mark McBeth's "Arrested Development: Revising Remediation at John Jay College of Criminal Justice" [2006]). On the other hand, the diversity of the BW student population and the dispersal of instructional sites can loom as a teaching challenge pervading the curriculum (as in Stephen Fishman and Lucille McCarthy's *Whose Goals, Whose Aspirations? Learning to Teach Underprepared Writers Across the Curriculum* [2002] or Vivian Zamel and Ruth Spack's "Teaching Multicultural Learners: Beyond the ESOL Classroom and Back Again" [2006]).

Issues of basic writing's definition, of teaching methods and approaches, have never seemed more complicated, never less susceptible to the direction and definition of BW teachers. Legislative mandates and admission restrictions seem to have taken over decisions about who BW students are (or even whether such students exist). Yet such radical redefinitions of circumstance, like those that led to the beginning of open admissions and basic writing, are also opportunities for rethinking and innovation. Mainstreaming is an excellent example of this kind of productive redefinition. Rhonda Grego and Nancy Thompson devised their "studio" approach in response to the decision of South Carolina's Commission on Higher Education to discontinue credit for basic writing. Redefining both assessment and instruction, Grego and Thompson responded by creating special support for students who might find regular composition tough going without it. The small-group approach they developed was, for them, an improvement on the institutionally subverted status quo for BW students and not just a substitute for it. Those small groups provided students with mutual support while they worked on actual college-level assignments rather than simply preparing for some future time when they might be called on to do such work. Grego and Thompson's project has served as a model for what basic writing can become in the crucible of the new pressures on the field and its students: an opportunity for rethinking and restructuring, an application of new methods and alternative pedagogies (for descriptions of other innovative models, see Tassoni and Lewiecki-Wilson, Huse et al., Rigolino and Freel, Glau, "*Stretch at 10*," and Adams et al.).

That challenges to the existence of basic writing can also be opportunities is what Deborah Mutnick concludes in her overview of basic writing pedagogy ("On the Academic Margins" [2001]), but she stresses that such opportunities are not easily seized. Redefining BW pedagogy in effective ways requires the kind of knowledge making and sharing that the straitened situations of BW teachers militate against. It means making sound, informed decisions when in a position to make them, and it necessarily means scrambling for the leverage to make decisions at all. The onus, writes Mutnick, is

> to know the history of remedial instruction if we are to deal with the larger implications of current trends in higher education, not only the elimination of remedial courses but also attacks on affirmative action and other equal opportunity programs designed to give masses of people access to higher education. We will need to understand linguistic theories of error, the relationship between language and meaning, and approaches to teaching and learning in diverse cultural contexts. And we will need to continue to research literacy acquisition and the writing process of adult writers, a project that, as numerous scholars have suggested, illuminates the complexities of written language for us all. But we will also, I believe, have to become more savvy, more politically astute and active, if we are to be the ones to decide which courses best serve the students we teach. (198)

That's a tall order, and a big "if." But it certainly underscores the way research needs to inform teaching, which is the subject of the next chapter.

4 Research

Research on basic writing is in short supply. Chronic marginalization of BW faculty is the chief cause of the dearth of scholarship. Michael Bérubé (with specific reference to his experience as a placement director in English) has referred to the reliance on part-timers as the "adjunctification" of academic labor (355). No branch of academia has been more adjunctified than composition, no subset of that more adjunctified than BW. Marc Bousquet has noted that the reliance on adjunct labor means even those with full-time positions in writing, precisely those who would be expected to carry the research forward, "will frequently expect to serve the managed university as management" (232). Those in the field who aren't scrambling for sections to teach are usually scrambling for (or tending to) staff, with the consequence that no one has much time for research and writing. Even Mina Shaughnessy had to get out from under administering her writing program at City College to find the time to write *Errors and Expectations*. Like Shaughnessy, who became a university dean, many in basic writing find success means moving up and out, leaving BW behind.

The other great challenge for the field, particularly for its undersized research arm, has been what to focus on. The burning need for BW instruction is to "fix" things. With this urgency investing BW research, there could be no disinterested way of establishing priorities; the need was to focus on problems that could be solved—or at least grappled with. Ultimately, it did not matter that the larger world seemed the locus of the most important causes and effects of the conditions for students and teachers. Ever aware of the societal implications of the work she undertook, Mina Shaughnessy felt "the 'new' remedial English" that she termed basic writing could be dated from the mid-1960s acknowledgment of the "cultural deprivation" of the population it served ("Basic Writing" 178). She concluded *Errors and Expectations*, published in 1977, with the hope for "reforms which over the next decade may close the shocking gaps in training between the poor and the affluent, the minority and the majority" (291).

In her diagnosis of why "academically ill-prepared young adults" have difficulty with writing, she stressed that three explanations are needed: "One explanation focuses on what the student has not internalized in the way of *language patterns* characteristic of written English [in other words, error], another on his unfamiliarity with the *composing process* and another on his *attitude* toward himself within an academic setting" (72–73). Much of the research conducted over the next thirty years dealt with these three broad concerns. But they are all directly related to a fourth. In basic writing, as in real estate, what *really* matters is location, location, location. As David Bartholomae said, "We know who basic writers are . . . because they are the students in classes we label 'Basic Writing' ("Writing on the Margins" 67). Everything turns on BW placement or, more especially, the assessment that determines it. In this chapter, then, we focus on research in basic writing through the lenses of these four critical categories: *error, assessment, process,* and *attitudes and identities.*

Error

Following Shaughnessy's lead, the first research challenge taken up by the field was that of error in student writing. Error as a research topic circumscribes (without specifying) a vast territory of causes and concerns and questions. Why do errors occur? Which ones really matter? What's to be done about them? What are errors anyway? Are there, if not immutable standards, at least strong and wide points of agreement about errors? Attempting to answer such questions initially directed the attention of BW researchers to the many varieties of linguistics.

Insights from Linguistics

In *Errors and Expectations*, Shaughnessy suggested readings from theoretical linguistics (Jespersen, John Lyons), applied linguistics, and sociolinguistics (Labov, Wolfram). "Basic Writing," her bibliographic essay in *Teaching Composition*, included even the (then) new Chomskyan linguistics. Readings in linguistics were needed to understand where the problem lay as traditional prescriptive grammars had been discredited as a pedagogic failure. *Research in Written Composition* (Braddock, Lloyd-Jones, and Schoer) had long ago warned, "The teaching of formal grammar has a negligible or, because it usually displaces some instruction and practice in actual composition, even a harmful effect on the improvement of writing" (37–38).

Inflecting instruction in America from the time of Puritan hornbooks, prescriptive grammar still had many adherents among instructors, but researchers knew they had to look to something more modern and presumably more productive. There was plenty to look to. Structural grammar, represented in Shaughnessy's suggested readings by Charles Fries's *The Structure of English* (1952), was one point of reference and research, but it was really purely descriptive, and basic writing was too hungry for applications and solutions to pursue this approach to any important degree. A qualified exception would be tagmemics in the form offered by Kenneth Pike's *Language in Relation to a Unified Theory of the Structure of Human Behavior* (1954; 1967). Pike, who had also authored "A Linguistic Contribution to Composition" (1964), had always had designs on writing instruction, especially in the work he coauthored with Richard Young and Alton Becker, *Rhetoric: Discovery and Change* (1970). But tagmemics, with its reference to particle, wave, and field perspectives (epistemological/observer functions) and contrastive, variable, and distributive features (ontological functions), has a daunting vocabulary, leading Ronald Lunsford to a conclusion in 1990: "While tagmemic grammars have been rather fertile ground for rhetoricians in the last twenty-five years, the one consistent complaint against applications based on tagmemics is that they require a good deal of sophistication with language. Thus, tagmemics has not led to applications for basic writers" ("Modern Grammar and Basic Writers" 81).

A similar fate awaited BW research on transformational grammar. Noam Chomsky's *Syntactic Structures* (1957) created an alternative to structural grammar, one that was not purely descriptive but, by definition, generative. The problem was that transformational or generative grammar was focused on explaining language behaviors, not on changing them. Studying transformational grammar would, by Chomsky's own principles, have scarcely more effect on language use than study of the digestive process would have on digestion. The one real contribution transformational grammar had to make to instruction was based on Chomsky's idea of linguistic competence—the language user's ability to form grammatical structures in consistent and systematic ways despite the user's inability to articulate them. As

Donald Freeman showed in "Linguistics and Error Analysis" (1979), this notion applies even and especially to language uses labeled "ungrammatical" (in terms of prescriptive grammars). Their internal consistency—what Shaughnessy called (and was originally going to title her book) "the logic of error"—is attributable to linguistic competence. Errors of this internally consistent kind (for example, errors due to dialect difference) are actually proof of competence, not incompetence.

Error Analysis

While it is useful to the teacher, research in linguistics only provides a starting point, not a method. But the other half of Freeman's title, "Error Analysis," would provide richer ground. Error analysis began with work in English as a Second Language (ESL). The representative and seminal text is *Error Analysis: Perspectives on Second Language Acquisition* (1974), edited by Jack C. Richards. From the standpoint of error analysis, errors are signs of learning. They may be due to first-language interference, but they are at least as likely to appear as intermediate stages in language acquisition called "interlanguage," a point stressed by S. Pit Corder in "Error Analysis, Interlanguage, and Second Language Acquisition" (1975).

Whether they stem from such transitional accommodations or the deep structures of transformational grammar, errors proceed more from knowledge than ignorance. That was the critical realization: errors occur as applications of language systems learned, not from the absence of language learning. And the clash of different language systems, generating transferences from one system to another or hybrid approximations, must imbue errors, rightly understood, with an explicability—what Shaughnessy would call the logic of errors. This logic is also a trajectory, since language learning is very much a process rather than a static state.

Clearly, error analysis had important applications for work with error in basic writing. BW researchers came to see that students, in attempting standard English and academic discourse, were going through something very like second-language acquisition. This was the point emphasized in many of the 129 items in the annotated bibliography accompanying the NCTE's 1974 position statement "Students' Right to Their Own Language." Students whose oral competence outstripped but also interfered with their written competence, students whose home dialects were effectively different mother tongues than the standardized one they needed to master—these students were very much language learners, and their errors were ripe for the sort of analysis ESL teachers had given to *their* students.

Shaughnessy had recognized this kinship in the Introduction to *Errors and Expectations*, where she referred to early BW students as "strangers in academia" who spoke "other languages or dialects at home and never successfully reconciled the worlds of home and school" (3). More than a plea for sympathy, this is a description of BW students as much more like ESL students than like native students at an earlier or lower level of instruction. The appreciation of how maturity is combined with limited proficiency, of how the attempt to acquire discourse and assimilate to a culture is combined with a profound sense of not belonging (or belonging elsewhere), is a constant in Shaughnessy's description of the BW student.

Most of the pieces in the initial, error-themed issue of the *Journal of Basic Writing* (1975) could be called instances of error analysis, most notably Barbara Quint Gray's "Dialect Interference in Writing: A Tripartite Analysis," Patricia Laurence's "Error's Endless Train: Why Students Don't Perceive Errors," Nancy Lay's "Chinese Language Interference in Written English," and Betty Rizzo and Santiago Villafane's "Spanish Influence on Written English." Of course, it was Shaughnessy herself who best represented such methods.

In "Error-Analysis and the Teaching of Composition," Barry Kroll and John Schafer invoked a range of sources, especially those that supported the viewing of errors "in much the same way that Freud regarded slips of the tongue or that Kenneth Goodman views 'miscues' in reading[,] as clues to inner processes, as windows into the mind" (209). In addition to Goodman's *Miscue Analysis: Applications to Reading Instruction* (1973), these sources included M. A. K. Halliday and Ruqaiya Hasan's *Cohesion in English* (1976), which saw cohesion not as a grammatical but a semantic phenomenon reliant on contextual as well as textual features. What mattered, even and especially with errors, was not only what was happening on the page but also in the writer's mind and, indeed, in the writer's world.

This interest in the whys and wherefores for error led to further milestones in error analysis research, notably David Bartholomae's "The Study of Error" and Glynda Hull's "Acts of Wonderment," both of which placed special emphasis on "talk-aloud" protocols, allowing students to reveal their thoughts as they made errors or met with them in rereading their writing. Such work provided an enriched understanding of errors and their origins. What it did not offer was an ability to generalize about much more than the complexity of the processes, psychological and social, that gave rise to errors. Rather than providing a simple guideline of what needed to be taught, error analysis offered strikingly labor-intensive procedures of individualized instruction that had no place for prefabricated exercises or recycled lessons. It was a tough trade-off.

Upholding the Standard

Given the labor-intensive nature of error analysis, it is not surprising that not all BW researchers agreed that it was a productive direction to take. From the first, some held that grammar instruction had more potential than emergent research suggested. In the inaugural issue of *JBW* devoted to error, Sarah D'Eloia advocated "Teaching Standard Written English" (1975) and, in a later issue, elaborated on her methods in "The Uses—and Limits—of Grammar" (1977). An extended battery of grammar exercises made it clear that she was more focused on the uses than the limits. In 1985, even as Patrick Hartwell published his argument against the teaching of formal grammar ("Grammar, Grammars, and the Teaching of Grammar"), Mary Epes, in "Tracing Errors to Their Sources: A Study of the Encoding Processes of Adult Basic Writers," was concluding that "direct instruction in the grammar of standard written English is essential for nonstandard dialect speakers" (31). An extreme variant on this view was "IQ and Standard English" (1983), in which Thomas Farrell argued that "the mean IQ scores of black ghetto students will go up when they learn to speak and write Standard English" (481). Holding an opposite position but still noting the connection between standard dialect and standard assessment in "Doublespeak: Dialectology in the Service of Big Brother" (1972), James Sledd held that teaching standard English, even as a second dialect, was part of a white supremacist program, something underscored by the title of his earlier article: "Bi-Dialecticalism: The Language of White Supremacy" (1969).

The collective effect of such work was to project a profound lack of consensus among researchers about the attainable or acceptable goals of instruction that focused on errors. Grammar instruction might or might not work to standardize students' language, which might or might not be a good idea. Frankly, the right goal was really less in question than the ability to reach it. Arguments like Sledd's and Farrell's would certainly have achieved more attention if there had been a strong sense that standardization of students' language was something that could be accomplished effectively, even with great effort. But the work on error that seemed most persuasive seemed to suggest that students' language habits were difficult to uncover, much less change. Discerning patterns of error and means of correction seemed to be so labor-intensive and student-specific as to be beyond the capacities of teachers with dozens of students and little class time.

Changing Attitudes toward Error

The potential efficacy that research on error might hold for teaching, and especially for ways teachers might address error, was further undercut by the pursuit of still larger questions. As Glynda Hull wrote in "Research on Error and Correction" (1985), "Attitudes toward error in writing are now changing, and they are changing, in part, because we have come to value things other than sentence-level correctness in the writing of our students" (163). The field needed to address matters of process (processes of writing and of thought), for instance, and questions raised about levels and types of literacy were particularly vexing. In 1979, Harvey Graff had gone so far as to say that the idea that there was a stable and singular thing we could call "literacy" was in fact a "literacy myth" (the title he gave his book): "We do not know precisely what we mean by literacy or what we expect individuals to achieve from their instruction in and possession of literacy. . . . We continue to apply standards of literacy that—owing to our uncertainties—are inappropriate and contradictory . . ." (323). And James C. Raymond, in his introduction to *Literacy as a Human Problem* (1982), urged that "we must be more cautious and less doctrinaire in our deliberations about literacy and its human consequences" (x). Here, too, consensus was lacking, but the message was clear on one major point: it was easy to make missteps by treading too confidently. Change was the one sure thing. Who could say what kinds and levels of literacy would be critical in the age of mass media and the thawing of a homogeneous, hegemonic notion of discourse, especially academic discourse?

Oddly, one major error study, Robert Connors and Andrea Lunsford's "Frequency of Formal Errors in Current College Writing, or Ma and Pa Kettle Do Research" (1988), suggested that such big questions didn't seem to matter much in composition classrooms, a conclusion that may, in effect, have helped to quell research on error. The subtitle presumably was to give a lighthearted air to their work, but the article reported on a massive study, undertaken to provide a scholarly basis for the treatment of error in the handbook they were coauthoring. Working from a stratified sampling of 20,000 college papers, Connors and Lunsford culled 3,000 and noted how instructors responded (or failed to respond) to a variety of errors. They discounted all but the 20 most frequent types, with the consequence that errors that were especially frequent and/or easy to mark loomed large in the study, regardless of their seriousness. In one sense, the upshot of the study was to suggest how little error research, at least of the purely quantified kind, had to tell instructors. Connors and Lunsford were frank about what the study could not determine; it said nothing about the relative seriousness of errors or even why those marked were marked. It could also say nothing about why they occurred. And, when the most frequent error turned out to be the absence of a comma after an introductory element—something many instructors might not even call an error—it seemed that error frequency, however much it might inform a handbook, could do little to inform instruction.

Some solace was found in the discovery that, though errors had changed over the years (Connors and Lunsford admitted they had no idea what errors some decades-old names for them might designate), error frequency had not. Gauging their findings (reported in 1988) against studies from the 1930s, Connors and Lunsford found that the frequency of errors remained remarkably constant; taking into account the mania for TV watching, video games, and other things that could most kindly be called extratextual literacies, they concluded, "In this case, not losing means we're winning" (406). A follow-up study modeled on the one reported in 1988 (conducted by Andrea Lunsford and Karen Lunsford and reported in 2008) confirms a remarkable consistency in the frequency of error in student writing over time: 2.26 in the 1986 sample and 2.45 in the 2006 sample. Even looking back at a study conducted in 1917, the frequency of error has remained essentially unchanged.

Error Recognition

If error frequency seemed stable, it was an illusory stability. The volatility it masked was another focus of research on error: error recognition. This instability was in fact a subtext of both the Connors and

Lunsford study reported in 1988 and the Lunsford and Lunsford study reported in 2008; what constituted an error changed over time (to such an extent that once-significant errors had become ciphers to present-day researchers), and errors in college papers turned out to be unmarked and unnoted more often than not. For instance, 15 of the 20 errors in the 1988 report were problems with commas, and the frequency with which they were marked ranged from 54% (comma splices) to 4% (missing commas in a series).

Like other quantifications, this does not begin to get at the variation among individuals, but other studies already had addressed this issue. In May 1981, *College Composition and Communication* had published a special issue on "Language Studies and Composing" with two especially important articles. Sidney Greenbaum and John Taylor found great variation in what composition instructors thought needed correction and what to do about it ("The Recognition of Usage Errors by Instructors of Freshman Composition"). Still more sweepingly, Joseph Williams's "The Phenomenology of Error" discussed the variability in how errors in various contexts are noted, defined, and judged, emphasizing his point by salting his text with errors, most *not* noted by the readership. When it comes to spotting errors, Williams demonstrated, we see what we expect to see, and we don't expect errors in scholarly publications.

At the other end of the decade, Susan Wall and Glynda Hull conducted a study of fifty-five English teachers, showing they did not share common conceptions and definitions of error ("The Semantics of Error: What Do Teachers Know?" [1989]). This lack of common ground was a problem Hull had struggled with in an earlier (1987) essay, "Constructing Taxonomies for Error (or Can Stray Dogs Be Mermaids?)." There she noted a variation not only in error recognition but also in whole taxonomies and categories of error. She had proposed a system based on the editing process, acknowledging that error recognition rests in the eye of the beholder.

Ultimately, the problem with error recognition could not be solved even with the most powerful and widely accepted taxonomy of error. As error analysis had demonstrated, understanding an error meant understanding not only the surface feature that seemed in error but also the process of thought and intention that gave rise to it. Hull had driven home the point in "Research on Error and Correction": "If the errors we count and tabulate have no reality besides the interpretation we give them, if, that is, our counts can't inform instruction (or can inform it only wrongly) because the errors we see don't represent the errors the students actually make, then tabulation research has limits we haven't yet considered" (170). Lest it be thought this shows the limits only of error frequency studies or error taxonomies, Hull recalls that changing attitudes toward error and controversies about the utility of teaching grammar or taking a "bidialectical" approach to instruction mean the pedagogical implications of error research are very much in question. That would remain true even if we settled the controversies about appropriate error categories and "readings" of error: "Once we have a taxonomy that satisfies, however, and once we have tabulated the frequency of errors in students' writing across grades, we still do not know how such information should inform pedagogies and curricula" (170).

A dilemma, to be sure—but Hull would call it "the dilemma that still counts": "We can choose to make it count less by continued scholarship on the processes of mind that govern error commission and correction" ("Research" 181). Drawing the title for their 1998 article "'The Dilemma That Still Counts': Basic Writing at a Political Crossroads" from Hull, Susanmarie Harrington and Linda Adler-Kassner wrote, "Despite Hull's conclusion, which outlined a broad research agenda, the study of error has not advanced much in succeeding years" (19). They even suggested that research like Hull's and that which she reviewed—research showing how unstable error taxonomies were, how little consensus there was on what constituted error, and how little error frequency studies could be expected to inform instruction—was responsible for dampening interest in further work on error. In a sense, Hull would have agreed with this assessment. Her overview of the research on error more than a decade earlier had concluded by saying that the real focus should be not on error, per se, but on issues of assessment and instruction:

> For many students, becoming an insider (like becoming "literate") will have, should have, little to do with learning to be correct; for them error is a minor matter. For other students, becoming an insider will, for a time, have everything to do with learning to edit; for them, error is a dilemma. The research that will aid the second group will pay respectful attention to a student's position as an outsider and will search for ways

> to ease his or her entry into the academic setting, even to make such a movement possible. It is such research that will, I expect, drive studies of error and editing for the next several years. ("Research" 184)

The real issues, Hull suggested, were matters of initiation and assimilation, respect and understanding and support. Errors themselves were symptoms and signs of much larger issues having to do with advantages (or the lack thereof), social placement (and not just writing placement), and kinds of public regard and civic enclosure. What had begun as a seemingly simple matter—looking into why students made mistakes—had led to vastly complex sets of questions about social identity and access. The gaze had turned from students' mechanical errors to the institutional mechanisms that noted them and made them matter. In research as well as in practice, academic structures would be called into question, above all, the structuring of basic writing. Though considerable attention would be given to the students, the harshest scrutiny would fall on the systems that defined them as outsiders—first and foremost systems of assessment.

Assessment

As attention to error waned, attention to assessment waxed, ultimately building to a kind of hue and cry in the 1990s. But assessment was always an especially problematic research problem, and the 1970s is the place to start to understand why. Part of the problem from the first seemed to be the lack of a solid research base. In 1978, the *Journal of Basic Writing* devoted an entire issue to evaluation. It concluded with a selected and annotated bibliography by Richard Larson, who found quite a bit of advice on responding to student writing but only two works worth including that bore on "decisions made about where to place student papers, and students, on scales that permit assigning the student to a particular class" (92). These were Paul Diederich's *Measuring Growth in English* and Richard Braddock's "Evaluation of Writing Tests." Larson reminded readers of what was at stake, saying that he hoped his bibliography would help teachers and "may fortify them against capricious efforts to adopt judgmental techniques that have not themselves been fully investigated and evaluated" (93). It was the fitting endpiece to a collection that was bracing in its frankness about what was lacking in the knowledge of assessments and the application of that knowledge.

The first two pieces in the issue set the tone. Rexford Brown, the director of publications for the National Assessment of Educational Progress, held that the tests in use were clearly inadequate and uninformative: "Like holistic essay scoring, multiple choice testing of writing is seldom diagnostic in any useful way" (3). Brown did hold out hope of improvement (even if it had a "nowhere to go but up" flavor), but Joseph Williams took a bleaker view. Ascribing a general "inability to find simple and reliable measures" to "some questions that I don't think we have attended to as carefully as we might have," he quickly added, "I wish I could say that I think the questions will help simplify this matter of evaluation, but in fact their answers, such as they are, seem to complicate it" ("Re-Evaluating" 8). Ultimately, according to Williams, the real issue is not even the ability to devise a viable system of assessment. It's who is doing the assessing. He tried to imagine a system that would be consistent, reliable, and objective—one that would "rationalize and defend admissions procedures," even result in "the adoption of better teaching methods":

> But it is not at all clear that such a system would be more than a self-justifying instrument that had taken its values and hence its measures from those who have not demonstrated any special competence in distinguishing competent writing in any world except their—our—own. That is a harsh charge to make against a whole profession and by no means includes every member in it. But I think it is essentially true. (8)

To a remarkable extent, Williams effectively articulated the problems that would, over the next decades, damage and defeat assessment programs that fed and shaped basic writing. For all their attention to matters of validity and reliability, all that was needed to render them invalid was a shift in political climate, one that raised the "right to judge" issue. Then these vast, carefully calibrated assessments would come to seem narrow gates made by the narrow-minded, determined to preserve their positions of privilege.

Foundational Work in Mass Testing

Though such suspicions were always in the air, not least of all in the 1970s, there was, at that time, a much greater, more pervasive sense of urgency about all the work to be done—and with it the hope that this work would vanquish the problems besetting the workers in the field. Looked at from another perspective, the problem raised by Williams was a kind of opportunity; English professors were invited to determine the values and measures that would distinguish writing competence. No one seized the opportunity like Edward M. White, Director of the English Equivalency Examination and Coordinator of English Testing Programs for California State Universities and Colleges (CSUC). White was the architect of the largest assessment program to date, and his contribution to the 1978 "Evaluation" issue of *JBW*, "Mass Testing of Individual Writing: The California Model," laid the groundwork for much organized assessment thereafter. The CSUC English Equivalency Examination, as its name would suggest, was originally designed to determine which students could skip college instruction, earning credit in composition simply by scoring high enough on the equivalency exam. But the scales were also designed to register, in addition to proficiency, minimal competency (and even performances below that). A happy marriage of carefully designed prompts that students could choose from and normative scales of performance that readers could refer to and apply holistically, the CSUC Equivalency Examination made evaluation, not least of all the "mass testing" of White's title, seem sufficiently fair and doable.

White's own work on assessment was invaluable in California and beyond. He was an indefatigable writer and researcher, with a special gift for practical synthesis, and he was there with a ready answer to the burning question. As Richard Lloyd-Jones emphatically put it in his bibliographic essay "Tests of Writing Ability" (1987), "The question is not whether to test but what kind to use" (159). Lloyd-Jones was no less emphatic about where to look for the answer; he said of White's *Teaching and Assessing Writing* (1985), "For most readers his book makes earlier works unnecessary except for historical reasons . . ." (160).

A variant on the CSUC English Equivalency Examination with its choice of prompts and six-point holistic scale was the CUNY Writing Assessment Test, and the CUNY Instructional Resource Center (IRC) would publish a series of monographs on testing (see chapter 3 for a more detailed account of this work). Some of the researchers from the IRC (notably Karen Greenberg, Harvey Wiener, and Virginia Slaughter) would create the National Testing Network in Writing (NTNW) to disseminate research and best practices. The Network's first two conferences, in 1983 and 1984, resulted in an important collection, *Writing Assessment: Issues and Strategies* (Greenberg, Wiener, and Donovan).

Assessment had clearly given rise to a rich discussion, but its main points were fairly clear and straightforward; the way to assess writing was through actual writing samples, scored holistically (hence White's 1984 manifesto "Holisticism"). The foe was what Rexford Brown had identified as the inexpensive but suspect way: multiple-choice, machine-scored tests that are "cheaper and easier to score" but have "glaring weaknesses" ("What We Know" 3). By the mid-1980s, the need to base assessment on actual student writing had become a kind of orthodoxy. As expressed in the preface to *Writing Assessment: Issues and Strategies*, "Multiple-choice tests cannot measure the skills that most writing teachers identify as the domain of composition: inventing, revising, and editing ideas to fit purpose and audience within the context of suitable linguistic, syntactic, and grammatical forms" (xiv).

In 1987, Lloyd-Jones could say that holistically scored testing was "now the system most used for mass testing" (165). A part that might stand for the whole is the story Harvey Wiener recounts in "Evaluating Assessment Programs in Basic Skills" (1989). In 1983, he and other CUNY colleagues had conducted a national survey of assessment in 1,200 institutions of higher education, discovering that 97% of them did assess entering students. But a subsequent survey done under the auspices of the National Testing Network in Writing showed that, beyond that basic reality, generalizations were difficult to come by. A variety of assessments, many of them homegrown, were used with little regard for reliability or validity. In consequence, Wiener and his colleagues created the College Assessment Evaluation Program to facilitate effective assessment design and evaluation. Without declaring the problem solved, Wiener's story was a clear account of progress toward clearly seen goals.

Disillusionment with Holistic Assessment

For some time, however, the clarity about assessment had been illusory, persisting for so long because of enormous intellectual and institutional investment. The real research basis for holistic writing assessment, largely unexamined and simply adopted, stretched back decades. Even before Paul Diederich published the 1974 manual, *Measuring Growth in English*, he had done research on assessment for the College Entrance Examination Board, work distilled in a 1961 research bulletin coauthored with John French and Sydell Carlton, *Factors in Judgments of Writing Ability*. It was this work that led Martin Nystrand, Stuart Greene, and Jeffrey Wiemelt to declare Diederich "the father of holistic essay evaluation" and to say his real coup was to decide to give all factors, from spelling to ideas, equal weight:

> This proposal was in effect a psychometric fiat; no validity studies were undertaken to determine appropriate weights. In 1961, then, Diederich could plausibly argue—and in so doing shape an entire generation of writing assessment—that writing could be effectively, reliably assessed by reading one sample on one topic in one genre per writer if—*mirabile dictu*—readers could only be made to agree. (276)

This is not the indictment of arbitrary judgment it might seem; on the contrary, Nystrand and his coauthors, in their "intellectual history" of composition, are stressing what the climate of the times could support—and very nearly dictate. Their point is that the same formalism that gave rise to New Criticism in literary studies supported this insistence on the stable, univocal text in assessment. Like New Criticism, assessment needed to insist on careful reading—without interference by interpretive questioning, worries about authorial intention, and contextual considerations. But this attempt to approach objectivity and stability in assessment was in fact the highly unstable product of its time. Literary studies, pushed by the need to find "original" readings of texts, broke from formalistic approaches much earlier. Assessment, whose twin lighthouses were reliability and validity, took longer to unravel its belief in the univocal text. But it really only took a few voices saying, so others could hear, that the emperor had no clothes.

One such voice came from Pat Belanoff, who labeled all the past certainties "The Myths of Assessment" in a 1991 *JBW* article by that name. According to Belanoff, assessment lacked a clear purpose and focus as well as a clear consensus and basis. Here's how she put the "four myths":

1. We know what we're testing for
2. We know what we're testing

3. Once we've agreed on criteria, we can agree on whether individual papers meet those criteria
4. And the strongest myth of all, that it's possible to have an absolute standard and apply it uniformly (55)

Pointedly recast, these were in fact the fundamental premises under which the great assessment enterprise had been operating.

Belanoff was not articulating a sudden and general change of heart (or mind), of course. This was also not a matter of postmodernism finally knocking on BW's door. There had been some rethinking even and especially within the assessment community. By coincidence, the lead piece for the same issue of *JBW* was the published version of the keynote for the 1989 National Testing Network in Writing conference. The speaker/author was Rexford Brown, the erstwhile director of publications for the National Assessment of Educational Progress who had led off the evaluation-themed issue of *JBW* in 1978. Now the director of communications for the Education Commission of the States, Brown had a different (though by no means uncritical) take on assessment. Perhaps thinking of the landscape he had surveyed over a decade earlier, he saw much accomplished: "You certainly see more and more people using writing samples, whether they score them holistically or analytically or through primary trait or error analysis" (11). But for Brown the use of writing samples was no longer the assessment grail. The big challenge, as he saw it now, was how to teach and test for something much more elusive than formal traits, something he was calling "thoughtfulness," which would become better known as critical thinking ("Schooling and Thoughtfulness" 3–15).

The changing views on assessment reflected more than just a change in the intellectual climate. The job of assessment research in the 1970s and 1980s had been to address an urgent need, to tell BW instructors and programs how to sort and place students. If anything, the job had been done too well. The burning need had been answered with what was feeling more and more like a calcifying imposition. Teachers for too long had felt that assessments were imposed on them, circumventing their own judgments (particularly when those assessments governed exit as well as placement). The blame could be (and was) placed on specific assessments, but in another sense no assessment could be good enough. The research question closed for much of the 1980s—not how to assess but whether to assess at all, at least in externally imposed and institutionalized ways—was once again opened.

Not How to Test, But Whether

For researchers, the empirical basis for questioning the vast (if various) assessment industry was to be through one of that industry's tenets: accountability. If assessments were necessary for placement and BW programs were salutary, could those salutary effects be documented?

The 1990s, and particularly the fourth National Conference on Basic Writing in 1992, offered a negative answer (see chapter 1 for an extended analysis of this conference and the resulting special issue of *JBW* in 1993). Suddenly the thought-leaders in the field like David Bartholomae were asking if BW placement ought to exist at all. There were even anecdotal accounts, like Peter Dow Adams's, that being placed in BW courses did more harm than good ("Basic Writing Reconsidered"). Assessment research in BW had to turn from the means to the ends, had to make a case for assessment. Edward White's "The Importance of Placement and Basic Studies: Helping Students Succeed Under the New Elitism" (1995) defended assessment by arguing that the attacks gave support to the "new elitists" on the right who saw remediation as beneath the task of higher education and an unwarranted drain on university budgets. "Nonetheless," White reasoned, "if faculty and administrators could be persuaded that the required course and placement testing do in fact help underprivileged students succeed, they would be less likely to join those seeking to limit opportunity for them" (78). To that end, White presented data from two statewide systems, and then, in his conclusion, conveyed his hope—but also his sense of the powerful forces aligned against it:

> Those of us concerned about preserving the hard-won higher education opportunities for the new students may not be able to stem the elitist tide, at least not immediately. But we can present the data and the arguments for basic writing programs and force those opposing them to confront the social biases they are endorsing. The argument that our programs do not work is baseless, as the California and New Jersey data show; given adequate support, we can help most low-scoring students succeed. (83)

Other, smaller scale studies, such as William Sweigart's account of pre- and post- testing (1996), showed in a more localized setting what White's review of whole state systems revealed: that, by and large (and in statistically significant ways), BW placement and instruction seemed to work. But BW placement was also being reworked with important consequences.

Alternatives to Established Assessments

Beginning in the 1990s, assessment research itself was reorganizing, becoming less unidirectional and univocal. Pat Belanoff of SUNY Stony Brook advocated portfolios. Eric Miraglia of Washington State proposed self-assessment. And Daniel Royer and Roger Gilles of Grand Valley State University favored self-directed placement (an idea that caught on widely enough to result in their edited collection titled *Directed Self-Placement: Principles and Practices* [2002]). Particularly important were mainstreaming experiments like those of Rhonda Grego and Nancy Thompson of the University of South Carolina and Mary Soliday and Barbara Gleason of CUNY's City College, since these helped to surface multifaceted longitudinal assessments, information-rich alternatives to the snapshot placements like the timed impromptu writing test. At about the same time, the 1993 CCCC Position Statement on Writing Assessment effectively indicted widespread practices like the timed writing sample without mandating specific alternatives. Research was opening new avenues that focused on tying assessment to the curriculum it potentially drove.

Not surprisingly, representatives of the established methods responded to the changing climate for research on assessment. In his "Apologia for the Timed Impromptu Essay Test," White argued that the lately maligned test was not only preferable to multiple-choice assessments but also more efficient and reliable than alternative forms like portfolio assessment. But the discourse had changed. White's arguments were about economy, efficiency, and efficacy. There was something utilitarian about his take—a kind of "greatest good for the greatest number" argument that worked best in large institutions that never could assess each student's individual situation. The case studies approach used by such scholars as Barbara Gleason in "When the Writing Test Fails: Assessing Assessment at an Urban College" (1997) or Deborah Mutnick in *Writing in an Alien World* (1996) functioned on a different principle—the belief that if assessments failed a single student unfairly, then that was one student too many—and the cost, at least for that student, was too great.

For the new research vanguard, there would also be ironic upsets. The mainstreaming experiment of Soliday and Gleason at CUNY's City College, the focus of so much attention for so long, is an illustrative example. A three-year, grant-funded project initiated in 1993, it established that BW students (or rather students who would ordinarily have had BW placement) could function and even flourish in "enriched" versions of regular writing courses (whose other students would also benefit from this enrichment). As documented in "From Remediation to Enrichment: Evaluating a Mainstreaming Project" (1997), the project used an impressive array of assessment tools: traditional assessments (as a kind of baseline), student self-assessments, cross-read portfolios, even a cadre of outside readers/consultants. But meeting its own goals was not enough to ensure the project's success. The students it was designed to serve were being denied access to City College by the time the project had run its course. In "Evaluating Writing Programs in Real Time: The Politics of Remediation" (2000), written as a retrospective and even a postmortem of the project in which she and Mary Soliday had invested so much, Barbara Gleason concluded, "The empirically verifiable account that we were striving for in this evaluation was fatally compromised by the socio-political forces that had gathered around the issue of remediation" (582). In *The Politics of Remediation* (2002), Soliday would add, "Empirical accounts remain central to arguing for the worth of programs, but evaluation is a political enterprise in many respects, which is merely to say that alone, data won't do the job of ideological justification" (142).

But Soliday would not stop there. Empirical accounts may not be enough, but she stressed that accounts focusing on case studies of individual students may have their own fatal flaw. If they show what often eludes the "big picture" perspective, then they can also elide the "big picture" itself. This is true whether the goal is to argue for reform in approaches to BW or to argue that attempts at remediation are doomed enterprises and wastes of money. It really does not matter if a critic of remediation is arguing that remediation is unfair or suggesting that it is impossible. The problem with focusing on BW students as special (and especially needy) cases is, as Soliday sees it, that they come to seem unusual and their problems intractable when the real issue is for institutions to ensure that such students are adequately supported: "By invoking the discourse of student need, critics of remediation often focus on students' agency, eluding or downplaying the roles that institutions do or could play in enhancing students' educational progress" (*Politics* 138).

With the help of hindsight, Soliday sees that it is the political context that matters most even and especially when it comes to matters of assessment and placement. More than this, she sees that both sides were focusing on student success or failure without taking the institutional context sufficiently into account. Yet as events unfolded, even that broader context proved too narrow a focus. By the time Soliday's book was published, students with remedial placement were no longer admitted to City College, her institution, and the assessment that determined their placement was no longer made by the CUNY WAT. The real assessment revolution had happened outside the academy altogether.

High Schools as Gatekeepers

From the early days of open admissions, basic writing students had been labeled as "underprepared" for college. But in the 1990s there was a growing conviction on the part of policy makers that students who were leaving high school without being ready for college simply shouldn't get a high school diploma. In 1998, the National Governors Association published, on the NGA website, an "Issues Brief" titled "High School Exit Exams: Setting High Expectations" (Otte, "High Schools as Crucibles" 109). That "Issues Brief" is no longer available, partly because this is no longer policy proposed but policy implemented. According to *State High School Exit Exams: A Challenging Year*,

> In 2006, 65% of the nation's public high school students and 76% of the nation's minority public high school students were enrolled in school in the 22 states with current exit exams. By 2012, an estimated 71% of public high school students and 81% of minority public high school students will be enrolled in school in the 25 states that expect to have exit exams in place. (Kober et al. 10)

As a consequence, BW students are disappearing from higher education because they are not completing secondary education. In *Time to Know Them: A Longitudinal Study of Writing and Learning at the College Level*, Marilyn Sternglass managed to combine statistics with case studies to show that BW students could succeed if given time—

something she could show only by tracking them over longer periods and with more in-depth attention than ever before. Yet even as *Time to Know Them* received the Mina P. Shaughnessy Award of the Modern Language Association in 1998 and the Outstanding Book Award of the Conference on College Composition and Communication in 1999, Sternglass's college and the focus of her study, City College of the City University of New York, was phasing out basic writing—or, more specifically, the students who would have taken it.

At this point, the most important work on assessment of BW students is quite possibly not about college assessments at all. *The Testing Trap: How State Writing Assessments Control Learning* (2002) by George Hillocks, Jr., is about the assessments going on in the high schools, where graduation is increasingly determined by state-mandated testing. Hillocks is careful and balanced in his conclusions and finds some practices much more estimable than others, but the overall picture he paints is effectively summed up by his title. However wise or unwise the states are in test design and administration, state-mandated assessments—created a world away and shaped by policy, expediency, and political decisions—now effectively control which students will eventually be admitted to college. The assessment and placement of BW students have never been further removed from those who design and teach in BW programs.

Thomas Hilgers, making a brief for the 1993 CCCC Position Statement on Assessment, wrote, "It is my belief that bad assessment is what gets most students labeled as 'basic writers'" (69). Many in the field agreed, and their research certainly challenged the assessments as well as the BW label. The students so labeled, however, may be a vanishing species now that state-mandated assessments at the pre-college level have become more like a wall than a gate.

Process

When basic writing students first appeared on the scene, the task was simply (or not so simply) to describe these students, initially seen as "strangers in academia" in Shaughnessy's Introduction to *Errors and Expectations* (3). Five years later, taking a national rather than a local perspective, Lynn Quitman Troyka expanded: these students were generally older, often with children and jobs. Many were from the first generation in their family to attend college. An increasing number of them were foreign born. And most important for this discussion, they arrived at college "without strong literacy skills" ("Perspectives on Legacies and Literacy in the 1980's" 253). In the descriptions of the time, BW students were seen as less prepared, less acclimated, and less literate. But such descriptions had a subtext: the definition had to be a diagnosis; the description had to be a prescription.

Generally speaking, this description/prescription could take two forms. One, largely observational or theoretical and quasi-objective, was to define the BW student in terms of needs, leaving those for the teacher to address. The other was to give a narrative of an attempt to meet those needs. This was most often done in the form of what the field learned to call the "teacher as hero" story (and sometimes the "program as hero"), though a variant could be the story of a failure to meet needs, a kind of confessional that offered enlightenment instead of a full teaching program.

Mina Shaughnessy encapsulated both of these forms in *Errors and Expectations*. Hers was largely a success story; after five years she could say of the students whose essays had inspired her book that more than a few "of those 'ineducable' students have by now been graduated" (3). Yet her book was more diagnostic than prescriptive. It was certainly a revelation in how to make sense of the writing of BW students, but just where to go from there was less than certain. As exercises in definition that were also ineluctably diagnostic (and prescriptive), they could be generally described as attempts to define how BW students thought as well as how BW students thought about themselves (but also, importantly, how others thought about them). Attention to the thought processes of basic writers would dominate research in the 1980s.

The groundbreaking work on process was done by Janet Emig. In 1971, Emig published *The Composing Processes of Twelfth Graders*, which Mina Shaughnessy approvingly cited in *Errors and Expectations* as important "for the contrast it offers between the ways students behave as writers and the ways textbooks and teachers often have assumed they ought to behave" (299). By having students talk through their acts of composing, Emig was able to show how their thinking got translated into writing and how their thoughts about that process bore on the process itself. But hers was a double revelation. She would show not only how thought processes influenced writing processes but also how writing, in turn, influenced thought. She would become an important formative and informing influence on work in writing across the curriculum with research like "Writing as a Mode of Learning" (1977), arguing that writing fostered analytical and relational thinking important to academic work (and discourse). From the beginning, then, the focus on process was never only on the writing process but also on the thought process, and the teaching goals that came of this focus were as much about teaching students how to think as teaching them how to write.

Writing Process(es)

Initially, BW research focused more on the writing process. Mina Shaughnessy had warned, in her bibliographic essay "Basic Writing," about the "rigorous and informed thinking that must take place before there is any substantial yield for writing from current learning theory" (206). That was of course a challenge as well as a caution, and many in the field would soon rise to it. Adopting and developing Emig's methods, especially the approach of having students talk through their composing processes, Sondra Perl based her dissertation on intensive work with five students. She published the findings in several important articles. "A Look at Basic Writers in the Process of Composing," published in 1980, was keyed specifically to basic writing. Accessible yet still detailed in terms of primary research, "A Look at Basic Writers" dispelled the persistent myth that BW students "do not know how to write" by showing each had stable and consistent composing processes. Their chief problem in fact seemed be an arsenal of self-imposed constraints and counterproductive strategies that reined in the writing and often interrupted the flow for the sake of correction (or hypercorrection): "Seen from this point of view, teaching basic writers how to write needs to be conceived of in a new way, in part, by 'loosening' the process rather than 'tightening' it" (31). Perl's great strength was also the great challenge to applications of her research; because she regarded composing processes as individualized if not idiosyncratic, due attention to these processes would logically need to be the kind that she paid. She would not generalize about steps and stages. She would not make the composing process singular and schematized.

Taking the schematic approach meant turning away from individuals (and all their problematic differences) and turning to theory. Of those who did just that, the most influential was Linda Flower, who often partnered in her research and publication with John Hayes, a cognitive psychologist. In "Writer-Based Prose: A Cognitive Basis for Problems in Writing" (1979), she used cognitive theory to argue that the root of many writing problems—writing that is self-focused, associative rather than logical, and insufficiently considerate of its audience—is that it has not met the cognitive challenges of reader-based prose, which is considerate, thought-through, literate, logical, and propositional—in short, writing which takes various needs of the reader into account.

In a number of subsequent articles coauthored with Hayes—among them "The Cognition of Discovery" (1980), "Identifying the Organization of Writing Processes" (1980), "A Cognitive Process Theory of Writing" (1981), and "Images, Plans, and Prose: The Representation of Meaning in Writing" (1984)—Flower would delineate a sense of what the general writing process was, often with the help of diagrams and flow charts. There would be caveats about how the process was recursive, context-bound, even unpredictable. But what the work of Flower and Hayes communicated first and foremost was that the writing process was knowable (if complex), step-by-step (if recursive), and consistent across individuals and contexts (if only in its very general outlines). This was a powerful message for the beleaguered instructor. It didn't require an intimate knowledge of each student to teach process; what was needed—and at hand—was a model and a theory.

Thinking Process(es)

Cognitive theory, as its name implied, was about the very process of thought, and it became important well beyond its application to the writing process. After all, from the beginning, the writing process had never been only about writing but also about the thinking brought to bear on that writing. And the aspect focused on by most BW researchers was its longitudinal, developmental nature—less the act of cognition than the development of cognition over time. For better or worse (it would be both), this development was fundamentally seen as a matter of maturation.

Initially, this view was embraced. No one assumed that first-year college students, BW students in particular, were especially mature. As a political project, basic writing was concerned with democratizing education, opening up higher education to those who had not had access until now. The fear, not least of all from those who opposed such access, was that these students would prove to be ineducable.

Seen through the lens of cognitive or developmental theory, they were not unintelligent, just cognitively immature—largely a consequence of being underexposed to the tasks and settings that would spur their mental maturation. That made their intellectual growth, now that they were in college, seem not only possible but almost inevitable.

There were scholarly bases for this assertion of the possibility of intellectual growth. Of the thinkers who figured in developmental or cognitive research, particularly as it applied to BW, there were four principals: Lawrence Kohlberg, William Perry, Lev Vygotsky, and Jean Piaget. Kohlberg was primarily concerned with moral and ethical development, not intellectual growth per se. Perry had the virtue of focusing on college students—a focus problematically lacking in Piaget and Vygotsky—but his sampling had largely been restricted to Harvard males back before Harvard had gone coed; that had to seem an unfortunately restricted sampling, particularly to the BW research community indisposed to use yardsticks associated with privilege and power. Vygotsky, like Piaget, was concerned principally with childhood development; he had his arguments with Piaget, most rooted in his greater attention to social context, but he also resisted the neat schematizing that Piaget accommodated. Piaget was the main informant for cognitivists. In "Cognitive Studies and Teaching Writing," Andrea Lunsford effectively summed up why:

> The work of Swiss psychologist Jean Piaget is of particular significance to our field in that it represents a turning away from the rigid focus of behaviorism and logical empiricism and toward the ways in which people "know" the world and hence construct both knowledge and reality. For Piaget, knowing is an action or, more explicitly, an *inter*action between the self and its environment, and development occurs as we alter mental structures in order to make sense out of the world. Piaget categorizes this mental development into four "stages": the sensori-motor stage, the preoperational stage, the concrete-operational stage, and the formal operational stage, which is characterized by the ability to abstract, synthesize, and form coherent, logical relations. . . . (147)

Culminating in a stage that sounds like the great desideratum, not only of BW instruction but also of college instruction generally, the attraction of this scheme is immediately apparent. But the great problem with it becomes no less apparent as Lunsford continues:

> At the stage of concrete operations, the child's thought is still closely linked to concrete data; completely representational, hypothetical thought still eludes the child. As the child moves through the stages of cognitive development, he or she relies less and less on such concrete data and direct physical experience and more and more on general, abstract, representational systems. . . . (147)

What is most problematic is that this is a *maturational* scheme of development—specifically, of child development. The concrete-operational stage is characteristic of children from six to eleven years of age. What's more, Piaget had grave doubts about the ability of formal education to accelerate the developmental process. His whole theory was, in fact, an alternative to the (for him repugnant) idea that the growth of knowledge and thought is merely additive, the accretion of information. Instead, knowledge structures restructure themselves to accommodate new concepts, new logics. These new ways of thinking cannot be imposed from the outside, though they do result, as Lunsford affirms, from complex interactions between the self and the environment. Cognitive growth is not an easy or smooth process. It tends to work by disruptive interactions of the sort that overturn long-held conceptual frameworks. Creating such interactions in a classroom might be a dubious enterprise, supposing it was possible.

Initially, such problems did not stop the cognitivists. They were prepared to make adjustments, not least of all in regard to Piaget, as Karl Taylor did in explaining the genesis of his DOORS program (for the Development of Operational Reasoning Skills) in 1979: "Despite Piaget's hypothesis that 17- or 18-year-olds should be at the formal level, I concluded that my students might not have fully arrived at that point" (53). How far such notions would take some in a fairly short space of time is strikingly instanced by the opening sentence of Anna Berg and Gerald Coleman's *JBW* article "A Cognitive Approach to Teaching the Developmental Student" (1985): "There is a growing consensus among developmental researchers that a substantial number, perhaps even a majority, of the freshmen admitted into colleges and universities in the United States approach the academic task of college-level courses on the concrete operational level of cognitive functioning" (4). For anyone who knows this is the preadolescent stage in the Piagetian scheme, this pronouncement has to seem alarming, but for the BW community, it gets worse: "The undereducated, urban community college student lags far behind the average college or university freshman in the ability to deal with intellectually complex operations called for in college courses" (4). The latter statement was made with specific reference to the authors' home institution, "Passaic County Community College, an inner-city school with a large enrollment of educationally disadvantaged students" (4). Berg and Coleman go on to describe their "remedial curriculum, The 'Cognitive Project,'" which provides "underprepared, nontraditional students an opportunity to actively experience ways of acquiring, solidifying, and using knowledge while acquiring the basic reading and writing skills necessary for college work" (4–5). This hardly seems a solution commensurate with the problem, but any prescription has to pale in the face of the damning diagnosis.

Berg and Coleman's "Cognitive Approach" was the leadoff article in the last of the themed issues of *JBW* under the old editorial board, billed "Basic Writing and Social Science Research II." In fact, the first several articles of that issue used a cognitivist approach; in addition to Berg and Coleman's piece, there was Joan M. Elifson and Katharine R. Stone's "Integrating Social, Moral, and Cognitive Developmental Theory" and Annette Bradford's "Applications of Self-Regulating Speech in the Basic Writing Program" (though the latter used "the early research of Piaget, Vygotsky, and Luria" [41] only as a starting point). The journal's recourse to this theme (for the second of two issues) highlighted the tendency of researchers at the time to cloak themselves in the vestments of other disciplines, notably psychology, sociology, and linguistics.

Cognition or Discourse Conventions?

A glimmering of what lay beyond cognitivists' explanations of the deficiencies of BW students appeared in the very next issue of *JBW*, the first under Lynn Quitman Troyka's editorship. Here is the opening sentence of Myra Kogen's article on "The Conventions of Expository Writing" (1986): "A number of composition researchers in the past few years have come to the conclusion that students cannot think" (24). The shift away from the specialized vocabulary of the Piagetian model to the bald and false-sounding claim that "students cannot think" is the first clue that this is not another such researcher. Kogen cites a number of developmental researchers, including the author of "Cognitive Development and the Basic Writer" (1979): "Andrea Lunsford asserts that basic writers 'have not attained that level of cognitive development which would allow them to form abstractions or conceptions' (38)" (24). Other researchers making such striking and damning charges against basic writers come in for citation and disputation—notably Janice Hays, an editor of the collection *The Writer's Mind* (1983) and author of a piece in that collection titled "The Development of Discursive Maturity in College Writers." Hays was a special target for Kogen not because she was making more damning or dramatic claims about student writers than other cognitive researchers had but because she provided, as evidence of these claims, samples of student writing. Kogen maintained that, like other developmental researchers, ". . . Hays is asserting that poor writers have not developed the ability to think abstractly and conceptually" (34). But the writing samples given by Hays offered the opening for an alternative interpretation: "Looking at the same student samples," Kogen concluded that "freshman writers certainly can think abstractly but they have not yet learned to present their ideas in accordance with conventional expectations" (34). The next year, Hays published an apologia of cognitivism called "Models of Intellectual Development and Writing: A Response to Myra Kogen et al." But even this spirited defense was rendered irrelevant. Kogen's turn of thought had introduced reasonable doubt about cognitivists' claims.

In finding the argument that "students do not have sufficient cognitive maturity to argue successfully in academic discourse" muddled and in claiming that the real issue was not students' maturity but adequate knowledge of discourse conventions, Kogen was making a point whose time had come. She was certainly not the only one, not even the first. Ann Berthoff had clearly expressed her exasperation with developmental theorists two years before in "Is Teaching Still Possible? Writing, Meaning, and Higher Order Reasoning" (1984). Two years before that, in "Cognition, Convention, and Certainty" (1982), Patricia Bizzell had argued that cognitivists were too focused on inner processes and needed to be more attentive to social context, a notion put forth even more emphatically that same year by Janet Emig in "Inquiry Paradigms and Writing" (1982), an article that had nothing nice to say about composition researchers who proceeded "a-contextually, with no consideration or acknowledgement of setting" (71). It seems ironic that this rebuke came from the researcher who had done so much to focus attention on composing processes and, concomitantly, thought processes.

A shift of attention for basic writing research was in the works, and *JBW*, under the editorship of Troyka, helped to bring it forward. In the "Editor's Column," she announced several changes. Now a national refereed journal, *JBW* would move away from issues with a single theme to issues on various topics, a move calculated to encourage more timely publication of new material (1). Despite this emphasis on new material, the leadoff piece of the reincarnated *JBW* was an abridged reprint of David Bartholomae's "Inventing the University," published the year before in Mike Rose's collection *When a Writer Can't Write* (1985). The Bartholomae piece is famous for insisting that the challenge for his students is "to know what I know and how I know what I know . . . ; they have to learn to write what I would write . . ." (9). What is less well known is that this is simply Bartholomae's way of putting in memorable phrasing what he quotes Bizzell's "Cognition, Convention, and Certainty" as saying—that the challenge faced by basic writers is not so much a matter of cognitive development as a lack of familiarity with academic discourse: "What is undeveloped is their knowledge both of the ways experience is constituted and interpreted in the academic discourse community and of the fact that all discourse communities constitute and interpret experience" (Bizzell, "Cognition" 230, qtd. in Bartholomae, "Inventing" 11–12).

That Bartholomae's piece immediately precedes Kogen's in this issue is a small indication of how much was coming together in this seismic realignment of perspectives, the collective suggestion that conventions trump cognition in explaining the challenges that basic writers face in the academy. Some of this realignment was truly subterranean, like the fact that Bizzell's criticism in the cited piece ("Cognition, Convention, and Certainty") is focused less on the developmentalists who claim that "students cannot think" than on the chief cartographers of the writing process, Flower and Hayes, who are (Bizzell argues) too schematic, linear, inner-directed, and a-contextual in their mappings of that process. The tracers of process, whether writing or thinking, were charged with being blinded by theory, ignoring context and difference, and reducing the life and individuality of what individuals do to stages of growth and flow charts of process.

There were many other instances of this realignment. In a widely discussed typology (and judgment) of what his title called "The Major Pedagogical Theories" (1982), James Berlin would exclude the cognitivists from what he called "the New Rhetoric" (a.k.a. "social epistemic" rhetoric) for being too inattentive to social context and the social construction of knowledge. The extent to which Linda Flower, at least, took this to heart may be seen in her eventual publication of *The Construction of Negotiated Meaning: A Social Cognitive Theory of Writing* (1994). And there were other conversions, notably that of Mike Rose, who could sum up the major research shift of the decade by publishing a piece subtitled *A Cognitivist Analysis of Writer's Block* at the start of the decade (1980) and, before it was out (1988), writing an article that in its title leveled a charge of "Cognitive Reductionism" and gave high praise to the contextual focus of Bartholomae and Bizzell.

Academic Literacy

In teaching practice, the shift away from cognitive approaches and toward academic literacy is nowhere better captured than in Bartholomae and Petrosky's *Facts, Artifacts, and Counterfacts* (see chapter 3 for a discussion of this book's impact). In the field's research, however, the work to look to is that of Patricia Bizzell. She was campaigning against the cognitivists at a time when they seemed to hold the field. One of her earliest articles was "Thomas Kuhn, Scientism, and English Studies" (1979). It was a reaction to Maxine Hairston's speech at the 1978 convention of the Conference on College Composition and Communication, the gist of which was published three years later as "The Winds of Change: Thomas Kuhn and the Revolution in the Teaching of Writing" (1982). Both Hairston and Bizzell were drawing on *The Structure of Scientific Revolutions* (1962, 1970), Thomas Kuhn's argument that significant scientific discoveries are conceptual crises forcing new ways of thinking (with Copernican astronomy the paradigmatic example). Hairston was arguing for a new empirical rigor in composition studies, something less like the fuzziness of literary methods and more like the problem-solving strategies and reliance on "hard" evidence found in the social sciences. Bizzell would have it quite the other way. The apparatus of literary/critical methods and rhetorical analysis should be just the thing to help the struggling student as well as to feed research; there was no need to appeal to scientific (but really just scientistic) modes of observation and verification. She also noted (with special attention to Kuhn's lengthy postscript to his second edition) that Kuhn himself resisted claims of objectivity or empiricism, holding instead to the importance of structures and contexts of thought.

It is easy to see the seeds of later attacks on cognitivism in Bizzell's "Thomas Kuhn," but she is not just arguing against a "scientistic" redefinition of her discipline. She is arguing *for* something, and it is a sense of continuity she traces through Shaughnessy. In her first published article, "The Ethos of Academic Discourse" (1978), Bizzell credits Shaughnessy with being the one who began the project Bizzell herself would commit to for so long. In arguing for "making the ethos of academic discourse available to beginning adult writers," she was quick to say that the project did not begin with her: "By calling for a 'taxonomy' of academic discourse, Shaughnessy has suggested how we might begin to make the academic ethos available to these students" (36). In her "Thomas Kuhn" essay, Bizzell says that students and teachers don't need empirical methods and claims of proof but persuasive methods and rhetorical strategies. Again she sees Shaughnessy pointing the way:

> . . . Shaughnessy suggests that the study of these rhetorical strategies should be the special province of English studies—to make accessible in our composition classes what I have called the ethos of academic discourse. . . . If we can uncover the rhetorical conventions that help us, in our own professional work, to establish this ethos and make our arguments respectable, we can cease to make the insulting claim that a badly argued essay contravenes universal standards of rationality verified by simple inspection of the natural order. (770)

This uncovering of "the rhetorical conventions" was a research program that more and more would join. The fact that these conventions inhere "in our own professional work" had to help. What also helped was that this was cast not as a new method but as an ongoing disciplinary project. By the end of the 1980s, the ascendant research project for basic writing and composition generally was so far from the paradigm shift Hairston demanded and predicted as to seem its opposite: not a vanquishing of the old by the new but something quite the reverse. The invasion of methods and concepts from the social sciences had obscured an older, deeper tradition and chain of influences now re-manifested. The presence of assorted literary theorists in the introduction to *Facts, Artifacts, and Counterfacts* has been duly noted (see chapter 3), but no less important—probably more important—than the invocations of deconstruction by way of Jonathan Culler and of German hermeneutics by way of Hans-Georg Gadamer is the acknowledgment of I. A. Richards, whose *How to Read a Page* (1942) is cited as well as his *Philosophy of Rhetoric* (1936). What conquered cognitivism (besides time and that movement's own inherent weaknesses) was actually a return to a discipline's tradition, one comprising the literary/critical as well as the rhetorical. That tradition (and conjunction) had been incarnated in Richards, carried on and amplified by his fiercely loyal and brilliant student Ann Berthoff, and, with Patricia Bizzell, taken up by a new generation. Looking back, in fact, Bizzell said that

> the Kuhn essay was important because it got me the attention of Ann Berthoff. At the 1979 Conference on College Composition and Communication, one of the first meetings I attended, I sat in a large lecture hall listening to Ann give a major address and suddenly heard her praise my Kuhn essay, which had appeared only the month before. I experienced a feeling of pure pleasure I thought was only available to little girls being praised by their mothers. (*Academic Discourse* 10)

Bizzell went on to say that the two were introduced by David Bartholomae, who had been a graduate student with Bizzell at Rutgers. Reflecting on this meeting, Bizzell says that she "can't overemphasize the importance" (10) of this connection—this sense of kinship, approval, and alliance.

Bizzell would go on to map out the program of initiating students into academic discourse while people like Bartholomae would be the popularizers and demonstrators, taking the theory into application. If Bizzell did less of the latter it was not because she was a "pure" researcher—BW never had one—but because she was consistently more attentive to knotty problems rather than their solutions, to the distance to travel rather than the steps to take. "College Composition: Initiation into the Academic Discourse Community" (1982), for example, is very far from taking the subject of its title as an accomplished fact; on the contrary, Bizzell's sense is that she and her colleagues have scarcely begun to account for

> the nature of academic discourse as a form of language use that unites a particular community, and we have not examined the relationship between the academic discourse community and the communities from which our students come: communities with forms of language use shaped by their own social circumstances. We have not demystified academic discourse. (108)

Seeing such challenges, Bizzell also imagined that students would rise to meet them, even and especially the BW students who were her initial and ongoing concern. She concludes "What Happens When Basic Writers Come to College?" (1986) with the proposition that they would be especially willing and even able to adopt "the comparative deliberative stance of the academic world view" precisely because of their struggles and disadvantages:

> The basic writers already know that their home communities' standards are not the only ones possible—they learn this more immediately and forcefully when they come to college than do students whose home world views are closer to the academic, when they experience the distance between their home dialects and Standard English and the debilitating unfamiliarity they feel with academic ways of shaping thoughts in discourse. . . . But precisely because of the hegemonic power of the academic world view, my hypothesis is that they will also find its acquisition well worth the risks. (173)

Bizzell, like others who made initiation into academic literacy the great project of the 1980s, wasn't interested in mere conversion. Like Berthoff, she was influenced by the work of Paulo Freire, the liberatory educator who had done so much to bring literacy to the Brazilian peasantry. And the project of demystifying academic discourse was not only to give access to it, as Bizzell stresses in *Academic Discourse and Critical Consciousness*, the retrospective account she published in 1993 but also to make sure that it didn't seem something generalized and "natural"—the discourse of the "right" way to write and think rather than a socially constructed network of conventions:

> Thus academic discourse is not allowed to masquerade as the clearest or most rational or most efficient form of language use, to the detriment of the students' home languages, and the students are encouraged to relativize their acquisition of academic discourse, to see it as one more addition to their discursive repertoires, useful for specific purposes, rather than to see it as a means of growing up or learning to think. Nevertheless, like Freire, I assume here that with the critical detachment academic discourse affords when it is acquired in a (supposedly) liberatory manner will more or less automatically come insight into social injustices and the will to correct them. (*Academic Discourse* 20)

The problem Bizzell hints at she then makes explicit. It really isn't that initiation into academic discourse is a form of indoctrination, though she admits that

> the idea that teaching academic discourse could *cause* critical consciousness in students . . . was somewhat exaggerated. I was more dissatisfied with critical consciousness itself as a goal for pedagogy. I began to doubt that critical detachment in the Freirean sense could be achieved. . . .
>
> I think this doubt began to grow due to my continued contact with postmodern and deconstructive theories of literary interpretation, which implied that one could not get "out of" the cultural text by any critical means. (*Academic Discourse* 21)

This realization is crucial. It represents the downside of what saved BW research from marching steadily to the empirical "certainties" of "scientistic" research. When Bizzell and others had argued for turning away from that path, the resources they recommended instead were those "native" to the discipline of English, notably the tools of literary theory and interpretation. But these afforded something very far from easy certainties or clear pedagogical procedures. Given the way they themselves were (re)structured over this time, with the growing attention to postmodern takes on texts and culture, they were more or less guaranteed to stoke doubts about pedagogies of initiation. The long-term effect might be traced as the arc Bartholomae traveled from saying in 1985 that his students must "know what I know and how I know what I know " (in "Inventing the University" 9) to worrying, in his keynote for the fourth National Conference on Basic Writing in 1992, that he and basic writing as a field had effectively turned BW students into "the 'other' who is the incomplete version of ourselves, confirming existing patterns of power and authority, reproducing the hierarchies we had meant to question and overthrow" ("The Tidy House" 18).

Attitudes and Identities

In research, the move away from pedagogies of academic initiation had the effect of shifting attention increasingly from the teacher's methods (and what might make them seem appropriate) to the student's situation. The researcher's gaze was redirected from what might be said about or done for the students to what the students might say for themselves. This redirection came with its own set of problems, of course. One of those was necessarily how students long defined as inarticulate could give accounts of themselves. There were basically two answers, and they became the two new important research trends of the1990s: the case study and the literacy narrative.

The student's literacy narrative was always more important as a pedagogical strategy than as a research tool, but it had its complement (and to some extent its impetus) in the teacher's literacy narrative. (See chapter 1 for a discussion of the literacy narratives of the 1990s.) Especially important were the literacy narratives of those whose racial, ethnic, class, and/or language backgrounds made them the supreme (because they became highly successful) exemplars of the very students basic writing was designed to serve: teacher/scholars now situated on the other side of the literacy divide. These included not only writers of color like Keith Gilyard (*Voices of the Self* [1991]) and Victor Villanueva (*Bootstraps* [1993])) but also writers with working-class origins like Linda Brodkey ("Writing on the Bias" [1994]) and Mike Rose (*Lives on the Boundary* [1989]). Influential as they proved, these of course had their antecedents, in works like Richard Rodriguez's *Hunger of Memory* (1982)—oft-excerpted and anthologized (in Bartholomae and Petrosky's *Ways of Reading*, for instance)—and like Rodriguez's explicitly acknowledged precursor, Richard Hoggart (*The Uses of Literacy* [1959]). What made the latter-day literacy narratives especially important was their explicit determination to make autobiography a means to a scholarly end, a way of plumbing more deeply into the educational lives and struggles of BW students. As Rose put it in the preface to *Lives on the Boundary*,

> I've worked for twenty years with children and adults deemed slow or remedial or underprepared. And at one time in my own educational life, I was so labeled. But I was lucky. I managed to get redefined. The people I've tutored and taught and the people whose lives I've studied . . . hadn't been so fortunate. They lived for many of their years in an educational underclass. In trying to present the cognitive and social reality of such a life—the brains as well as the heart of it—I have written a personal book. The stories of my work with literacy interweave with the story of my own engagement with language. *Lives on the Boundary* is both vignette and commentary, reflection and analysis. I didn't know how else to get it right. (xi-xii)

For all their differences, these scholarly literacy narratives had this much in common: getting it right meant getting personal—but never "merely" personal. The turning inward was also a turning outward, a means of using the self as the measure of institutionalized rigidity and resistance, social pressures and social injustice. The bifocal nature of the literacy narrative is perfectly captured by the title of an early instance: "The Classroom and the Wider Culture: Identity as a Key to Learning English Composition" (1989). And though the title seems to promise a pedagogical program, it is actually Fan Shen's personal account of the need to become bicultural as well as bilingual as a native Chinese learning to write in English.

The Conflict Within, the Conflict Without

Since what Shen and others described was effectively a clash of cultures (experienced on a personal level), an apt and compelling definition for what might be appropriate pedagogical approaches came in the form of a metaphor for just such a clash. In 1991, Mary Louise Pratt published "Arts of the Contact Zone," an account of what teaching might mean in contexts where cultures are not only coming together but also confronting each other on unequal terms. Though two examples are drawn from the education of her own children, Pratt's most sustained example comes from classic colonialism, specifically the confrontation of an Incan with the culture of the Spanish conquistadores. As she sees it, the problem of the classroom is to some extent the problem of colonization. The context for interaction is defined in terms of lopsided power relations; consequently,

> only legitimate moves are actually named as part of the system, where legitimacy is defined from the point of view of the party in authority, regardless of what other parties might see themselves as doing. Teacher-pupil language, for example, tends to be described almost entirely from the point of view of the teacher and teaching, not from the point of view of pupils and pupiling (the word doesn't even exist, though the thing certainly does). (38)

To some extent, the situation Pratt described exists in any classroom, a danger she immediately went on to warn against: "If a classroom is analyzed as a social world unified and homogenized with respect to the teacher, whatever students do other than what the teacher specifies is invisible or anomalous to the analysis" (38). This description had a special aptness for the BW classroom, a "social world" that was so obviously like a war of the worlds of home and academic culture, of difference from the dominant—a point made even before Pratt's "Contact Zone" by Tom Fox in "Basic Writing as Cultural Conflict" (1990). What's more, this conflict was very much an internalized one, a war comprising any number of wars (or at least border skirmishes) within, as so many literacy narratives had come to proclaim. Each BW student might well present, it seemed, a variant on Gloria Anzaldúa's famous description of her "border identity" (from the Preface to *Borderlands/La Frontera: The New Mestiza* [1987]):

> I am a border woman. I grew up between two cultures, the Mexican (with a heavy Indian influence) and the Anglo (as a member of a colonized people in our own territory). I have been straddling that *tejas*-Mexican border, and others, all my life. It's not a comfortable territory to live in, this place of contradictions. Hatred, anger and exploitation are the prominent features of this landscape. (19)

There is a strong sense of social injustice here, one that would be declaimed against and addressed in a parallel track of BW research stretching from the inspiration derived from Freire's *Pedagogy of the Oppressed* (1970) to Tom Fox's arguments leavening the students' stories in *Defending Access* (1999) and beyond. But Anzaldúa is describing not only a plight but also an opportunity:

> However, there have been compensations for this mestiza, and certain joys. Living on borders and in margins, keeping intact one's shifting and multiple identity and integrity, is like trying to swim in a new element, an "alien" element. There is an exhilaration in being a participant in the further evolution of humankind, in being "worked" on. (iii)

Significantly, though the sense of struggle is what she highlights in an epigraph from Anzaldúa, Min-Zhan Lu concludes her "Conflict and Struggle: The Enemies or Preconditions of Basic Writing?" (1992) with the compensatory perspective and what it should mean for and to researchers:

> We need more research which critiques portrayals of Basic Writers as belonging to an abnormal—traumatized or underdeveloped—mental state and which simultaneously provides accounts of the "creative motion" and "compensation," "joy," or "exhilaration" resulting from Basic Writers' efforts to grapple with the conflict within and among diverse discourses. We need more research analyzing and contesting the assumptions about language underlying teaching methods which offer to "cure" all signs of conflict and struggle, research which explores ways to help

students recover the latent conflict and struggle in their lives which the dominant conservative ideology of the 1990s seeks to contain. (911)

Case Studies of Conflict and Struggle

Research of the type Lu was calling for was forthcoming, and not all of it in the form of literacy narratives—for there were only so many who could write from the perspective of a Gilyard or an Anzaldúa. From those who couldn't, and even from some who could, there came a veritable explosion of case studies, an attempt on the part of BW researchers to have the BW students speak for themselves. In some cases, the focus was on a single student or a single student-teacher interaction. The extent to which these individual cases could be freighted with weighty, general arguments is evident from such titles as "Remediation as Social Construct: Perspectives from an Analysis of Classroom Discourse" (by Glynda Hull et al.) and "Warning: Basic Writers at Risk—The Case of Javier" (by Sally Barr Reagan). These single-case examples, both from 1991, were essentially cautionary tales, accounts of how predetermined ideas of what BW students are like can shut down possibilities for understanding on the teacher's part and learning on the student's.

As the decade advanced, more sustained ethnographic work made the case for such understanding and such learning. Sometimes, the focus was on the special trials and resources of a specific group, as in Valerie Balester's *Cultural Divide: A Study of African-American College-Level Writers* (1993) or Tom Fox's account of five African-American students in *Defending Access: A Critique of Standards in Higher Education* (1999). More often, the sampling was mixed, but the point was largely the same: students had unacknowledged, untapped competencies (like the oral skills of the students represented in Laura Gray-Rosendale's *Rethinking Basic Writing* [2000] or the reflective abilities of the student highlighted in Rebecca Mlynarczyk's "Personal and Academic Writing: Revisiting the Debate" [2006]). Some simply needed more time to show what they could learn and accomplish (as demonstrated in Marilyn Sternglass's *Time to Know Them* [1997]). The point of these studies, as emphasized by Eleanor Kutz, Suzy Groden, and Vivian Zamel in *The Discovery of Competence* (1993), was that students possessed competencies if only their teachers could find a way to acknowledge and foster these abilities. Part of the message was often that the learning and teaching could be mutual, something affirmed by Mlynarczyk's "Finding Grandma's Words: A Case Study in the Art of Revising" (1996), Howard Tinberg's "Teaching in the Spaces Between: What Basic Writing Students Can Teach Us" (1998), and Linda Adler-Kassner's "Just Writing, Basically: Basic Writers on Basic Writing" (1999). And there were, inevitably, searches for patterns, perhaps most comprehensively made by Richard Haswell in *Gaining Ground in College Writing: Tales of Development and Interpretation* (1991). Prefiguring Min-Zhan Lu's arguments in "Conflict and Struggle," Haswell sought to show that tension and instability in students' educational lives were preconditions of important steps forward in their learning and thought.

It was also true that these case studies had the cumulative effect of showing how hard the struggles of BW students were, how great the odds against them. This was especially true of Deborah Mutnick's *Writing in an Alien World: Basic Writing and the Struggle for Equality in Higher Education* (1996). Mutnick's exploration of four students' lives constituted a reminder that nothing defined BW students so much as their disadvantages in an unequal society. This was an essential shift in definition since it justified special support (as a means of redressing injustice) without prescribing the form that it would take.

The mid-1990s seemed to be a time of rethinking the instructional and institutional forms for providing BW support. A concentrated example of this type of rethinking was the February 1996 issue of *College Composition and Communication*. It contained two important accounts of mainstreaming, Rhonda Grego and Nancy Thompson's "Repositioning Remediation" and Mary Soliday's "From the Margins to the Mainstream: Reconceiving Remediation," along with shorter pieces in a section titled "Rethinking Basic Writing" that included Judith Rodby's "What's It Worth and What's It For? Revisions to Basic Writing Revisited," a report on another mainstreaming experiment, this one at Cal State Chico (for a fuller account of mainstreaming, see chapter 3).

Following hard upon these tales of restructuring basic writing instruction—in the very next issue of *College Composition and Communication*—Bruce Horner's "Discoursing Basic Writing" (1996) invited a conceptual restructuring of BW both as a field of research and a teaching endeavor. Arguing that BW had tried to become safe and self-enclosed, especially as a CUNY-centric formation conscious of its precarious position in the wake of open admissions, Horner cast BW—and particularly BW research—as too focused on teachers' methods and student texts, too inattentive to the social and material conditions that marginalized those students and teachers. As the sources cited earlier in this chapter indicate, case studies and programmatic overviews went on throughout the late 1990s and well into the new century, informed by the revisionist urgings of Horner and others. But social and material conditions also reasserted themselves in ways that such research could not adequately account for or counter. Reconceptualization and even restructuring quickly came to seem either luxuries or desperate acts as forces dismissive of remediation threatened to sweep away basic writing entirely.

In the next chapter, we will look more closely at the realm of public policy in light of such developments and the ways they have reshaped the terrain of basic writing. These putatively "external" forces are forcible reminders of the importance of the social and material conditions of BW students and teachers, and their vulnerability to these forces is impossible to ignore as we contemplate what the future may hold for them and for the field.

5 The Future of Basic Writing

As this book goes to press in 2010, the story of basic writing is far from resolved. The global economic downturn that began in 2008 echoes on a huge scale the New York City financial crisis that eviscerated BW programs in the City University of New York in the mid-1970s. Mina Shaughnessy, speaking at the 1976 Conference of the CUNY Association of Writing Supervisors (CAWS) to those who had lived through budget cuts and retrenchments, struggled to find a way of seeing something good come of such hardship. She found some consolation in the solidarity that was forged during these shared struggles:

> I cannot imagine a group of teachers who have ever had more to say to one another. It is a special fraternity joined not only by our common purposes and problems as teachers but by our having come to know, through our students, what it means to be an outsider in academia. Whatever our individual political persuasions, we have been pedagogically radicalized by our experience. . . .
>
> Such changes, I would say, are indestructible, wherever we go from here. ("The Miserable Truth" 269)

Basic writing came back from that scene of devastation, and it may once again in a new century, but not as a unified project. Coherence, if it ever exists in academic research or its application, is a property of beginnings. Maturity breeds complexity. What research has disclosed about basic writing—whether as a teaching project, a population of students taught, or a context for such teaching and learning—is that its incarnations differ from one site and time to the next.

Recognizing that basic writing will continue to evolve in the years ahead, in this final chapter we assess the current situation and suggest some possible future directions for the field. In order to contextualize this discussion, we will first review the political climate that has led us to this point.

POLITICAL PORTENTS

Questioning the Value of Remediation

Throughout the 1990s, the debate over whether BW students had any business being in college was reopened with a vengeance. An early warning shot came in the form of a "Point of View" piece in the *Chronicle of Higher Education* in 1991. Marc Tucker, then president of the National Center on Education and the Economy, effectively made his point with his title: "Many U.S. Colleges Are Really Inefficient and High-Priced Secondary Schools." His elaboration of the point basically outlines a program that would be followed throughout the decade:

> Remediation is a poor substitute for prevention. Nonexistent standards are a part of the problem, not the solution. Colleges that take whomever they can get in order to fill seats are in no position to complain about the schools. If some part of the current capacity of higher education has to be shut down if we institute appropriate standards, then so be it—if the funds released can be made available to the schools to do the job properly the first time. If colleges want to keep that money to do what they should have been doing all along—both to help the beleaguered schools and to run their own part of the "secondary" system effectively—then legislatures and the federal government should be ready to listen. It is time to be honest about these issues and to do something about them. (A38)

Many of the politically charged attacks against basic writing that surfaced in the 1990s were inspired by the publication of James Traub's *City on a Hill: Testing the American Dream at City College* (1994), a journalistic account of the trials and tribulations of BW students and teachers at CUNY's City College, one that calls the whole enterprise into question. Largely anecdotal, the book purports to let its readers draw their own conclusions, but its effect is to make the critical question it begins with rhetorical: "How powerful are our institutions in the face of economic and cultural forces that now perpetuate inner-city poverty?" (5). As Nathan Glazer would write in an approving review of the book (but one with seams of sympathy for City College and its students), "Remedial education, even the best kind, can only do so much." Why? Because, though both the commitment of the students and the school's ability to match it once seemed so high, "Now the students have changed because the city has changed, and because the society has changed. It has not been a change to which many institutions have successfully adapted" (41).

As Glazer's comment suggested, the issues raised rippled well beyond one college in New York City—and one book, albeit one named a *New York Times* Notable Book of the Year. For a variety of reasons— social and demographic changes, increasing numbers of high school students enrolling in college (see Otte, "High Schools as Crucibles of College Prep"), and ongoing efforts to democratize and diversify higher education—remediation had become a vast industry. Attention to it was growing as both costs and enrollments in higher education grew. This was particularly true at the time of Traub's book, a period of significant economic downturn, which led to a budget crisis for CUNY and City College. Especially in a difficult economic climate, the BW enterprise was ripe for downsizing. As Mary Soliday later showed in *The Politics of Remediation* (2002), the representations of the actual extent of remediation varied considerably: "Estimates on the numbers of institutions that offered remediation in the '90s range from 40 to 81 percent" (124). The U.S. Department of Education's National Center for Education Statistics (NCES) estimated that, at the beginning of the 1990s, a third of college students took at least one remedial course; by the end of the decade, that number was 28 percent, with about three-quarters of all post-secondary institutions offering such courses. Significantly, the one area of decline was "remedial writing": institutions offering such courses fell from 71 percent to 68 percent from 1995 to 2000 (Parsad and Lewis).

What matters more than the exact numbers is what people made of them. There could be numerous explanations for the prevalence of remedial college courses at the end of the twentieth century: high schools were not doing their job, assessments were too strict or unreliable, culturally different students were resistant to assimilation, and so on. Of all the explanations, one seemed to have particular power for those looking at the remedial enterprise from the outside: the problem was to be found in the high schools, which were ripe for reform. Public dissatisfaction with the high schools led to demands for higher standards and more testing. By the end of the decade, legislatively mandated exit exams would be imposed for public high schools in most states, and in some states (California, New York, and Virginia, for example) colleges were required to help high schools meet the new standards (Otte, "High Schools as Crucibles of College Prep").

Basic writing, as a field, had some complicity in the conclusion that the high schools were not doing their job since it had, from the beginning, cast students as "underprepared." From this perspective, basic writing was the place to address the problems of a special population in need of special support. In one of the many defenses of BW in the 1990s (this one from 1995), Mary Sheridan-Rabideau and Gordon Brossel argued, "Basic writing classrooms . . . provide safe spaces where students are encouraged to address their writing difficulties within a supportive environment" (24). In explaining why basic writers needed such "safe spaces," these authors reasoned, "Unfamiliar with and underprepared for fulfilling the university's writing expectations, basic writers are often exploring writing practices that more experienced writers may already be quite comfortable with" (23–24).

But that is also a milder way of stating a conclusion that Shaughnessy had come to a couple of decades before when she refused to validate a type of education that had failed to properly educate millions of young adults. In *Errors and Expectations*, she expressed her wish that programs such as the one she established and ran would help to "close the shocking gaps in training between the poor and the affluent" (291). She and those who followed her lead in attempting to compensate for these gaps—especially in the absence of the needed reforms—eventually came in for critique. For example, in "The 'Birth' of Basic Writing" (an expanded version of "Discoursing Basic Writing," which appeared as the first chapter of *Representing the "Other"* [Horner and Lu]), Bruce Horner noted that rising to such pedagogical challenges in the absence of called-for social changes could actually entrench rather than address the inequities Shaughnessy inveighed against: "Unfortunately, pedagogies labeled as 'effective' at producing results within the constraints of degrading material conditions work in tandem with such reports and protests to legitimize those conditions—conditions of crisis that seem somehow never to be relieved" (27).

Real-World Repercussions

Horner's analysis effectively explains as well as excoriates the way, in the 1990s, politicians seemed concerned less with relieving "the constraints of degrading material conditions" than with reducing the cost of programs that had been attacked as ineffective. Assuming an increasingly activist stance toward postsecondary "remediation," state legislatures across the country began to pass laws limiting the availability of remedial programs. Different states have taken different approaches to "the remediation problem," but a common thread is to force students judged to need remediation in reading, writing, or mathematics into community colleges or adult education programs rather than admitting them to baccalaureate programs in four-year schools (Greene and McAlexander 15).

At the same time that states were placing restrictions on remediation, colleges and universities interested in raising their standards and status began to look critically at their entrance requirements, student retention rates, and progress toward the all-important baccalaureate degree. They soon saw that students initially classified as basic writers had a negative effect on these numbers—coming in with lower placement scores and often taking longer to graduate. The 1999 decision by CUNY's Board of Trustees to end open admissions at its four-year colleges, sending all students needing remediation to its community colleges, was an early example of this trend. Citing similar concerns about the erosion of standards, the Board of Trustees of the California State University system (the middle tier of that state's system, which also includes community colleges and research universities) ruled in the late 1990s that students must complete all remediation in English and mathematics within one year (Goen-Salter 83).

For those concerned with basic writing and basic writers, there was worse to come. In the new millennium, several of the oldest and most highly esteemed open admissions units attached to universities were phased out. In 2003, the University of Cincinnati (UC) decided to do away with University College, a two-year open admissions unit at the main campus. For decades, University College had offered developmental work within a supportive environment to underprepared students with the goal of helping them make the transition to a regular baccalaureate program at the University. Michelle Gibson and Deborah T. Meem, professors at the University of Cincinnati who taught basic writing at University College for many years, explain the rationale behind the decision to eliminate University College: "The goal of our university has been to remove nearly all underprepared students from the main campus's degree-granting units in order to bolster UC's academic ratings in such publications as *US News and World Report*" (64). In the summer of 2009, the University of Cincinnati announced that, beginning in 2010, the main campus will admit only "those students who meet the university's academic success criteria" (Hand). Students who seem less likely to "succeed" will be referred to the university's regional campuses or to programs at Cincinnati State Technical and Community College.

In 2005, the Regents of the University of Minnesota made a similar move, voting to eliminate the University's General College, which had a distinguished history of offering basic writing and other support services to underprepared students. This decision, like the one at Cincinnati, was motivated by the institution's desire to move into the top tier of research universities. Administrators at the University of Minnesota pointed out that students who began in General College took much longer to graduate, thus increasing the average time to attain the baccalaureate degree, one of the standards used to assess the quality of research universities (University of Minnesota). As of 2009, students who formerly would have entered the General College could take courses in the College of Education and Human Development, but the University's goal is eventually to reduce the number of students in need of remedial work by 60 percent (Greene and McAlexander 16).

Although a baccalaureate degree has become an increasingly important credential in today's society, access to basic writing and other compensatory programs for underprepared students is not a high priority for state legislators and university officials. And, as we will see in the next section, at the end of the 1990s, basic writing came under fire from within as well as from without.

Basic Writing Under Siege from Within

Arguing for Abolition

As legislators and university officials were questioning remedial efforts such as basic writing, scholars within the field were also taking a close look at BW programs and practices. This scrutiny became especially intense in the 1990s, with some saying that the whole structure of tracking and teaching BW students was unacceptable and needed to be jettisoned. The most dramatic expression of this was Ira Shor's "Our Apartheid: Writing Instruction and Inequality" (1997). Arguing that regular composition, instituted at Harvard in the last decade of the nineteenth century to control and gentrify a rising middle class, was itself a mechanism of "containment," Shor argued that basic writing was essentially more of the same:

> BW has added an extra sorting-out gate in front of the comp gate, a curricular mechanism to secure unequal power relations in yet another age of instability, the protest years of the 1960s and after. To help secure the status quo against democratic change in school and society, a BW language policy producing an extra layer of control was apparently needed to discipline students in an undisciplined age. At the time of BW's explosive birth, the system was under siege by mass demands for equality, access, and cultural democracy. Since then, the economy, short in graduate labor until about 1970, has been unable to absorb the educated workers produced by higher education in the past 25 years. In this scenario, BW has helped to slow the output of college graduates. BW, in sum, has functioned inside the larger saga of American society; it has been part of the undemocratic tracking system pervading American mass education, an added layer of linguistic control to help manage some disturbing economic and political conditions on campus and off. (92-93)

Even in its strong words (like the "apartheid" of the title), Shor's analysis was essentially an elaboration of David Bartholomae's claim, in his 1992 Conference on Basic Writing keynote address, that BW was guilty of "confirming existing patterns of power and authority, reproducing the hierarchies we had meant to question and overthrow" ("The Tidy House" 18). Shor's claims were rebutted by Karen Greenberg ("Response"), Terry Collins ("Response"), and Deborah Mutnick ("The Strategic Value of Basic Writing"). In fact, the debate overshadowed other BW research throughout the decade and into the next. The whole Spring 2000 issue of *JBW* was essentially devoted to the debate, and even Gerri McNenny's collection *Mainstreaming Basic*

Writers (2001) is less about mainstreaming than it is about the debate over mainstreaming.

The dissensus was evidence of a turning point in the history of basic writing. Controversies had always existed in the field, but in the past they had focused on how best to proceed with BW instruction, not on whether to do so. The 1990s changed that irrevocably. Only part of this critique was mounted by those present at the creation like Bartholomae and Shor. There was also a generational shift producing scholars who argued for a wholesale rethinking of basic writing, not as a logical curricular offering but as a social, historical, and, perhaps now, outdated construction. The concerns of this new generation were effectively articulated by two prominent voices, Bruce Horner and Min-Zhan Lu. In their introduction to *Representing the "Other": Basic Writers and the Teaching of Writing* (1999), they wrote:

> We see ourselves as part of a generation of compositionists trained in the late 1980s whose experience of basic writing was shaped by the canonical reception of certain texts on basic writing in graduate programs and professional journals. The gap between official accounts of basic writing and our day-to-day experience as writing teachers and students resulted in a dissatisfaction with what we saw as the occlusion of attention from the social struggle and change involved in the teaching and learning of basic writing, and representations of the "problems" of basic writers and basic writing in ways that risked perpetuating their marginal position in higher education. (xiv)

Distinguishing between "basic writing" and "the specific sociopolitical and intellectual contexts of both the production and reception of a discourse dominating the field ('Basic Writing')" (xi) allowed Horner and Lu to distinguish between the "heterogeneity of basic writing" and the "hegemonic position of Basic Writing" (xii), between the field's voices of dissent and complexity on the one hand and BW as the Establishment on the other.

The Great Unraveling

With or without "cultural materialist" critique and whether upper-cased or not, basic writing was looking far from hegemonic as the 1990s came to an end. This was not just due to debates over its abolition but to its actually being abolished or downsized, as attested to in accounts like Gail Stygall's 1999 article "Unraveling at Both Ends: Anti-Undergraduate Education, Anti-Affirmative Action, and Basic Writing at Research Schools." Stygall, like Gibson and Meem, Greene and McAlexander, and Soliday, recounted a political as well as a politicized deconstruction in which forces from within the institution joined with forces from without to bring basic writing down.

Horner and Lu were by no means oblivious to the consequences for BW students and teachers of such unraveling. In "Some Afterwords: Intersections and Divergences," the piece concluding *Representing the "Other,"* Horner writes:

> Certainly our insistence on the historicity of Basic Writing challenges the construction of "basic writing" into an objective, unified, and stable entity, represented as a "course," "student," or "writing." To teachers concerned with their own and their students' immediate institutional survival, however, any suggestions that "basic writing" is a construction may seem an elitist gesture from those situated to afford engagement in fine theoretical distinctions, at best an irresponsible admission, but in any event likely to provide additional fodder to those on the New Right attacking basic writing programs, teachers, and students. For if "basic" writing does not signify a "real" phenomenon, a concrete body of students with self-evident needs that must be met, then one may legitimately question whether or not to preserve basic writing programs. Similarly, given existing power relations in the United States, any emphasis on the political import of the teaching of basic writing may well seem to threaten to encourage those in positions of dominance to exercise that dominance more conclusively by putting an end to basic writing programs. Even teachers who agree that representations of basic writing are constructs that have functions strategically but problematically may well argue that such theoretical critiques are not worth the immediate, perhaps long-term, and significant material losses that such critiques may cost. (191–92)

In light of this litany of objections, the recourse Horner and Lu offer—at least in the capsule form provided in the introduction to *Representing the "Other"*—may seem small consolation: "By recognizing the heterogeneity of basic writing at any given time and place, teachers can draw on the full range of positions and forces—dominant, alternative, and oppositional as well as residual or emergent—with some of which we might align ourselves and with all of which we must contend" (xiii). Given their own insistent focus on basic writing's "marginal position in higher education," this recognition seems to call for a remarkable resourcefulness from a harried and insecure cadre of largely part-time instructors and out-on-a-limb administrators.

Around the turn of the century, it began to seem that any efforts by teachers and administrators (no matter how resourceful they might be) to improve or even preserve their basic writing programs would be doomed to failure. Debates were roiling, programs closing. But in the midst of this disarray, two of the most significant testaments to the importance of basic writing since *Errors and Expectations* were published, reporting on research at CUNY's City College—the same site where Shaughnessy had done her groundbreaking work. Using the most carefully collected longitudinal evidence ever seen in BW research, Marilyn Sternglass's *Time to Know Them* (1997) gave compelling evidence of basic writers' ability to succeed. Although this research demonstrated that educational opportunity coupled with academic support could transform students' lives, ultimately it didn't seem to matter much. The elimination of basic writing from City College was imminent. By the time Mary Soliday's *Politics of Remediation* (2002) was published, the erasure of basic writing at that college was an accomplished fact, despite the success of Soliday and Gleason's own mainstreaming experiment there.

Basic Writing Revised

Public Policy and Basic Writing

Yet as basic writing was being phased out at many four-year colleges, BW programs were being preserved, or even transformed, at other institutions. One place where questions about the future of basic writing were raised was in the special Fall 2006 issue of the *Journal of Basic Writing*, which celebrated the publication of the journal's twenty-fifth volume. It seems significant, in light of CUNY's decision to shift BW into the community colleges, that by this time in the journal's history the editors were both community college professors—Bonne August and Rebecca Mlynarczyk. In 2007, when August stepped down, Hope Parisi, another community college professor, became coeditor.

In the special issue of 2006, the editors asked some of the leaders of the field to analyze the current state of basic writing. In their contribution titled "In the Here and Now: Public Policy and Basic Writing," Linda Adler-Kassner and Susanmarie Harrington assert that BW researchers must contend with "three themes that run through contemporary discussion of education generally, and writing specifically: that students aren't prepared for college or work during their high school years; that this lack of preparation is costing institutions and, directly or indirectly, taxpayers; and that these first two problems are rooted in a system that requires outside agents to come in and repair it" (30). They propose countering these three themes with carefully crafted rhetoric, empirical data, and a resolve to reach those beyond as well as within the academy: ". . . we need to *make* the decisions, *do* the research, and *use* the data we collect in strategic ways. It's time to move beyond academic discussion. We need to take our perspectives and our programs public: it's time to take data in hand, with rhetorical fierceness" (45). If this seems utopian, Adler-Kassner and Harrington would stress that it is nevertheless necessary given how the problem of the "underprepared" student is currently framed: "Unless compositionists of all stripes—those teaching basic writing, those who work with first-year composition and graduate students—are able to shift the direction of this discussion, it will have significant and deleterious effects on our work, affecting everything from the students who sit in our classes to the lessons that we design" (30).

But such urgency does not assure that what is needed is also what is possible. At this point, says Laura Gray-Rosendale (also writing in the special 2006 issue of *JBW*), the field has become so context-focused, so concerned with local/institutional circumstances and individual cases that

> we may have lost some of our ability to describe relevant institutional, political, and social trends in broader, general terms within basic writing scholarship. . . . While focusing on the minute specifics of basic writers' situations has allowed us to gather a great deal of crucial local knowledge, focusing so much of our energies

> on these projects may leave us in danger of abandoning the important national and global concerns that have defined our discipline for many years and have been fundamental to making successful arguments on behalf of our students. ("Back to the Future" 20)

Recent developments concerning basic writing have certainly confirmed the point made by the authors of these articles: BW professionals need to communicate more effectively with college administrators, politicians, and the general public about what they do in basic writing and why these endeavors are worthy of continued support. In order to do this, they need to publicize how BW programs have evolved to meet students' (and society's) changing needs. In introducing the special issue of 2006, Mlynarczyk and August emphasize the ways in which this evolution was already happening: "In response to legislative mandates banning 'remediation' from four-year institutions, faculty committees are developing creative and academically sound programs to offer students BW support as well as academic credit" ("Editors' Column" 1). Two such programs were featured in the issue. Mark McBeth describes a new approach to basic writing developed at CUNY's John Jay College of Criminal Justice that offers students a rich academic experience while at the same time helping them to pass the ACT exam required for exit from the course. In "Redefining Literacy as a Social Practice," Shannon Carter details the comprehensive approach developed at her institution, Texas A&M University at Commerce, in which BW students begin by analyzing a discourse they know well and gradually apply what they have learned to understand the relatively unfamiliar features of academic discourse.

Alternative Program Structures

The changing structures of basic writing programs are summarized in William Lalicker's "A Basic Introduction to Basic Writing Program Structures" (1999). In this report based on a survey Lalicker conducted on the Writing Program Administrators (WPA) listserv, he groups existing BW programs into six broad categories. The first, which he terms the "baseline" or "prerequisite model," is the traditional non-credit "skills" course in which basic writing is viewed as a prerequisite to be completed before taking "college-level" composition. Although some programs using this model have adopted more progressive pedagogies and practices, the prerequisite model often causes resentment among students, who fail to see the relevance of these required non-credit courses. The five alternatives listed by Lalicker seek to avoid this problematic aspect of the prerequisite model by integrating BW instruction more completely into regular college course structures—often granting some academic credit for this work. In the stretch model (such as the well-known approach used at Arizona State University), BW students are given two semesters to complete a regular one-semester composition course (see Glau, "*Stretch* at 10," "The 'Stretch Program'"). In the studio model first developed at the University of South Carolina, basic writers take regular first-year composition along with a required studio workshop in which they receive additional help with their writing (see Grego and Thompson). Other colleges have opted for directed self-placement. With this model, entering students are advised of the availability of basic writing courses and left to make their own decision as to whether to take BW or regular composition (see Royer and Gilles, "Basic Writing and Directed Self-Placement," *Directed Self-Placement*). A fourth alternative is the intensive model in which students who are judged to need basic writing are assigned to a composition course in which students meet for more hours than required for regular composition and receive extra support (see Seagall). The intensive model, which is similar to the studio approach in many respects, differs from it in that students remain with the same teacher and student group for all the required hours of instruction whereas with the studio model students from several different composition classes attend the same studio session. The final category listed by Lalicker is mainstreaming. Strictly speaking, this option does away with BW, placing all students in regular composition. However, Mary Soliday and Barbara Gleason, directors of a successful mainstreaming project at CUNY's City College, point out that teachers who are not trained in teaching basic writing need extra resources and support in the form of professional development workshops, mentoring programs, and tutoring services for students. In effect, according to Soliday and Gleason, if mainstreaming is to succeed, then it must offer an enriched approach to teaching composition.

Other models for offering basic writing that are not mentioned in Lalicker's report include service learning, WAC (Writing Across the Curriculum) and WID (Writing in the Disciplines), and learning communities. In service-learning programs, students perform community service, which becomes the basis for their academic learning and reflection. In recent years, basic writing programs at many institutions have implemented courses that include a community service component. In *Writing Partnerships: Service-Learning in Composition* (2000), Thomas Deans states that, at its best, service learning is "a pedagogy of action and reflection, one that centers on a dialectic between community outreach and academic inquiry" (2). Based on his analysis of a variety of service-learning projects, Deans has developed a taxonomy of three paradigms that operate in these courses: (1) writing *about* the community (in which students use their community involvement as a subject to think and write about for their academic course), (2) writing *with* the community (in which students, professors, and community members collaborate in writing about issues and concerns relevant to that community), and (3) writing *for* the community (in which students create written products for the community such as flyers or newsletter articles) (15–20).

The response to service learning from participants—teachers, students, and community members—has, on the whole, been positive (Deans 2), but descriptions of service learning in basic writing classes also allude to possible pitfalls. For example, in "Servant Class: Basic Writers and Service Learning," Don J. Kraemer takes a critical look at "the tensions and contradictions between the process-oriented, learning-centered pedagogy" usually associated with BW courses and "the product-based, performance-centered moment" emphasized in writing-for-the-community projects (92). After an analysis of his students' experiences in a writing-for project, Kraemer concludes: "When writing for the community, students do good—but very little seeking, describing, naming, acting, and changing" (108). These activities, which help students develop their rhetorical abilities, are, in Kraemer's view, more important goals for basic writing.

Even in the writing-about version of service learning, in which students use their community service to analyze a social issue, problems can arise if students do not feel personally invested in their service experience. In an article analyzing a qualitative research project focused on a basic writing course requiring students to tutor in a local elementary school, Nancy Pine found that only one student—the one who had elected to take this course because of the tutoring component—chose to include his tutoring experiences as part of the mix of sources for the required research essay. While acknowledging the complexities involved in helping basic writers to acquire academic literacy through analyzing their service experiences, Pine believes that "in writing-about composition service learning classes, it is crucial that connections between the service and course content be made explicit by and for students in multiple forms of writing and speaking" (53). Service learning has the potential to make coursework in basic writing more meaningful, but it requires careful planning of program structures and pedagogies.

When basic writing is offered as Writing Across the Curriculum (WAC) or Writing in the Disciplines (WID), the concern for helping students become better writers moves beyond "remedial" programs and into mainstream courses. With WAC and WID, professors in a variety of disciplines work to encourage the development of students' academic literacies (see Bazerman et al. for a comprehensive discussion of these approaches). While it is certainly desirable for students placed in BW to receive writing support in their mainstream classes, it may be problematic if WAC or WID is seen as a replacement for basic writing. Faculty in disciplines other than English may lack the desire, the fundamental knowledge of BW theory and practice, or the time needed to help basic writers become successful writers in their subject areas.

Another way of expanding the responsibility for teaching basic writing beyond the confines of the English department is seen in the growing trend toward learning community (LC) programs for students with BW placement. First developed in the 1920s and 1930s as enrichment programs for the most academically prepared students (Gabelnick et al.), in recent years learning community programs have also proved effective for students classified as basic or ESL writers. The rationale behind learning communities is to "purposefully restructure the curriculum to link together courses or coursework so that students find greater coherence in what they are learning as well as increased intellectual interaction with faculty and fellow students" (Gabelnick et al. 5). In learning community programs for basic writers, a cohort of students takes a BW course and one or more courses in other disciplines. Faculty members in the learning community collaborate to design and implement a curriculum that will help students see the interconnections between ideas from the different courses, sometimes developing joint syllabi and shared assignments.

Like other alternative approaches to basic writing, learning community programs have potential problems—most notably the "hyperbonding" that sometimes occurs when students in the same learning cohort "gang up" to engage in disruptive classroom behavior or to sabotage an instructor or a project ("The Impact"). These negative behaviors are the exception, however, rather than the rule. For the most part, BW students who participate in learning communities are more engaged in their learning and have higher retention rates in the course and in the college, higher graduation rates, and higher grades than control groups of basic writers who do not have this experience (see Darabi, Heaney, Mlynarczyk and Babbitt for results at different colleges). Such positive, statistically significant outcomes are certainly important for the students and faculty participating in these programs. Perhaps equally important in this data-driven environment, they offer a way to convince college administrators and state legislators of the value of well-designed approaches to basic writing. Rachelle Darabi explains:

> Positioning basic writing courses within learning communities may lead not only to positive outcomes like greater student success but also relief of some of the tensions surrounding remediation at the university level. By increasing students' opportunities to succeed, universities can spotlight these successes rather than being defined by failures, allowing faculty and students alike to focus their attention on learning. (71)

The recent development of new models for providing basic writing instruction at many U.S. colleges is a hopeful sign. Program directors and professors across the country are using what they have learned about basic writing over the years to design innovative programs that better meet students' needs while also conforming to the requirements imposed by politicians or university administrators. For the most part, these redesigned programs are an improvement on the old prerequisite model of remediation, where students first had to complete basic writing to certify that they were ready for "college-level writing." Instead, students are developing the academic literacies needed for college coursework while actually taking "college-level" courses. Whether such programs will survive in the face of mounting pressure to cut costs and raise "standards" in higher education remains to be seen.

Basic Writing for the Twenty-First Century

Anticipating the Need

In discussing the fate of basic writing in the years to come, one question that arises is whether the need for this type of support at the college level will decrease, increase, or remain relatively stable. Several indicators suggest that the need will increase substantially. Since the 1990s, many states' efforts have focused on eliminating the need for "remediation" in higher education. But the success of these efforts has been negligible. In fall 1995, the National Center for Education Statistics (NCES) surveyed two- and four-year institutions. Of those that offered remedial courses, about 47 percent reported that the number of students enrolled in these courses had remained about the same over the past five years. For 39 percent of the institutions, the number had increased. Only 14 percent of the schools surveyed said the number had declined (Parsad and Lewis).

The experiences of the California State University system illustrate the difficulty of trying to reduce the need for remediation in higher education. In a *JBW* article titled "Critiquing the Need to Eliminate Remediation: Lessons from San Francisco State" (2008), Sugie Goen-Salter takes a historical approach. Beginning in the 1980s when about 42 percent of entering students were judged to be in need of remediation by the system's English placement test, the California Postsecondary Education Commission began to develop complex and expensive approaches to try to reduce, and eventually eliminate, the need for English remediation at the Cal State campuses (Goen-Salter 81). These measures have included many well-designed and well-implemented programs such as requiring that all students applying to the system take four years of English in high school, tightening the requirements of teacher education programs in the state, developing innovative partnerships between high school and college teachers, and inviting eleventh graders from under-represented minorities to take a mock placement test and attend Saturday workshops to improve their academic writing (81-82).

Despite these well-conceived and well-intentioned measures, by 1990 the number of incoming students to the Cal State system in need of English remediation had climbed to 45 percent. California continued to pour resources and energy into a variety of programs to solve "the remediation problem" before students arrived on its college campuses, but by 1997 the number had climbed once again—to 47 percent of new students. In this same year, the Cal State Board of Trustees enacted new initiatives designed to reduce the number of students needing remediation to 10 percent by 2007 (83). They also imposed a one-year limit on the time students could take to complete remedial courses in English and mathematics. Those who failed to meet this limit would be "disenrolled" and required to complete the requisite courses at a community college before returning to the Cal State system (83). Despite these measures, in 2007, the year when it was hoped only 10 percent of new students would require remediation, the percentage of students who needed remediation after enrolling at Cal State remained at 46.2 percent (96).

Goen-Salter outlines this somewhat discouraging history of attempts to eliminate the need for remediation in order to highlight the success of the Integrated Reading/Writing Program (IRW) developed at her own campus, San Francisco State University. This program, which currently enrolls more than 1,000 students each year, provides integrated support in both reading and writing and enables students to complete the required English remediation as well as first-year composition in their first year on campus. The success of the IRW Program strengthens Goen-Salter's central argument that college is the appropriate place to help students develop the academic literacy required in today's society:

> To perform its democratic function, basic writing sits not at the point of exit from high school, but at the *entry* point to higher education. Historically, basic writing has served to initiate students to the discourses of the academic community, which may be far distant from and even alien to those of their home communities. But basic writing doesn't just initiate students to a more privileged language; it also offers them the opportunity and instructional practice to critically reflect on a variety of discourses, of home, school, work and the more specific public discourses of the media, the law, the health care system, and even of the college writing classroom itself. (98)

It is appropriate to invoke the ideals of a democracy in defending the notion that college should be the place to help students master the various discourses they will need in our increasingly complex society. This, of course, was the central argument that fueled demands for open admissions in the late 1960s. And there are signs that, in the years to come, enrollment in American colleges and universities will increase dramatically to accommodate growing numbers of nontraditional students, many of whom are likely to be judged "underprepared" for college-level writing.

One development that will undoubtedly increase the size of the college population—and also the need for remedial support—is the new GI bill passed in May 2008. Under this law, veterans who completed at least three years of active-duty service in the U.S. military after September 10, 2001, are eligible to receive thirty-six months of full tuition at public institutions of higher education in their states (for specific details on the new law, see "GI Bill 2008: Frequently Asked Questions"). The greatly expanded availability of educational funding for veterans will result in large increases in college enrollments. And because of the demographics of the U.S. military, many of these new students will be first-generation college students who have been out of school for years—a group that has historically needed basic writing or other types of remediation to succeed in college.

Another indicator of the likelihood of a growing need for remediation is the Obama administration's commitment to increasing the percentage of Americans attending college. In February 2009 in his first address to a joint session of Congress, President Barack Obama pointed out that 75 percent of present-day jobs require more than a high school education but that only slightly more than half of all Americans actually graduate from high school. Obama expressed the hope that by 2020 the United States would have the highest percentage of college graduates of any country in the world, and he asked "every American to commit to at least one year or more of higher education or career training" at a four-year college, a community college, or a vocational program or apprenticeship ("Address"). In his first major education address (March 10, 2009), Obama pledged increased support for higher education, and his proposed 2009 budget included substantial increases in federal Pell grants as well as a tuition tax credit for students from working families ("Remarks"). The stimulus law that Obama signed in February 2009 acknowledges "the remediation problem" and requires states that receive stabilization money to improve high school courses and testing in order to reduce the number of students who need remedial courses in college (Dillon). But California's failure to significantly reduce the need for remediation (described earlier in this chapter) suggests that in the future many students will continue to arrive at college in need of appropriate remedial programs.

As U.S. college enrollments increase significantly among veterans and nontraditional students, the need for basic writing is also likely to increase, as it did in the early days of open admissions. And there is an accumulating body of evidence that remedial programs—including basic writing—can have substantial benefits not only for the students enrolled in them but also for U.S. society at large.

Examining Costs and Benefits

Although coverage in the mainstream media has tended to focus on the supposed failings of remedial programs at the college level, many of these claims are not supported by well-designed research. One scholar who has taken a rigorous approach to the question of how remedial courses affect students is Bridget Terry Long, professor of education and economics at the Harvard Graduate School of Education. In a 2005 article titled "The Remediation Debate: Are We Serving the Needs of Underprepared College Students?" (in *National Crosstalk*, an online publication of the National Center for Public Policy and Higher Education), Long described the motivation for her research:

> While the policy debate about college remediation focuses on where it should be offered and who should pay for it, more careful thought should be given to what impact remediation has on students. Do the courses help remedial students perform better and remain in higher education longer? Is the investment in remedial programs worthwhile?

To address these questions in a reliable way, Long felt it was important to compare students with similar family backgrounds, high school programs and grades, and demographics—some of whom had taken remedial courses while others had not. She found a suitable student population in Ohio, where public colleges are allowed to set their own standards for assigning students to remedial courses. Looking at the results of remediation from this more nuanced perspective, Long found that "students in remediation have better educational outcomes than do students with similar backgrounds and preparation who do not take remedial courses." She believes that curtailing remedial programs or insisting that all such support be provided in community colleges could have serious negative consequences: "Lower levels of education are associated with higher rates of unemployment, government dependency, crime and incarceration." What may initially look like a cost-saving measure—eliminating remedial programs from American colleges and universities—could end up costing society much more in the long run.

Assessing the costs and benefits of open access to higher education has been the longstanding research interest of sociologist David Lavin. In studies conducted over many years, he has focused on the student population that entered the City University of New York under open admissions in the early 1970s, the same population that inspired Mina Shaughnessy to write *Errors and Expectations*. Lavin's most recent book, coauthored with Paul Attewell and titled *Passing the Torch: Does Higher Education for the Disadvantaged Pay Off Across the Generations?* (2007), provides a fascinating glimpse of the lives of these students thirty years later. The book addresses two broad research questions: (1) when viewed over a long time span (thirty years), how have the students who entered CUNY under open admissions fared in terms of college graduation and later earning power? and (2) how have the educational achievements of the first generation affected their children's educational careers? (Attewell and Lavin xvii). After extensive, multifaceted statistical analysis of data from a sample of about 2,000 of these former CUNY students along with a much larger national sample (for purposes of comparison), Attewell and Lavin reach conclusions that confirm the value of making higher education widely available:

> A broad population of students, including those with poor high school preparation, enters the doors of public colleges. In response, these institutions have extended remedial courses—which were always offered to wealthy students in Ivy League colleges—to any students who need them. Is that remediation a bad investment? Contrary to critics' contentions, our analyses suggest that remedial courses do not depress graduation rates for most students, and that remediation may reduce college dropout rates in the short term.
>
> Taken as a whole, the evidence presented in this book indicates that the democratization of public

> higher education has not generated hordes of unemployable graduates or worthless degrees. Those who graduate with a college degree from public universities earn significantly more than high school graduates, net of background characteristics. For hundreds of thousands of underprivileged students, a college education is the first step up the ladder of social mobility and their college attendance generates an upward momentum for most of their children. (7)

One of the most surprising facts this study revealed was that most students who started college at CUNY during open admissions eventually earned a degree. When Attewell and Lavin examined the educational outcomes of 2,000 female students from this group over a long time period (thirty years), 71 percent had completed a degree, and three-quarters of those who earned a degree received a bachelor's degree (4–5). Obviously, studies that assess graduation rates by looking at a period of four or six years miss many of the students who eventually graduate from nonselective public institutions.

How does remediation—specifically basic writing—influence students' chances of graduation? Statistics reported in *Passing the Torch* show that students who take remedial courses do take longer to graduate (Attewell and Lavin 173). However, in recent studies that tease apart the effect of taking remedial courses from other influences such as family economic status and high school preparation, it appears "that most of the gap in graduation rates has little to do with taking remedial classes in college, but instead reflects pre-existing skill differences carried over from high school" (174).

In a related study titled "New Evidence on College Remediation" (Attewell et al. [2006]), there was evidence that community college students who took and passed remedial courses were more likely to graduate than were their peers who had not taken such courses (Attewell et al. 912; Attewell and Lavin 174). In fact, community college students who took and passed remedial writing were 13 percent more likely to graduate than students with similar high school backgrounds who did not take remedial writing (Attewell et al. 912). Four-year college students who took one or more remedial courses had lower graduation rates, but students who took only remedial writing graduated at the same rate as students who took no remedial courses (Attewell et al. 909). The statistics on graduation rates from four-year schools are especially important if one considers the students' ethnicity. Nationwide, a large proportion of African-American and Hispanic students who eventually earned a BA took one or more remedial courses—50 percent for African-Americans and 34 percent for Hispanics. If these students had been denied admission to four-year colleges, a large number of the minority high school graduates from the class of 1992 would never have earned a bachelor's degree (Attewell and Lavin 173–74).

Attewell and Lavin conclude their discussion of remediation by emphasizing what is gained from providing remedial support: "Currently, college remediation functions both as a second-chance policy for poorly prepared students and as a form of institutional quality control that prevents students from graduating unless and until they demonstrate basic skills. Critics of remedial education seem to overlook the importance of remedial education for maintaining academic standards" (*Passing the Torch* 175). Attacks on remediation that have gained widespread attention in the media often ignore the subtleties revealed by thoughtful, statistically-based research. A closer look reveals that this type of instruction has important benefits not only for individual students but also for the institutions they attend and the society of which they are a part.

The children of those students also stand to benefit from the educational opportunities offered to their parents. It is well established that children born to mothers with a college education do much better educationally than those whose mothers did not go to college (Attewell and Lavin 72). In order to get a more nuanced understanding of this phenomenon, Attewell and Lavin looked at seven possible educational outcomes for children such as vocabulary, reading and math achievement, and (eventually) college attendance (74–75). For five of the seven outcomes, "the effect of a mother's having a B.A. was a highly statistically significant predictor of the child's educational performance" (74). Although the authors emphasize that class and race still have a big effect on children's educational achievement, they also feel that "increased entry to higher education weakens the cycle of disadvantage" (78).

Breaking the cycle of disadvantage is a primary concern in this age of economic uncertainty. Increasing educational opportunity for previously underrepresented groups has definite economic benefits for society at large. After looking carefully at income figures for people who attended CUNY during open admissions, Attewell and Lavin concluded that "[m]ass education has not made a degree worth less" (5) as critics of open access had feared. There were substantial increases in earnings for every higher degree achieved, from the associate's degree through graduate degrees (36). If open admissions had not enabled the women in this study to attend college, then their overall lifetime earnings would have been much lower. Given the women's actual income figures from 2000 and a hypothetical calculation of what their income would have been if they had not gained admission to CUNY, the researchers estimated that the women would have earned about $7,700 less a year (192).

Income projections are also provided in Lavin's 1996 book *Changing the Odds* (coauthored with David Hyllegard). When Lavin and Hyllegard examined the earnings of the cohort of students from the first three classes that entered CUNY under open admissions in the early 1970s, they estimated that during one year in the 1980s, these people made nearly sixty-seven million dollars more than they would have if they had not attended college. Using conservative estimates of their earning power over the next thirty years, Lavin and Hyllegard predict that the long-term aggregate increase in earnings for this group would be more than two billion dollars (197–98). By increasing the earnings of people who would not previously have gone to college, CUNY's open admissions policy has broadened the tax base, contributing not only to the well-being of the individuals involved but also to society at large.

The statistically-based conclusions of scholars such as Bridget Terry Long and David Lavin and his colleagues are highly relevant to this discussion of the future of basic writing. In the face of attacks on remediation as a dangerous and costly experiment, views that were widely expressed in the 1990s and early 2000s, there is increasing evidence that, in the long run, providing access to higher education along with appropriate forms of academic support such as basic writing pays off for individuals and for society. This is not only an economic issue but also a moral one, a point that is stressed by Michelle Gibson and Deborah T. Meem in their description of the demise of University College, the open access arm of the University of Cincinnati:

> The way a culture treats its non-elites serves as a benchmark of the culture's moral authority. Our country has sold the myth of the American Dream to generations of its poor and disenfranchised—a myth

> that has traditionally revolved around access to education. If state support of higher education results in public universities providing less and less access to underprepared, working class, poor, or otherwise marginalized students, then our sense of who is able to pursue that dream—and who is not—is dramatically altered. (50)

In his 2009 book titled *Why School? Reclaiming Education for All of Us* (excerpted in *The Chronicle of Higher Education*), Mike Rose also emphasizes the role of American colleges and universities in offering students a second chance and, thus, fulfilling the promises of our democracy. "It is terrible," Rose acknowledges, "that so many students—especially those from poorer backgrounds—come to college unprepared." But, he goes on,

> colleges can't fold their arms in a huff and try to pull away from the problem. Rather than marginalize remediation, they should invest more intellectual resources in it, making it as effective as it can be. The notion of a second chance, of building safety nets into a flawed system, offers a robust idea of education and learning: that we live in a system that acknowledges that people change, retool, grow, and need to return to old mistakes, or just to what is past and forgotten.
>
> Remediation may be an unfortunate term for all this, as it carries with it the sense of disease, of a medical intervention. "Something that corrects an evil, a fault, or an error," notes *The American Heritage Dictionary*. But when done well, remediation becomes a key mechanism in a democratic model of human development. ("Colleges Need to Re-Mediate Remediation" A76)

Despite Rose's inspirational words encouraging colleges and universities to invest more of their financial and intellectual resources in effective remedial programs such as basic writing, the future of the field is far from certain. There is no way to determine whether research will lead to dramatic advances in pedagogy or further fragmentation. It is possible but by no means certain that current threats to basic writing may be trumped by future needs as economic forces reconfigure the political landscape. More powerful models for providing BW instruction may emerge, as well as more unified support for an under-supported field. Predictions are always dubious, particularly in a time of upheaval. So the fate of basic writing—and of basic writers—in the decades to come is an open question. What is not questionable is that the country needs an increasing number of well-educated, literate citizens to compete in the economy of the twenty-first century. Past experience suggests that many students will continue to arrive at colleges and universities lacking the writing abilities and habits of thought needed to succeed in college and the workplace. Well-designed and carefully implemented basic writing programs can enhance these students' chances for success. But this will happen only if the concerted effort to displace these students from the nation's institutions of higher education is itself displaced. What is needed is a sustained national commitment to fully educate this vital but vulnerable student population. The fate of those who would need basic writing is tied to the larger society, a society that has to decide whether to do the right thing by them and expand its commitment or contract its own chances by curtailing educational opportunity.

Of course, a society never really decides to do anything. That falls to individuals, to their resolve and their initiative. The future of basic writing, like its past, will depend on how external forces combine with initiative from within, often resulting in moments of extraordinary leadership and fragile consensus as well as incremental progress and stunning setbacks. There are lessons to be learned from that history, some hard and some inspiring. Some may have lost their relevance with the passage of time. But some may make the past of basic writing a guide to building its future.

Appendix: Basic Writing Resources

In addition to the many books and articles on basic writing discussed in this book, other resources are available to those interested in BW programs and practices. Some of these offer opportunities for networking with people in the BW community through organizations such as the Conference on Basic Writing (CBW) or the National Association for Developmental Education (NADE) or through internet listservs and blogs. Others are current publications of interest, many of which are available online. The resources in this appendix (listed in alphabetical order) were selected on the basis of importance to the field, currency, comprehensiveness, and ease of access. For the sake of quick reference, here is a list of the resources included with annotations and elaborations to follow:

> Bedford Bibliographies for Teachers of Basic Writing
> CompPile (and CompFAQs)
> Conference on Basic Writing (including its *Basic Writing e-Journal*)
> Conference on College Composition and Communication
> Council of Writing Program Administrators
> International Writing Centers Association
> *Journal of Basic Writing*
> *Journal of Developmental Education*
> National Association for Developmental Education
> Teaching Basic Writing
> *Teaching Developmental Writing: Background Readings*
> The WAC Clearinghouse

BEDFORD BIBLIOGRAPHIES FOR TEACHERS OF WRITING

Adler-Kassner, Linda, and Gregory R. Glau, eds. *The Bedford Bibliography for Teachers of Basic Writing*. 2nd ed. Boston: Bedford/St. Martin's, 2005. Print and Web. 12 Feb. 2010.

Glau, Gregory R., and Chitralekha Duttagupta, eds. *The Bedford Bibliography for Teachers of Basic Writing*. 3rd ed. Boston: Bedford/St. Martin's, 2010. Print.

These bibliographies provide a comprehensive, annotated listing of the most influential works of scholarship related to basic writing. The second edition, which was published in the same year as the 25th anniversary of the Conference on Basic Writing, includes Karen Uehling's historical overview titled "The Conference on Basic Writing, 1989–2005" (http://www.bedfordstmartins.com/basicbib/content/conference.html). The third edition is larger, with more than four hundred entries by two hundred teachers from around the country, reflecting the growing amount of basic writing scholarship; it includes expanded coverage in a more complete section on "Second-Language Learners/Special Populations." The *Bibliography* is available free from all Bedford/St. Martin's sales representatives, and the second edition is also online at http://www.bedfordstmartins.com/basicbib/.

CompPile

CompPile (http://comppile.org/) is a searchable database that provides important resources related to all aspects of composition, rhetoric, and writing studies. The Basic Writing section of CompFAQs (that part of CompPile done as a wiki) is available at http://comppile.tamucc.edu/wiki/BasicWriting/Home and includes the following links:

> Teaching Basic Writing,
> Basic Writing Resources (including lists of syllabi, texts, and online resources)
> Personal Writing in Basic Writing Courses
> Course Credit
> Theme-Based Courses
> Best Practices
> Reading List: Teaching Basic Writing
> Basic Writing Syllabi (for graduate courses in basic writing)
> Basic Writing Graduate Courses

Because these sections of "Basic Writing@CompFAQs" (like the rest of CompFAQs) are all parts of a wiki (a collaboratively authored and edited collection of web-based documents), contributions to the growing body of resources can be made at any time and are welcome.

Conference on Basic Writing

The Conference on Basic Writing (http://orgs.tamu-commerce.edu/cbw/cbw/News.html), often referred to as CBW, is a special interest group of NCTE's Conference on College Composition and Communication (CCCC). CBW's goal is to provide a forum for professional and personal conversations on pedagogy, curriculum, administration, and social issues affecting basic writing. CBW offers a variety of resources for those interested in basic writing:

Basic Writing e-Journal

An electronic publication of the Conference on Basic Writing designed to broaden conversations about basic writing, BWe is a refereed journal (http://orgs.tamu-commerce.edu/BWe/index.htm) that publishes articles, book reviews, and announcements and welcomes submissions in traditional or multimedia formats. Current editors are Shannon Carter of Texas A&M University at Commerce (Shannon_Carter@tamu-commerce.edu) and Susan Naomi Bernstein (susan.naomi@gmail.com). Electronic submissions are preferred.

CBW Facebook Page

An open group sponsored by the Conference on Basic Writing, the CBW Facebook Page (http:/www.facebook.com/group.php?gid=50538806660) serves as a venue for discussions of issues related to basic writing and a site for posting announcements, photographs, and general information. The Facebook page aims to engage BW students and teachers in discussions of the processes and practices of writing in order to enhance academic success across the curriculum.

CBW-L

This e-mail listserv (http:/orgs.tamu-commerce.edu/CBW/Listserv.html) is open to anyone who would like "to participate in an ongoing discussion of basic writing as it is studied and practiced in its historically rich and varied contexts." To subscribe, send an e-mail message to: listserv@umn.edu. Leave the subject line blank, and be sure to remove your signature from the e-mail. The content of the message should read:

> subscribe CBW-L Firstname Lastname.
> For example: subscribe CBW-L Jane Doe.

After subscribing, you will receive an e-mail confirmation of your subscription and instructions for sending messages, setting up your account in digest form (if you prefer), accessing the CBW-L archive, or receiving a complete index of CBW-L messages.

CBW SIG at CCCC

The Conference on Basic Writing is a Special Interest Group (SIG) of the Conference on College Composition and Communication and holds an evening meeting on the Thursday or Friday of the CCCC annual convention. This is an open meeting, and all who are interested in basic writing are welcome to attend. For information about how to register for CCCC, go to http://www.ncte.org/cccc/conv.

CBW Workshop on Basic Writing

An all-day workshop on current issues in basic writing is held each spring on the day before the beginning of the national Conference on College Composition and Communication (CCCC). For information about how to register or topics being discussed, go to http://www.ncte.org/cccc/conv.

National Survey of Basic Writing Programs

Sponsored by the Conference on Basic Writing, the National Survey of Basic Writing Programs is intended to gather information nationwide about basic writing programs, policies, teaching practices, demographics, and the effects of state and local legislation on them. The resulting database will provide national information for teachers, researchers, and program administrators about the history, structures, and practices of basic writing in the U.S. The Survey, consisting of only ten questions, is available on Survey Monkey. To fill out the Survey for your institution, go to http://www.surveymonkey.com/s.aspx?sm=xH qm3g7tYx7ildvliwJMMg_3d_3d.

Conference on College Composition and Communication (CCCC)

A constituent group of the National Council of Teachers of English (NCTE), the Conference on College Composition and Communication (http://ncte.org/cccc) promotes best practices in the teaching of writing by sponsoring conferences and workshops, publishing books and journals, supporting research on composition, and advocating for language and literacy education. Over the years, the CCCC Executive Committee has approved position statements in many areas such as National Language Policy, Students' Right to Their Own Language, Writing Assessment, and Ethical Conduct of Research in Composition Studies. Current versions of all CCCC position statements are available online at http://ncte.org/cccc/resources/positions.

Council of Writing Program Administrators (WPA)

WPA (http://www.wpacouncil.org/) is a national association open to all who are involved with or interested in directing writing programs. The Council publishes a newletter and semi-annual refereed journal (*WPA: Writing Program Administration*) and newsletter and hosts an annual workshop and conference. WPA also develops position statements, makes grants and awards, and provides consultations and evaluations of writing programs.

International Writing Centers Association

The Association (http://writingcenters.org/) provides a variety of resources for all who direct or work in writing centers. IWCA publishes books as well as *The Writing Center Journal* and *The Writing Lab Newsletter*. The Association also hosts national and regional conferences and offers research grants to encourage scholarship related to writing centers.

Journal of Basic Writing (JBW)

The *Journal of Basic Writing* (http://orgs.tamu-commerce.edu/cbw/cbw/JBW.html) is a fully refereed journal published since 1975 by the City University of New York with support from its Office of Academic Affairs. *JBW* is published twice a year and features research reports and articles that are original, well-grounded in theory, and clearly related to practice. Since 2003, full-text versions of its articles are available electronically through Communication and Mass Media Complete (EBSCO) (http://www.ebscohost.com/thisTopic.php?topicID=56&marketID=1) and the Education Resources Information Center (ERIC) (http://www.eric.ed.gov/).The current editors of *JBW* are Rebecca Mlynarczyk (rebecca.mlynarczyk@gmail.com) and Hope Parisi (HopeKCC@aol.com).

Journal of Developmental Education

Published three times a year by the National Center for Developmental Education (NCDE) at Appalachian State University in Boone, NC, the journal (http://www.ncde.appstate.edu/jde.htm) seeks to disseminate information about such topics as placement, assessment, and program evaluation as well as best practices in developmental education across the curriculum.

National Association for Developmental Education (NADE)

Founded in 1976 as the National Association for Remedial/Developmental Studies in Postsecondary Education, the organization (http://www.nade.net/) adopted its current name in 1984. It now has more than 3,000 members and includes chapters in many different states. NADE holds an annual conference and sponsors several publications such as the *Journal of Developmental Education*, *NADE Digest*, and the *NADE Newsletter*. Its stated purpose is to focus on "the academic success of students by providing professional development, supporting student learning, providing public leadership, disseminating exemplary models of practice, coordinating efforts with other organizations, facilitating communication among developmental edu-

cation professionals, and anticipating trends" (http://www.nade.net/
NADEdocuments/FactSheet.pdf).

Teaching Basic Writing

Sponsored by McGraw-Hill, Teaching Basic Writing (http://www.
mhhe.com/socscience/english/tbw/) asks experienced college professors to write about current topics in BW for the benefit of others in the field including new instructors, part-timers, and teaching assistants. Recent topics include "Basic Writers' Responses to Teacher Comments" and "Digging, Exploring, and Recording Family Histories in Academic Spaces." The archive of these discussions can be viewed at http://www.mhhe.com/socscience/english/tbw/prevtopics.html.

Teaching Developmental Writing: Background Readings

Bernstein, Susan, ed. *Teaching Developmental Writing: Background Readings*. 3rd ed. Boston: Bedford/St. Martin's, 2007. Print.

Intended as a resource for classroom teachers, this volume includes classic essays by such scholars as Mina Shaughnessy and June Jordan as well as more recent chapters on the uses of technology in teaching writing and working with non-native speakers of English. Examination copies are available by contacting a Bedford/St. Martin's sales representative or by filling out an online order form at http://www.bedfordstmartins.com/newcatalog.aspx?search=developmental&isbn=0312432836 (click on the "Exam & Desk Copies" icon).

The WAC Clearinghouse

Hosted by Colorado State University's Composition Program, this site (http://wac.colostate.edu/) offers valuable resources for those interested in Writing Across the Curriculum (WAC). The Clearinghouse publishes books, journals, and other resources for teachers in all subject areas who use writing in their courses. One feature on this site is a link to abstracts of relevant theses and dissertations, including those related to basic writing (available at http://wac.colostate.edu/theses/index.cfm?category=18). Books published by the Clearinghouse (including this one) are available free of charge online and can be accessed at http://wac.colostate.edu/books/.

Works Cited

Adams, Peter Dow. "Basic Writing Reconsidered." *Journal of Basic Writing* 12.1 (1993): 22–35. Print.
—. Rev. of *Facts, Artifacts and Counterfacts*, ed. David Bartholomae and Anthony Petrosky. *CBW Newsletter* 7.1 (1988): 1–3. Print.
Adams, Peter, Sarah Gearhart, Robert Miller, and Anne Roberts. "The Accelerated Learning Program: Throwing Open the Gates." *Journal of Basic Writing* 28.2 (2009): 50-69. Print.
Adler-Kassner, Linda. "Just Writing, Basically: Basic Writers on Basic Writing." *Journal of Basic Writing* 18.2 (1999): 69–90. Print.
Adler-Kassner, Linda, and Gregory R. Glau, eds. *The Bedford Bibliography for Teachers of Basic Writing*. 2nd ed. Boston: Bedford/St. Martin's, 2005. Web. 12 Feb. 2010.
Adler-Kassner, Linda, and Susanmarie Harrington. "In the Here and Now: Public Policy and Basic Writing." *Journal of Basic Writing* 25.2 (2006): 28–49. Print.
Angelo, Thomas A. "Seven Promising Shifts and Seven Powerful Levers: Developing More Productive Learning (and Writing) Communities Across the Curriculum." *Journal of Language and Learning Across the Disciplines* 2.2 (1997): 56–75. Print.
Anokye, Akua Duku. "Oral Connections to Literacy: The Narrative." *Journal of Basic Writing* 13.2 (1994): 46–60. Print.
Anzaldúa, Gloria. *Borderlands/La Frontera: The New Mestiza*. San Francisco: Aunt Lute, 1987. Print.
Apple, Michael W. *Cultural Politics and Education*. New York: Teachers College P, 1996. Print.
Arenson, Karen W. "In Shift, CUNY Says It Will Use Standardized Tests in Admissions and Placement." *NYTimes.com*. New York Times, 9 Sept. 1999. Web. 4 June 2008.
Ashley, Hannah. "The Art of Queering Voices: A Fugue." *Journal of Basic Writing* 26.1 (2007): 4–19. Print.
Ashley, Hannah, and Katy Lynn. "Ventriloquism 001: How to Throw Your Voice in the Academy." *Journal of Basic Writing* 22.2 (2003): 4–26. Print.

Attewell, Paul, and David E. Lavin. *Passing the Torch: Does Higher Education for the Disadvantaged Pay Off Across the Generations?* New York: Russell Sage Foundation, 2007. Print.

Attewell, Paul, David Lavin, Thurston Domina, and Tania Levey. "New Evidence on College Remediation." *Journal of Higher Education* 77.5 (2006): 886–924. Web. 19 Apr. 2009.

Balester, Valerie M. *Cultural Divide: A Study of African-American College-Level Writers.* Portsmouth, NH: Boynton/Cook, 1993. Print.

Bartholomae, David. "Facts, Artifacts and Counterfacts: A Basic Reading and Writing Course for the College Curriculum." *A Sourcebook for Basic Writing Teachers.* Ed. Theresa Enos. New York: Random House, 1987. 275–306. Print.

—. "Inventing the University." *Journal of Basic Writing* 5.1 (Spring 1986): 4–23. Print. Abridged version of a chapter by the same name in *When a Writer Can't Write: Studies in Writer's Block and Other Composing-Process Problems.* Ed. Mike Rose. New York: Guilford, 1985. 134–65. Print.

—. "Teaching Basic Writing: An Alternative to Basic Skills." *Journal of Basic Writing* 2.2 (1979): 85–109. Print.

—. "The Study of Error." *College Composition and Communication* 31.3 (1980): 253–69. Print.

—. "The Tidy House: Basic Writing in the American Curriculum." *Journal of Basic Writing* 12.1 (1993): 4–21. Print.

—. "Writing Assignments: Where Writing Begins." *Forum: Essays on the Theory and Practice of Writing.* Ed. Patricia L. Stock. Upper Montclair, NJ: Boynton/Cook, 1983. 300–12. Print.

—. "Writing on the Margins: The Concept of Literacy in Higher Education." *A Sourcebook for Basic Writing Teachers.* Ed. Theresa Enos. New York: Random House, 1987. 66–83. Print.

—. "Writing with Teachers: A Conversation with Peter Elbow." *College Composition and Communication* 46.1 (1995): 62–71. Print.

Bartholomae, David, and Anthony Petrosky, eds. *Facts, Artifacts and Counterfacts: Theory and Method for a Reading and Writing Course.* Portsmouth, NH: Boynton/Cook, 1986. Print.

—. *Ways of Reading: An Anthology for Writers.* 8th ed. New York: Bedford/St. Martin's, 2008. Print.

Bazerman, Charles, Joseph Little, Lisa Bethel, Teri Chavkin, Danielle Fouquette, and Janet Garufis. *Reference Guide to Writing Across the Curriculum.* West Lafayette, IN: Parlor Press and WAC Clearinghouse, 2005. Print.

Belanoff, Pat. "The Myths of Assessment." *Journal of Basic Writing* 10.1 (1991): 54–66. Print.

Belanoff, Pat, and Peter Elbow. "Using Portfolios to Increase Collaboration and Communication in a Writing Program." *WPA: Writing Program Administration* 9.3 (1986): 27–40. Print.

Belanoff, Pat, and Marcia Dickson, eds. *Portfolios: Process and Product.* Portsmouth, NH: Heinemann-Boynton/Cook, 1991. Print.

Berg, Anna, and Gerald Coleman. "A Cognitive Approach to Teaching the Developmental Student." *Journal of Basic Writing* 4.2 (1985): 4–23. Print.

Berger, Mary Jo. "Funding and Support for Basic Writing: Why Is There So Little?" *Journal of Basic Writing* 12.1 (1993): 81–89. Print.

Berlin, James. "Contemporary Composition: The Major Pedagogical Theories." *College English* 44.8 (1982): 765–77. Print.

—. *Rhetoric and Reality: Writing Instruction in American Colleges, 1900–1985.* Carbondale, IL: Southern Illinois UP, 1987. Print.

—. *Writing Instruction in Nineteenth-Century American Colleges.* Carbondale, IL: Southern Illinois UP, 1984. Print.

Berman, Robert. "Stricter Standards at CUNY." *Chronicle of Higher Education* 6 Aug. 1999: B11. Print.

Bernhardt, Bill, and Peter Miller. "Editors' Column." *Journal of Basic Writing* 12.1 (1993): 1–3. Print.

Bernhardt, Stephen A., and Patricia G. Wojahn. "Computers and Writing Instruction." *Research in Basic Writing: A Bibliographic Sourcebook.* Ed. Michael G. Moran and Martin Jacobi. New York: Greenwood, 1990. Print.

Bernstein, Susan Naomi. "Teaching and Learning in Texas: Accountability Testing, Language, Race, and Place." *Journal of Basic Writing* 23.1 (2004): 4–24. Print.

Bernstein, Susan Naomi, ed. *Teaching Developmental Writing: Background Readings.* 3rd ed. Boston: Bedford/St. Martin's, 2007. Print.

Berthoff, Ann E. "Is Teaching Still Possible? Writing, Meaning, and Higher Order Reasoning." *College English* 46.8 (1984): 743–55. Print.

Bérubé, Michael. Afterword. *On the Market: Surviving the Academic Job Search.* Ed. Christine Boufis and Victoria C. Olson. New York: Riverhead, 1997. 348–63. Print.

Bizzell, Patricia. *Academic Discourse and Critical Consciousness.* Pittsburgh: U of Pittsburgh P, 1993. Print.

—. "Arguing about Literacy." *College English* 50.2 (1988): 141–53. Print.

—. "Basic Writing and the Issue of Correctness, Or, What to Do With 'Mixed' Forms of Academic Discourse." *Journal of Basic Writing* 19.1 (2000): 4–12. Print.

—. "Cognition, Convention, and Certainty: What We Need to Know About Writing." *Pre/Text* 3.3 (1982): 213–43. Print.

—. "College Composition: Initiation into the Academic Discourse Community." *Curriculum Inquiry* 12.2 (1982): 191–207. Print.

—. "The Ethos of Academic Discourse." *College Composition and Communication* 29.4 (1978): 351–55. Print.

—. "Literacy in Culture and Cognition." *A Sourcebook for Basic Writing Teachers*. Ed. Theresa Enos. New York: Random House, 1987. 125–37. Print.

—. "Thomas Kuhn, Scientism, and English Studies." *College English* 40.7 (1979): 764–71. Print.

—. "What Happens When Basic Writers Come to College?" *College Composition and Communication* 37.3 (1986): 294–301. Print.

—. "William Perry and Liberal Education." *College English* 46.5 (1984): 447–54. Print.

BMCC. "The CUNY/ACT Writing Sample." *The CUNY Skills Assessment Program*. The City University of New York Office of Assessment, n.d. Web. 4 June 2008.

Boegeman, Margaret Byrd. "Lives and Literacy: Autobiography in Freshman Composition." *College English* 41.6 (1980): 662–69. Print.

Boiarsky, Carolyn R. "Working Class Students in the Academy: Who Are They?" *Academic Literacy in the English Classroom: Helping Underprepared and Working Class Students Succeed in College*. Ed. Carolyn R. Boiarsky. Portsmouth, NH: Boynton/Cook, 2003: 1–21. Print.

Bousquet, Marc. "Tenured Bosses and Disposable Teachers." *Minnesota Review* n.s. 58–60 (2003): 231–41. Print.

Boyer, Ernest L., and Arthur Levine. "The Spare Room." *A Quest for Common Learning*. Ed. Ernest Boyer and Arthur Levine. Washington, DC: Carnegie Foundation, 1981. 1–4. Print.

Braddock, Richard. "Evaluation of Writing Tests." *Reviews of Selected Published Tests in English*. Urbana, IL: NCTE, 1974. 118–26. Print.

Braddock, Richard, Richard Lloyd-Jones, and Lowell Schoer. *Research in Written Composition*. Champaign, IL: NCTE, 1963. Print.

Bradford, Annette. "Applications of Self-Regulating Speech in the Basic Writing Program." *Journal of Basic Writing* 4.2 (1985): 38–47. Print.

—. "Cognitive Immaturity and Remedial College Writers." *The Writer's Mind: Writing as a Mode of Thinking*. Ed. Janice Hays et al. Urbana, IL: NCTE, 1983. 15–24. Print.

Brereton, John C., ed. *The Origins of Composition Studies in the American College, 1875–1925: A Documentary History*. Pittsburgh: U of Pittsburgh P, 1995. Print.

Brodkey, Linda. "Writing on the Bias." *College English* 56.5 (1994): 527–47. Print.

—. *Writing Permitted in Designated Areas Only*. Minneapolis: U of Minnesota P, 1996. Print.

Brown, Rexford G. "Schooling and Thoughtfulness." *Journal of Basic Writing* 10.1 (1991): 3–15. Print.

—. "What We Know Now and How We Could Know More about Writing Ability in America." *Journal of Basic Writing* 1.4 (1978): 1–6. Print.

Bruch, Patrick. "Moving to the City: Redefining Literacy in the Post-Civil Rights Era." *City Comp: Identities, Spaces, Practices.* Ed. Bruce McComisky and Cynthia Ryan. Albany, NY: State U of New York P, 2003. 217–33. Print.

Campbell, Dianna S., and Terry Ryan Miller. "A Design for a Developmental Writing Course for Academically Underprepared Black Students." *Journal of Basic Writing* 1.2 (Fall/Winter 1976): 20–30. Print.

Carter, Shannon. "Redefining Literacy as a Social Practice." *Journal of Basic Writing* 25.2 (2006): 95–126. Print.

—. *The Way Literacy Lives: Rhetorical Dexterity and Basic Writing Instruction.* Albany, NY: State U of New York P, 2008. Print.

Chomsky, Noam. *Syntactic Structures.* The Hague: Mouton, 1957. Print.

"The City University of New York: An Institution Adrift." Report of the Mayor's Advisory Task Force on the City University of New York." 7 June 1999. Web. 12 Feb. 2010.

Clark, J. Milton, and Carol Peterson Haviland. "Language and Authority: Shifting the Privilege." *Journal of Basic Writing* 14.1 (1995): 57–66. Print.

Cohen, Samuel. "Tinkering Toward WAC Utopia." *Journal of Basic Writing* 21.2 (2002): 56–72. Print.

Collins, Terence G. "A Response to Ira Shor's 'Our Apartheid: Writing Instruction and Inequality.'" *Journal of Basic Writing* 16.2 (1997): 95–100. Print.

Collins, Terence G., and Kim Lynch. "Mainstreaming? Eddy, Rivulet, Backwater, Site Specificity." *Mainstreaming Basic Writers: Politics and Pedagogies of Access.* Ed. Gerri McNenny. Mahwah, NJ: Erlbaum, 2001. 73–84. Print.

Collins, Terence G., and Melissa Blum. "Meanness and Failure: Sanctioning Basic Writers." *Journal of Basic Writing* 19.1 (2000): 13–21. Print.

Conference on College Composition and Communication. "Writing Assessment: A Position Statement." 2006 (revised 2009). Web. 10 Feb. 2010.

Connors, Robert J. "Basic Writing Textbooks: History and Current Avatars." *A Sourcebook for Basic Writing Teachers.* Ed. Theresa Enos. New York: Random House, 1987. 259–74. Print.

—. *Composition-Rhetoric: Backgrounds, Theory, and Pedagogy.* Pittsburgh: U of Pittsburgh P, 1997. Print.

—. "Mechanical Correctness as a Focus in Composition Instruction." *College Composition and Communication* 36.1 (1985): 61–72. Print.

—. "The Rhetoric of Mechanical Correctness." *Only Connect: Uniting Reading and Writing.* Ed. Thomas Newkirk. Upper Montclair, NJ: Boynton/Cook, 1986. 27–58. Print.

Connors, Robert, and Andrea Lunsford. "Frequency of Formal Errors in Current College Writing, or Ma and Pa Kettle Do Research." *College Composition and Communication* 39.4 (1988): 395–409. Print.

Corder, S. Pit. "Error Analysis, Interlanguage, and Second Language Acquisition." *Language Teaching & Linguistics: Abstracts* 8.4 (1975): 201–18. Print.

Crouch, Mary Kay, and Gerri McNenny. "Looking Back, Looking Forward: California Grapples with Remediation." *Journal of Basic Writing* 19.2 (2000): 44–71. Print.

Crowley, Sharon. "Response to Edward M. White's 'The Importance of Placement and Basic Studies.'" *Journal of Basic Writing* 15.1 (1996): 88–91. Print.

"CUNY: An Institution Adrift." *Report of the Mayor's Advisory Task Force*. (7 June 1999): n. pag. Print.

"CUNY: An Institution Affirmed." *Report of the CUNY Faculty Senate*. The City University of New York, July 1999. Web. 12 Feb. 2010.

D'Angelo, Frank J. "Literacy and Cognition: A Developmental Perspective." *Literacy for Life: The Demand for Reading and Writing*. Ed. Richard W. Bailey and Robin Melanie Fosheim. New York: MLA, 1983. Print.

Darabi, Rachelle L. "Basic Writers and Learning Communities." *Journal of Basic Writing* 25.1 (2006): 53–72. Print.

Deans, Thomas. *Writing Partnerships: Service-Learning in Composition*. Urbana, IL: NCTE, 2000. Print.

DeGenaro, William, and Edward M. White. "Going Around in Circles: Methodological Issues in Basic Writing Research." *Journal of Basic Writing* 19.1 (2000): 22–35. Print.

D'Eloia, Sarah. "Teaching Standard Written English." *Journal of Basic Writing* 1.1 (1975): 5–13. Print.

—. "The Uses—and Limits—of Grammar." *Journal of Basic Writing* 1.3 (1977): 1–48. Print.

DeMott, Benjamin. "Mina Shaughnessy: Meeting Challenges." *Nation* 9 Dec.1978: 645–48. Print.

Desy, Jeanne. "Reasoned Writing for Basic Students: A Course Design." *Journal of Basic Writing* 1.2 (Fall/Winter 1976): 4–19. Print.

Dewey, John. *Democracy and Education: An Introduction to the Philosophy of Education*. New York: Macmillan, 1916. Print.

Diederich, Paul B. *Measuring Growth in English*. Urbana, IL: NCTE, 1974. Print.

Diederich, Paul B., John W. French, and Sydell T. Carlton. *Factors in Judgments of Writing Ability*. Princeton, NJ: Educational Testing Service, 1961. Print.

Dillon, Sam. "New Push Seeks to End Need for Pre-College Remedial Classes." *NYTimes.com*. New York Times, 28 May 2009. Web. 28 May 2009.

DiPardo, Anne. *A Kind of Passport: A Basic Writing Adjunct Program and the Challenge of Student Diversity.* Urbana, IL: NCTE, 1993. Print.

Douglas, Wallace. "Rhetoric for the Meritocracy: The Creation of Composition at Harvard." *English in America: A Radical View of the Profession.* Ed. Richard Ohmann. Hanover, NH: Wesleyan UP, 1976. 97–132. Print.

Elbow, Peter. "Being a Writer vs. Being an Academic: A Conflict in Goals." *College Composition and Communication* 46.1 (1995): 72–83. Print.

—. "Reflections on Academic Discourse: How It Relates to Freshmen and Colleagues." *College English* 53.2 (1991): 135–55. Print.

Elifson, Joan M., and Katharine R. Stone. "Integrating Social, Moral, and Cognitive Developmental Theory." *Journal of Basic Writing* 4.2 (1985): 24–37. Print.

Emig, Janet. *The Composing Processes of Twelfth Graders.* Urbana, IL: NCTE, 1971. Print.

—. "Inquiry Paradigms and Writing." *College Composition and Communication* 33.1 (1982): 64–75. Print.

—. "Mina Pendo Shaughnessy." *College Composition and Communication* 30.1 (1979): 37–38. Print.

—. "Writing as a Mode of Learning." *College Composition and Communication* 28.2 (1977): 122–28. Print.

Epes, Mary. "Tracing Errors to Their Sources: A Study of the Encoding Processes of Adult Basic Writers." *Journal of Basic Writing* 4.1 (1985): 4–33. Print.

Faigley, Lester. *Fragments of Rationality: Postmodernity and the Subject of Composition.* Pittsburgh: U of Pittsburgh P, 1992. Print.

Farr, Marcia, and Harvey Daniels. *Language Diversity and Writing Instruction.* Urbana, IL: NCTE, 1986. Print.

Farrell, Thomas J. "Developing Literate Writing." *Journal of Basic Writing* 2.1 (1978): 30–51. Print.

—. "IQ and Standard English." *College Composition and Communication* 34.4 (1983): 470–84. Print.

Fasold, Ralph W., and Roger W. Shuy, eds. *Teaching Standard English in the Inner City.* Washington, DC: Center for Applied Linguistics, 1970. Print.

Fish, Stanley. *Doing What Comes Naturally: Change, Rhetoric, and the Practice of Theory in Literary and Legal Studies.* Oxford, UK: Clarendon, 1989. Print.

Fishman, Judith. "Do You Agree or Disagree: The Epistemology of the CUNY Writing Assessment Test." *WPA: Writing Program Administration* 8.1–2 (1984): 17–25. Print.

Fishman, Stephen M., and Lucille McCarthy. *Whose Goals? Whose Aspirations?: Learning to Teach Underprepared Writers Across the Curriculum.* Logan, UT: Utah State UP, 2002. Print.

Fitzgerald, Sallyanne H. "The Context Determines Our Choice: Curriculum, Students, and Faculty." *Mainstreaming Basic Writers: Politics and Pedagogies of Access*. Ed. Gerri McNenny. Mahwah, NJ: Erlbaum, 2001. 215–23. Print.

Flower, Linda. *The Construction of Negotiated Meaning: A Social Cognitive Theory of Writing*. Carbondale, IL: Southern Illinois UP, 1994. Print.

—. "Writer-Based Prose: A Cognitive Basis for Problems in Writing." *College English* 41.1 (1979): 19–37. Print.

Flower, Linda, and John R. Hayes. "The Cognition of Discovery: Defining a Rhetorical Problem." *College Composition and Communication* 31.1 (1980): 21–32. Print.

—. "A Cognitive Process Theory of Writing." *College Composition and Communication* 32.4 (1981): 365–87. Print.

—. "The Dynamics of Composing: Making Plans and Juggling Constraints." *Cognitive Processes in Writing*. Ed. Lee Gregg and Erwin Steinberg. Hillsdale, NJ: Erlbaum, 1979. 31–50. Print.

—. "Problem Solving and the Cognitive Processes of Writing." *Writing: The Nature, Development, and Teaching of Written Communication*. Ed. Carl H. Fredericksen, et al. Hillsdale, NJ: Erlbaum, 1981. 39–58. Print.

—. "Problem Solving Strategies and the Writing Process." *College English* 39.4 (1977): 19–37. Print.

Fox, Tom. "Basic Writing as Cultural Conflict." *Journal of Education* 172.1 (1990): 65–83. Print.

—. *Defending Access: A Critique of Standards in Higher Education*. Portsmouth, NH: Boynton/Cook, 1999. Print.

—. "Standards and Access." *Journal of Basic Writing* 12.1 (1993): 37–45. Print.

Freeman, Donald C. "Linguistics and Error Analysis: On Agency." *Linguistics, Stylistics and the Teaching of Composition*. Ed. Donald McQuade. Akron, OH: L&S Books, 1979. 135–50. Print.

Freire, Paulo. *Pedagogy of the Oppressed*. Trans. Myra Bergman Ramos. New York: Continuum, 1970. Print.

Freire, Paulo, and Donaldo Macedo. *Literacy: Reading the Word and the World*. Westport, CT: Bergin and Garvey, 1987. Print.

Fries, Charles Carpenter. *The Structure of English: An Introduction to Construction of English Sentences*. New York: Harcourt, 1952. Print.

Fuller, Robert G., ed. *Multidisciplinary Piagetian-Based Programs for College Freshmen*. 3rd ed. Lincoln, NE: ADAPT, 1978. Print.

Gabelnick, Faith, Jean MacGregor, Roberta S. Matthews, and Barbara L. Smith. *Learning Communities: Creating Connections among Students, Faculty, and Disciplines*. San Francisco: Jossey-Bass, 1990. Print.

"GI Bill 2008: Frequently Asked Questions." n.d. Web. 18 Apr. 2009.

Gibson, Michelle, and Deborah T. Meem. "The Life and Death and Life of a College, a Department, & a Basic Writing Program." *Basic Writing in America: The History of Nine College Programs*. Ed. Nicole Pepinster Greene and Patricia J. McAlexander. Cresskill, NJ: Hampton P, 2008. 49–70. Print.

Gilyard, Keith. "Basic Writing, Cost Effectiveness, and Ideology." *Journal of Basic Writing* 19.1 (2000): 36–42. Print.

—. *Voices of the Self: A Study of Language Competence*. Detroit: Wayne State UP, 1991. Print.

Gilyard, Keith, and Elaine Richardson. "Students' Right to Possibility: Basic Writing and African American Rhetoric." *Insurrections: Approaches to Resistance in Composition Studies*. Ed. Andrea Greenbaum. Albany, NY: State U of New York P, 2001. 37–51. Print.

Glau, Gregory R. "*Stretch* at 10: A Progress Report on Arizona State University's *Stretch Program*." *Journal of Basic Writing* 26.2 (2007): 30–48. Print.

—. "The 'Stretch Program': Arizona State University's New Model of University-Level Basic Writing Instruction." *WPA: Writing Program Administration* 20.1 (1996): 79–91. Print.

Glau, Gregory R., and Chitralekha Duttagupta. *The Bedford Bibliography for Teachers of Basic Writing*. Boston: Bedford/St. Martin's, 2010. Print.

Glazer, Nathan. "Unsentimental Education." *New Republic* 211.25 (19 Dec. 1994): 38–41. Print.

Gleason, Barbara. "Evaluating Writing Programs in Real Time: The Politics of Remediation." *College Composition and Communication* 51.4 (2000): 560–88. Print.

—. "When the Writing Test Fails: Assessing Assessment at an Urban College." *Writing in Multicultural Settings*. Ed. Carol Severino, Juan C. Guerra, and Johnnella E. Butler. New York: MLA, 1997. 307–23. Print.

Goen-Salter, Sugie. "Critiquing the Need to Eliminate Remediation: Lessons from San Francisco State." *Journal of Basic Writing* 27.2 (2008): 81–105. Print.

Goen, Sugie, and Helen Gillotte-Tropp. "Integrating Reading and Writing: A Response to the Basic Writing 'Crisis.'" *Journal of Basic Writing* 22.2 (2003): 90–113. Print.

Goodman, Kenneth S., ed. *Miscue Analysis: Applications to Reading Instruction*. Urbana, IL: NCTE, 1973. Print.

Goto, Stanford. "Basic Writing and Policy Reform: Why We Keep Talking Past Each Other." *Journal of Basic Writing* 21.2 (2002): 4–20. Print.

Gould, Stephen Jay. *The Mismeasure of Man*. New York: Norton, 1981. Print.

Graff, Harvey. *The Literacy Myth: Cultural Integration and Social Structure in the Nineteenth Century*. New York: Academic Press, 1979. Print.

Gray, Barbara Quint. "Dialect Interference in Writing: A Tripartite Analysis." *Journal of Basic Writing* 1.1 (1975): 14–22. Print.

Gray-Rosendale, Laura. "Back to the Future: Contextuality and the Construction of the Basic Writer's Identity in *Journal of Basic Writing* 1999–2005." *Journal of Basic Writing* 25.2 (2006): 6–27. Print.

—. *Rethinking Basic Writing: Exploring Identity, Politics, and Community in Interaction*. Mahwah, NJ: Erlbaum, 2000. Print.

Gray-Rosendale, Laura, Loyola K. Bird, and Judith F. Bullock. "Rethinking the Basic Writing Frontier: Native American Students' Challenge to Our Histories." *Journal of Basic Writing* 22.1 (2003): 71–106. Print.

Greenbaum, Sidney, and John Taylor. "The Recognition of Usage Errors by Instructors of Freshman Composition." *College Composition Communication* 32.2 (1981): 169–74. Print.

Greenberg, Karen L. "The Politics of Basic Writing." *Journal of Basic Writing* 12.1 (1993): 64–71. Print.

—. "A Response to Ira Shor's 'Our Apartheid: Writing Instruction and Inequality.'" *Journal of Basic Writing* 16.2 (1997): 90–94. Print.

Greenberg, Karen, and Trudy Smoke. "Editors' Column." *Journal of Basic Writing* 14.1 (1995): 1–6. Print.

—. "Editors' Column." *Journal of Basic Writing* 14.2 (1995): 1–2. Print.

Greenberg, Karen L., Harvey S. Wiener, and Richard A. Donovan, eds. *Writing Assessment: Issues and Strategies*. New York: Longman, 1986. Print.

Greene, Nicole Pepinster, and Patricia J. McAlexander. *Basic Writing in America: The History of Nine College Programs*. Cresskill, NJ: Hampton P, 2008. Print.

Greene, Stuart. "Composing Oneself through the Narratives of Others in Writing an Academic Argument." *ED* 382956 (Mar. 1995): n. pag. Web. 12 Feb. 2010.

Gregg, Lee, and Erwin Steinberg, eds. *Cognitive Processes in Writing*. Hillsdale, N.J: Erlbaum, 1979. Print.

Grego, Rhonda, and Nancy Thompson. "Repositioning Remediation: Renegotiating Composition's Work in the Academy." *College Composition and Communication* 47.1 (1996): 62–84. Print.

Grubb, W. Norton. "From Black Box to Pandora's Box: Evaluating Remedial/Developmental Education." *Community College Research Center, Teachers College*. University of California, Berkeley Aug. 2000. Web. 12 Feb. 2010.

Gunner, Jeanne. "Iconic Discourse: The Troubling Legacy of Mina Shaughnessy." *Journal of Basic Writing* 19.2 (1998): 25–42. Print.

—. "The Status of Basic Writing Teachers: Do We Need a 'Maryland Resolution'?" *Journal of Basic Writing* 12.1 (1993): 57–63. Print.

Hairston, Maxine. "The Winds of Change: Thomas Kuhn and the Revolution in the Teaching of Writing." *College Composition Communication* 33.1 (1982): 76–88. Print.

Hake, Rosemary. "With No Apology: Teaching to the Test." *Journal of Basic Writing* 10.1 (1991): 39–55. Print.

Halasek, Kay, and Nels P. Highberg. "Introduction." *Landmark Essays on Basic Writing*. Ed. Kay Halasek and Nels P. Highberg. Mahwah, NJ: Erlbaum, 2001: xi-xxix. Print.

Halliday, M. A. K., and Ruqaiya Hasan. *Cohesion in English*. London: Longman, 1976. Print.

Halsted, Isabella. "Putting Error in Its Place." *Journal of Basic Writing* 1.1 (Spring 1975): 72–86. Print.

Hand, Greg. "UC Admissions Changes Align with State Strategic Higher Education Plan." *University of Cincinnati News* (7 Aug. 2009): n. pag. Web. 14. Aug. 2009.

Harkin, Patricia. "The Postdisciplinary Politics of Lore." *Contending with Words: Composition and Rhetoric in a Postmodern Age*. Ed. Patricia Harkin and John Schilb. New York: MLA, 1991. 124–38. Print.

Harley, Kay, and Sally I. Cannon. "Failure: The Student's or the Assessment's?" *Journal of Basic Writing* 15.1 (1996): 70–87. Print.

Harrington, Susanmarie. "The Representation of Basic Writers in Basic Writing Scholarship, or Who is Quentin Pierce?" *Journal of Basic Writing* 18.2 (1999): 91–107. Print.

Harrington, Susanmarie, and Linda Adler-Kassner. "'The Dilemma That Still Counts': Basic Writing at a Political Crossroads." *Journal of Basic Writing* 17.2 (1998): 1–24. Print.

Harris, Joseph. "Negotiating the Contact Zone." *Journal of Basic Writing* 14.1 (1995): 27–42. Print.

Harris, Muriel. "Individual Diagnoses: Searching for Causes, Not Symptoms of Writing Deficiencies." *College English* 40.3 (1978): 318–23. Print.

Hartwell, Patrick. "Grammar, Grammars, and the Teaching of Grammar." *College English* 47.2 (1985): 105–27. Print.

Hartzog, Carol P. *Composition and the Academy: A Study of Writing Program Administration*. New York: MLA, 1986. Print.

Haswell, Richard H. *Gaining Ground in College Writing: Tales of Development and Interpretation*. Dallas, TX: Southern Methodist UP, 1991. Print.

Hays, Edna. *College Entrance Requirements in English: Their Effects on the High Schools*. New York: Teachers College P, 1936. Print.

Hays, Janice N. "The Development of Discursive Maturity in College Writers." *The Writer's Mind: Writing as a Mode of Thinking*. Ed. Janice N. Hays, Phyllis A. Roth, Jon R. Ramsey, and Robert D. Foulke. Urbana, IL: NCTE, 1983. 127-44. Print.

—. "Models of Intellectual Development and Writing: A Response to Myra Kogen et al." *Journal of Basic Writing* 6.1 (1987): 11–27. Print.
Hays, Janice N., Phyllis A. Roth, Jon R. Ramsey, and Robert D. Foulke. eds. *The Writer's Mind: Writing as a Mode of Thinking.* Urbana, IL: NCTE, 1983. Print.
Heaney, April. "The Synergy Program: Reframing Critical Reading and Writing for At-Risk Students." *Journal of Basic Writing* 25.1 (2006): 26–52. Print.
Heller, Louis G. *The Death of the American University: With Special Reference to the Collapse of the City College of New York.* New Rochelle, NY: Arlington, 1973. Print.
Hilgers, Thomas. "Basic Writing Curricula and Good Assessment Practices." *Journal of Basic Writing* 14.2 (1995): 68–74. Print.
Hill, Adams Sherman. *Our English.* New York: Chatauqua P, 1890. Print.
Hillocks, George, Jr. *The Testing Trap: How State Writing Assessments Control Learning.* New York: Teachers College P, 2002. Print.
Hirsch, E. D., Jr. *Cultural Literacy: What Every American Needs to Know.* Boston: Houghton, 1987. Print.
Hoggart, Richard. *The Uses of Literacy.* London: Chatto and Windus, 1959. Print.
Horner, Bruce. "Discoursing Basic Writing." *College Composition and Communication* 47.2 (1996): 199–222. Print.
—. "Rethinking the 'Sociality' of Error: Teaching Editing as Negotiation." *Rhetoric Review* 11.1 (1992): 172–99. Print.
—. "Some Afterwords: Intersections and Divergences." *Representing the "Other": Basic Writers and the Teaching of Writing.* Ed. Bruce Horner and Min-Zhan Lu. Urbana, IL: NCTE, 1999. 191–205. Print.
Horner, Bruce, and Min-Zhan Lu. *Representing the "Other": Basic Writers and the Teaching of Writing.* Urbana, IL: NCTE, 1999. Print.
Hourigan, Maureen M. *Literacy as Social Exchange: Intersections of Class, Gender, and Culture.* Albany: State U of New York P, 1994. Print.
Howe, Kenneth R. *Understanding Equal Educational Opportunity: Social Justice, Democracy, and Schooling.* New York: Teachers College P, 1997. Print.
Hull, Glynda. "Acts of Wonderment: Fixing Mistakes and Correcting Errors." *Facts, Artifacts and Counterfacts: Theory and Method for a Reading and Writing Course.* Ed. David Bartholomae and Anthony Petrosky. Upper Montclair, NJ: Boynton/Cook, 1986. 199–226. Print.
—. "Constructing Taxonomies for Error (or Can Stray Dogs Be Mermaids?)" *A Sourcebook for Basic Writing Teachers.* Ed. Theresa Enos. New York: Random House, 1987. 231–44. Print.

—. "Research on Error and Correction." *Perspectives on Research and Scholarship in Composition.* Ed. Ben W. McClelland and Timothy R. Donovan. New York: MLA, 1985. 162–84. Print.

Hull, Glynda, Mike Rose, Kay Losey Fraser, and Marisa Castellano. "Remediation as Social Construct: Perspectives from an Analysis of Classroom Discourse." *College Composition and Communication* 42.3 (1991): 299–329. Print.

Hungiville, Maurice. "Review of *Errors and Expectations*, by Mina P. Shaughnessy." *Chronicle of Higher Education* (4 Apr. 1977): 18. Print.

Hunter, Paul. "'Waiting for Aristotle': A Moment in the History of the Basic Writing Movement." *College English* 54.8 (1992): 914–27. Print.

Huse, Heidi, Jenna Wright, Anna Clark, and Tim Hunter. "It's Not Remedial: Re-envisioning Pre-First-Year College Writing." *Journal of Basic Writing* 24.2 (2005): 26–52. Print.

"The Impact of Hyper-bonding: Exploring Student Relations Within Courses." Learning Notes. University of Wyoming. Web. 11 Feb. 2010.

Jensen, George H. "The Reification of the Basic Writer." *Journal of Basic Writing* 6.1 (1986): 52–64. Print.

Jespersen, Otto. *Essentials of English Grammar.* University, AL: U of Alabama P, 1969. Print.

Jones, William. "Basic Writing: Pushing Against Racism." *Journal of Basic Writing* 12.1 (1993): 72–80. Print.

Kitzhaber, Albert. *Themes, Theories, and Therapy: The Teaching of Writing in College.* New York: McGraw Hill, 1963. Print.

Klages, Marisa A., and J. Elizabeth Clark. "New Worlds of Errors and Expectation: Basic Writers and Digital Assumptions." *Journal of Basic Writing* 28.1 (2009): 32-49. Print.

Knodt, Ellen Andrews. "Books That Have Stood the Test of Time." *Teaching English in the Two-Year College* 27.1 (1999): 118–23. Print.

Kober, Nancy, Dalia Zabala, Naomi Chudowsky, Victor Chudowsky, Keith Gayler, and Jennifer McMurrer. *State High School Exit Exams: A Challenging Year.* Washington, DC: Center on Education Policy, 2006. Web. 12 Feb. 2010.

Kogen, Myra. "The Conventions of Expository Writing." *Journal of Basic Writing* 5.1 (1986): 24–37. Print.

Kohlberg, Lawrence. *The Meaning and Measurement of Moral Development.* Worcester, MA: Clark UP, 1981. Print.

Kraemer, Don J. "Servant Class: Basic Writers and Service Learning." *Journal of Basic Writing* 24.2 (2005): 92–109. Print.

Kroll, Barry M., and John C. Schafer. "Error-Analysis and the Teaching of Composition." *College Composition and Communication* 29.3 (1978): 242–48. Print.

Kuhn, Thomas. *The Structure of Scientific Revolutions.* 2nd ed. Chicago: U of Chicago P, 1970. Print.

Kutz, Eleanor, and Hephzibah Roskelly. *An Unquiet Pedagogy: Transforming Practice in the English Classroom.* Portsmouth, NH: Boynton/Cook, 1991. Print.

Kutz, Eleanor, Suzy Q. Groden, and Vivian Zamel. *The Discovery of Competence: Teaching and Learning with Diverse Student Writers.* Portsmouth, NH: Boynton/Cook, 1993. Print.

Labov, William. *Language in the Inner City: Studies in the Black English Vernacular.* Philadelphia: U of Pennsylvania P, 1972. Print.

Lalicker, William B. "A Basic Introduction to Basic Writing Program Structures: A Baseline and Five Alternatives." *BWe: Basic Writing e-Journal* 1.2 (1999). Rept. *Teaching Developmental Writing.* Ed. Susan Naomi Bernstein. 3rd ed. Boston: Bedford/St. Martins, 2007. 15-25. Print.

Lamos, Steve. "Basic Writing, CUNY, and 'Mainstreaming': (De)Racialization Reconsidered." *Journal of Basic Writing* 19.2 (2000): 22–43. Print.

Larson, Richard L. "Selected Bibliography of Writings on the Evaluation of Students' Achievements in Composition." *Journal of Basic Writing* 1.4 (1978): 91–100. Print.

Laurence, Patricia. "Error's Endless Train: Why Students Don't Perceive Errors." *Journal of Basic Writing* 1.1 (1975): 23–42. Print.

Laurence, Patricia, et al. "Symposium on Basic Writing, Conflict and Struggle, and the Legacy of Mina Shaughnessy." *College English* 55.8 (1993): 879–903. Print.

Lavin, David E., and David Hyllegard. *Changing the Odds: Open Admissions and the Life Chances of the Disadvantaged.* New Haven, CT: Yale UP: 1996. Print.

Lavin, David E., Richard D. Alba, and Richard A. Silberstein. *Right Versus Privilege: The Open-Admissions Experiment at the City University of New York.* New York: Free Press, 1981. Print.

Lay, Nancy. "Chinese Language Interference in Written English." *Journal of Basic Writing* 1.1 (1975): 50–61. Print.

"Learning Notes #4: The Impact of Hyper-Bonding: Exploring Student Relationships Within Courses." *LEARN.* University of Wyoming, n.d. Web. 20 May 2009.

Leary, Chris. "When We Remix . . . We Remake!!!: Reflections on Collaborative Ethnography, The New Digital Ethic, and Test Prep." *Journal of Basic Writing* 26.1 (2007): 88–105. Print.

Lederman, Marie Jean. "Evolution of an Instructional Resource Center: The CUNY Experience." *ADE Bulletin* 82 (1985): 43–47. Print.

Lloyd-Jones, Richard. "Tests of Writing Ability." *Teaching Composition: 12 Bibliographic Essays.* Ed. Gary Tate. Fort Worth, TX: Texas Christian UP, 1987. 155–76. Print.

Long, Bridget Terry. "The Remediation Debate: Are We Serving the Needs of Underprepared College Students?" *National Crosstalk*. 13.4 (2005): n. pag. Web. 2 Feb. 2009.

Lu, Min-Zhan. "Conflict and Struggle: The Enemies or Preconditions of Basic Writing?" *College English* 54.8 (1992): 887–913. Print.

—. "From Silence to Words: Writing as Struggle." *College English* 49.4 (1989): 437–48. Print.

—. "Redefining the Legacy of Mina Shaughnessy: A Critique of the Politics of Linguistic Innocence." *Journal of Basic Writing* 10.1 (1991): 26–40. Print.

Lu, Min-Zhan, and Bruce Horner. "Expectations, Interpretations and Contributions of Basic Writing." *Journal of Basic Writing* 19.1 (2000): 43–52. Print.

Lunsford, Andrea A. "Assignments for Basic Writers: Unresolved Issues and Needed Research." *Journal of Basic Writing* 6.1 (1986): 87–99. Print.

—. "Basic Writing Update." *Teaching Composition: 12 Bibliographic Essays*. Ed. Gary Tate. Fort Worth, TX: Texas Christian UP, 1986. 207–26. Print.

—. "Cognitive Development and the Basic Writer." *College English* 41.1 (1979): 38–46. Print.

—. "Cognitive Studies and Teaching Writing." *Perspectives on Research and Scholarship in Composition*. Ed. Ben W. McClelland and Timothy R. Donovan. New York: MLA, 1985. 145–61. Print.

—. "Politics and Practices in Basic Writing." *A Sourcebook for Basic Writing Teachers*. Ed. Theresa Enos. New York: Random House, 1987. 246–58. Print.

Lunsford, Andrea A., and Patricia A. Sullivan. "Who Are Basic Writers?" *Research in Basic Writing*. Ed. Michael Moran and Martin Jacobi. New York: Greenwood, 1990. 17–30. Print.

Lunsford, Ronald F. "Modern Grammar and Basic Writers." *Research in Basic Writing: A Bibliographic Sourcebook*. Ed. Michael G. and Martin J. Jacobi. Westport, CN: Greenwood, 1990. Print.

Lyons, John. *Introduction to Theoretical Linguistics*. Cambridge, UK: Cambridge UP, 1968. Print.

Lyons, Robert. "Mina Shaughnessy." *Traditions of Inquiry*. Ed. John Brereton. New York: Oxford UP, 1985. 171–89. Print.

—. "Mina Shaughnessy and the Teaching of Writing." *Journal of Basic Writing* 3.1 (Fall/Winter 1980): 3–12. Print.

Maher, Jane. *Mina P. Shaughnessy: Her Life and Work*. Urbana, IL: NCTE, 1997. Print.

—. "Writing the Life of Mina P. Shaughnessy." *Journal of Basic Writing* 16.1 (1997): 51–63. Print.

Maxson, Jeffrey. "'Government of da Peeps, for da Peeps, and by da Peeps': Revisiting the Contact Zone." *Journal of Basic Writing* 24.1 (2005): 24–47. Print.

McBeth, Mark. "Arrested Development: Revising Remediation at John Jay College of Criminal Justice." *Journal of Basic Writing* 25.2 (2006): 77–96. Print.

McCrary, Donald. "Represent, Representin,' Representation: The Efficacy of Hybrid Texts in the Writing Classroom." *Journal of Basic Writing* 24.2 (2005): 72–91. Print.

McNenny, Gerri, ed. *Mainstreaming Basic Writers: Politics and Pedagogies of Access*. Mahwah, NJ: Erlbaum, 2001. Print.

Miller, Susan. "A Future for the Vanishing Present: New Work for Basic Writing." *Journal of Basic Writing* 19.1 (2000): 53–68. Print.

—. *Rescuing the Subject: A Critical Introduction to Rhetoric and the Writer*. Carbondale, IL: Southern Illinois UP, 1989. Print.

—. *Writing: Process and Product*. Cambridge, MA: Winthrop, 1976. Print.

Mills, Helen. "Language and Composition: Three Mastery Learning Courses in One Classroom." *Journal of Basic Writing* 1.2 (1976): 44–59. Print.

Miraglia, Eric. "A Self-Diagnostic Assessment in the Basic Writing Course." *Journal of Basic Writing* 14.2 (1995): 48–67. Print.

Mlynarczyk, Rebecca Williams. "Finding Grandma's Words: A Case Study in the Art of Revising." *Journal of Basic Writing* 15.1 (1996): 3–22. Print.

—. "Personal and Academic Writing: Revisiting the Debate." *Journal of Basic Writing* 25.1 (2006): 4–25. Print.

Mlynarczyk, Rebecca, and Bonne August. "Editors' Column." *Journal of Basic Writing* 25.2 (2006): 1–4. Print.

Mlynarczyk, Rebecca Williams, and Marcia Babbitt. "The Power of Academic Learning Communities." *Journal of Basic Writing* 21.1 (2002): 71–89. Print.

Mlynarczyk, Rebecca, and Steven B. Haber. *In Our Own Words: Student Writers at Work*. 3rd ed. New York: Cambridge UP, 2005. Print.

Moran, Michael G., and Martin J. Jacobi. *Research in Basic Writing: A Bibliographic Sourcebook*. New York: Greenwood, 1990. Print.

Mutnick, Deborah. "On the Academic Margins: Basic Writing Pedagogy." *A Guide to Composition Pedagogies*. Ed. Gary Tate, Amy Rupiper, and Kurt Schick. New York: Oxford UP, 2001. 183–202. Print.

—. "The Strategic Value of Basic Writing: An Analysis of the Current Moment." *Journal of Basic Writing* 19.1 (2000): 69–83. Print.

—. *Writing in an Alien World: Basic Writing and the Struggle for Equality in Higher Education*. Portsmouth, NH: Boynton/Cook, 1996. Print.

Myers, Nancy. "Citing/Siting/Sighting Ourselves: The Canon in Rhetoric and Composition Studies." *Journal of Teaching Writing* 14.1-2: (1997): 177-78. Print.

North, Stephen M. *The Making of Knowledge in Composition: Portrait of an Emerging Field*. Upper Montclair, NJ: Boynton/Cook, 1987. Print.

Obama, Barack. "Address to a Joint Session of Congress." *Top of the Ticket*. Los Angeles Times, 24 Feb. 2009. Web. 25 Feb. 2009.

—. "Remarks by the President to the Hispanic Chamber of Commerce on a Complete and Competitive American Education." *The White House*. Office of the Press Secretary, 10 Mar. 2009. Web. 18 Apr. 2009.

Odell, Lee. "Basic Writing in Context: Rethinking Academic Literacy." *Journal of Basic Writing* 14.1 (1995): 43–56. Print.

—. "Measuring Changes in Intellectual Processes as One Dimension of Growth in Writing." *Evaluating Writing: Describing, Measuring, Judging*. Ed. Charles R. Cooper and Lee Odell. Urbana, IL: NCTE, 1977. 107–34. Print.

Orfield, Gary, and Johanna Wald. "Testing, Testing." *The Nation* 270.22 (5 June 2000): 38–40. Print.

Otte, George. "Computer-Adjusted Errors and Expectations." *Journal of Basic Writing* 10.2 (1991): 71–86. Print.

—. "High Schools as Crucibles of College Prep: What More Do We Need to Know?" *Journal of Basic Writing* 21.2 (2002): 106–20. Print.

Otte, George, and Trudy Smoke. "Editors' Column." *Journal of Basic Writing* 19.1 (2000): 1–3. Print.

Parsad, Basmat, and Laurie Lewis. "Remedial Education at Degree Granting Postsecondary Institutions in Fall 2000." *National Center for Education Statistics*. U.S. Departmet of Education Institute of Education Sciences, Nov. 2003. Web. 12 Feb. 2010.

Patthey, Genevieve G., and Constance A. Gergen. "Culture as an Instructional Resource in the Multiethnic Composition Classroom." *Journal of Basic Writing* 11.1 (1992): 75–96. Print.

Perl, Sondra. "The Composing Processes of Unskilled College Writers." *Research in the Teaching of English* 13.4 (1979): 317–36. Print.

—. *Five Writers Writing: Case Studies of the Composing Processes of Unskilled College Writers*. Diss. New York University, 1978. Print.

—. "A Look at Basic Writers in the Process of Composing." *Basic Writing: Essays for Teachers, Research, Administrators*. Ed. Laurence W. Kasen and Daniel R. Hoeber. Urbana, IL: NCTE, 1980. 13–32. Print.

—. "Understanding Composing." *College Composition and Communication* 31.4 (1980): 389–99. Print.

Perry, William. *Forms of Intellectual and Ethical Development in the College Years: A Scheme*. New York: Holt, 1970. Print.

Petrie, Ann. "Teaching the Thinking Process in Essay Writing." *Journal of Basic Writing* 1.2 (1976): 60–67. Print.

Phipps, Ronald. "College Remediation: What It Is, What It Costs, What's at Stake." *Institute for Higher Education Policy*. Institute for Higher Education Policy, 1998. Web. 12 Feb. 2010.

Piaget, Jean. *The Child's Conception of the World*. New York: Humanities P, 1951. Print.

—. *The Construction of Reality in the Child*. New York: Basic Books, 1954. Print.

—. *Language and Thought of a Child*. Trans. Marjorie Bagain. New York: Free Press, 1965. Print.

Pierog, Paul. "Coaching Writing." *Journal of Basic Writing* 1.2 (1976): 68–77. Print.

Pike, Kenneth L. *Language in Relation to a Unified Theory of the Structure of Human Behavior*. 2nd rev. ed. The Hague: Mouton, 1967. Print.

—. "A Linguistic Contribution to Composition: A Hypothesis." *College Composition and Communication* 15.2 (1964): 82–88. Print.

Pine, Nancy. "Service Learning in a Basic Writing Class." *Journal of Basic Writing* 27.2 (2008): 29–55. Print.

Piro, Vincent P. "Renaming Ourselves." *Teaching English in the Two-Year College* 21.2 (1994): 114–19. Print.

Ponsot, Marie. "Total Immersion." *Journal of Basic Writing* 1.2 (1976): 31–43. Print.

Ponsot, Marie, and Rosemary Deen. *Beat Not the Poor Desk: What to Teach, How to Teach It, and Why*. Montclair, NJ: Boynton/Cook, 1982. Print.

Porter, Kevin. "A Pedagogy of Charity: Donald Davidson and the Student-Negotiated Composition Classroom." *College Composition and Communication* 52.4 (2001): 574–611. Print.

"Postsecondary Remedial Education." *National Conference of State Legislatures*. National Conference of State Legislatures, 2009. Web. 19 Apr. 2009.

Pratt, Mary Louise. "Arts of the Contact Zone." *Profession 91* (1991): 33–40. Print.

Ray, Brian. "A New World: Redefining the Legacy of Min-Zhan Lu." *Journal of Basic Writing* 27.2 (2008): 106–27. Print.

Raymond, James C., ed. *Literacy as a Human Problem*. Urbana, IL: NCTE, 1982. Print.

Reagan, Sally Barr. "Warning: Basic Writers at Risk—The Case of Javier." *Journal of Basic Writing* 10.2 (1991): 99–115. Print.

Reeves, LaVona L. "Mina Shaughnessy and Open Admissions at New York's City College." *Thought & Action: The NEA Higher Education Journal* (Winter 2001–2002): 117–28. Print.

Renfro, Sally, and Allison Armour-Garb. "Open Admissions and Remedial Education at the City University of New York." *The Official New York City Web Site*. The City of New York, June 1999. Web. 2 Feb. 2009.

Rich, Adrienne. "Teaching Language in Open Admissions." *Landmark Essays on Basic Writing*. Ed. Kay Halasek and Nels P. Highberg. Mahwah, NJ: Erlbaum, 2001. 1–13. Print.

Richards, I. A. *How to Read a Page: A Course in Effective Reading with an Introduction to a Hundred Great Words*. London: Routledge, 1942. Print.

—. *The Philosophy of Rhetoric*. London: Oxford UP, 1936. Print.

Richards, Jack C., ed. *Error Analysis: Perspectives on Second Language Acquisition*. London: Longman, 1974. Print.

Rigolino, Rachel, and Penny Freel. "Re-Modeling Basic Writing." *Journal of Basic Writing* 26.2 (2007): 49–72. Print.

Ritter, Kelly. "Before Mina Shaughnessy: Basic Writing at Yale, 1920–1960." *College Composition and Communication* 60.1 (2008): 12–45. Print.

Rizzo, Betty, and Santiago Villafane. "Spanish Influence on Written English." *Journal of Basic Writing* 1.1 (1975): 62–71. Print.

Robertson, Linda R., Sharon Crowley, and Frank Lentricchia. "The Wyoming Conference Resolution Opposing Unfair Salaries and Working Conditions for Post-Secondary Teachers of Writing." *College English* 49.3 (1987): 274–80. Print.

Rodby, Judith. "What's It Worth and What's It For? Revisions to Basic Writing Revisited." *College Composition and Communication* 47 (1996): 107–11. Print.

Rodby, Judith, and Tom Fox. "Basic Work and Material Acts: The Ironies, Discrepancies, and Disjunctures of Basic Writing and Mainstreaming." *Journal of Basic Writing* 19.1 (2000): 84–99. Print.

Rodriguez, Richard. *Hunger of Memory: The Education of Richard Rodriguez*. New York: Bantam, 1982. Print.

Rose, Mike. "Colleges Need to Re-Mediate Remediation." *The Chronicle of Higher Education* 55.43 (7 Aug. 2009): A76. Print.

—. "The Language of Exclusion: Writing Instruction at the University." *College English* 47.4 (1985): 341–59. Print.

—. *Lives on the Boundary: The Struggles and Achievements of America's Underprepared*. New York: Free Press, 1989. Print.

—. "Narrowing the Mind and Page: Remedial Writers and Cognitive Reductionism." *College Composition and Communication* 39.3 (1988): 267–300. Print.

—. "Rigid Rules, Inflexible Plans, and the Stifling of Language: A Cognitivist Analysis of Writer's Block." *College Composition and Communication* 31.4 (1980): 318–23. Print.

—. *Why School? Reclaiming Education for All of Us*. New York: New Press, 2009. Print.

Rossen-Knill, Deborah, and Kim Lynch. "A Method for Describing Basic Writers and Their Writing: Lessons from a Pilot Study." *Journal of Basic Writing* 19.2 (2000): 93–123. Print.

Rouse, John. "The Politics of Composition." *College English* 41.1 (1979): 1–12. Print.
Royer, Daniel J., and Roger Gilles. "Basic Writing and Directed Self-Placement." *Basic Writing e-Journal* 2.2 (2000): n. pag. Web. 2 Feb. 2009.
—. *Directed Self-Placement: Principles and Practices*. Cresskill, NJ: Hampton, 2002. Print.
Ruth, Leo, and Sandra Murphy. "Recommendations from Practice." *Designing Writing Tasks for the Assessment of Writing*. Norwood, NJ: Ablex, 1988. 17–38. Print.
Samuels, Marilyn Schauer. "Norman Holland's 'New Paradigm' and the Teaching of Writing." *Journal of Basic Writing* 2.1 (1978): 52–61. Print.
Scholes, Robert. *Textual Power: Literary Theory and the Teaching of English*. New Haven, CT: Yale UP, 1985. Print.
Schor, Sandra, and Judith Fishman. *The Random House Guide to Basic Writing*. New York: Random House, 1978. Print.
Scott, J. Blake. "The Literacy Narrative as Production Pedagogy." *Teaching English in the Two-Year College* 24.2 (1997): 108–16. Print.
Scott, Jerrie Cobb. "Literacies and Deficits Revisited." *Journal of Basic Writing* 12.1 (1993): 46–56. Print.
Seagall, Mary T. "Embracing a Porcupine: Redesigning a Writing Program." *Journal of Basic Writing* 14.2 (1995): 58–70. Print.
Shaughnessy, Mina P. "Basic Writing." *Teaching Composition: 12 Bibliographic Essays*. Ed. Gary Tate. Fort Worth, TX: Texas Christian UP, 1986. 177–206.
—. "Diving In: An Introduction to Basic Writing." *Mina P. Shaughnessy: Her Life and Work*. Ed. Jane Maher. Urbana, IL: NCTE, 1997. 255–62. Print.
—. *Errors and Expectations: A Guide for the Teacher of Basic Writing*. New York: Oxford UP, 1977. Print.
—. "Introduction." *Journal of Basic Writing* 1.1 (1975): 1–4. Print.
—. "Introduction." *Journal of Basic Writing* 1.2 (1976): 1–4. Print.
—. "The Miserable Truth" *Mina P. Shaughnessy: Her Life and Work*. Ed. Jane Maher. Urbana, IL: NCTE, 1997. 263–69. Print.
Shen, Fan. "The Classroom and the Wider Culture: Identity as a Key to Learning English Composition." *College Composition and Communication* 40.4 (1989): 459–66. Print.
Sheridan-Rabideau, Mary P., and Gordon Brossell. "Finding Basic Writing's Place." *Journal of Basic Writing* 14.1 (1995): 21–26. Print.
Shor, Ira. *Empowering Education: Critical Teaching for Social Change*. Chicago: U of Chicago P, 1992. Print.
—, ed. *Freire for the Classroom: A Sourcebook for Liberatory Teaching*. Portsmouth, NH: Boynton/Cook, 1987. Print.
—. "Illegal Literacy." *Journal of Basic Writing* 19.1 (2000): 100–112. Print.

—. "Our Apartheid: Writing Instruction and Inequality." *Journal of Basic Writing* 16.1 (1997): 91–104. Print.
Sledd, James. "Bi-Dialecticalism: The Language of White Supremacy." *English Journal* 58.9 (1969): 1307–15. Print.
—. "Doublespeak: Dialectology in the Service of Big Brother." *College English* 33.4 (1972): 439–56. Print.
Smith, Cheryl C. "Technologies for Transcending a Focus on Error: Blogs and Democratic Aspirations in First-Year Composition." *Journal of Basic Writing* 27.1 (2008): 35-60. Print.
Soliday, Mary. "From the Margins to the Mainstream: Reconceiving Remediation." *College Composition and Communication* 47.1 (1996): 85–100. Print.
—. *The Politics of Remediation: Institutional and Student Needs in Higher Education*. Pittsburgh: U of Pittsburgh P, 2002. Print.
—. "Translating the Self and Difference through Literacy Narratives." *College English* 56.5 (1994): 511–26. Print.
Soliday, Mary, and Barbara Gleason. "From Remediation to Enrichment: Evaluating a Mainstreaming Project." *Journal of Basic Writing* 16.1 (1997): 64–78. Print.
Sommers, Nancy. "Intentions and Revisions." *Journal of Basic Writing* 3.3 (1981): 41–49. Print.
Spear, Karen I. "Building Cognitive Skills in Basic Writers." *Teaching English in the Two-Year College* 9.2 (1983): 91–98. Print
Spellmeyer, Kurt. "Testing as Surveillance." *Assessment of Writing: Politics, Policies, Practices*. Ed. Edward M. White, William D. Lutz, and Sandra Kamusikiri. New York: MLA, 1996. 174–81. Print.
State High School Exit Exams: A Maturing Reform. Washington, DC: Center on Education Policy, 2004. Print.
Sternglass, Marilyn S. "Students Deserve Enough Time to Prove They Can Succeed." *Journal of Basic Writing* 18.1 (1999): 3–20. Print.
—. *Time to Know Them: A Longitudinal Study of Writing and Learning at the College Level*. Mahwah, NJ: Erlbaum, 1997. Print.
Stewart, Donald. "Harvard's Influence on English Studies: Perceptions from Three Universities in the Early Twentieth Century." *College Composition and Communication* 43.4 (1992): 455–71. Print.
Street, Brian V. "Autonomous and Ideological Models of Literacy: Approaches from New Literacy Studies." *Media Anthropology Network* (Jan. 2006). Web. 12 Feb. 2010.
"Students' Right to Their Own Language." *College Composition and Communication* 25.3 (1974). 1-32. Print.
Stygall, Gail. "Unraveling at Both Ends: Anti-Undergraduate Education, Anti-Affirmative Action, and Basic Writing at Research Schools." *Journal of Basic Writing* 18.2 (1999): 4–22. Print.

Sweigart, William. "Assessing Achievement in a Developmental Writing Sequence." *Research and Teaching in Developmental Education* 12.2 (1996): 5–15. Print.

Tassoni, John Paul, and Cynthia Lewiecki-Wilson. "Not Just Anywhere, Anywhen: Mapping Change through Studio Work." *Journal of Basic Writing* 24.1 (2005): 68–92. Print.

Taylor, Karl K. "DOORS English—The Cognitive Basis of Rhetorical Models." *Journal of Basic Writing* 2.2 (1979): 52–66. Print.

Tinberg, Howard. "Teaching in the Spaces Between: What Basic Writing Students Can Teach Us." *Journal of Basic Writing* 17.2 (1998): 76–90. Print.

Trachsel, Mary. *Institutionalizing Literacy: The Historical Role of College Entrance Examinations in English*. Carbondale, IL: Southern Illinois UP, 1992. Print.

Traub, James. *City on a Hill: Testing the American Dream at City College*. Reading, MA: Addison-Wesley, 1994. Print.

Trillin, Alice. *Teaching Basic Skills in College: A Guide to Objectives, Skills, Assessment, Course Content, Teaching Methods, Support Services, and Administration*. San Francisco: Jossey-Bass, 1980. Print.

Trimbur, John. "Articulation Theory and the Problem of Determination: A Reading of *Lives on the Boundary*." *JAC* 13.1 (1993): 33–50. Print.

—. "Taking the Social Turn: Teaching Writing Post-Process." *College Composition and Communication* 45.1 (1994): 108–118. Print.

Trimmer, Joseph F. "Basic Skills, Basic Writing, Basic Research." *Journal of Basic Writing* 6.1 (1987): 3–9. Print.

Troyka, Lynn Quitman. "Defining Basic Writing in Context." *A Sourcebook for Basic Writing Teachers*. Ed. Theresa Enos. New York: Random House, 1987. 2–15. Print.

—. "Editor's Column." *Journal of Basic Writing* 5.1 (1986): 1-3??. Print.

—. "How We Have Failed the Basic Writing Enterprise." *Journal of Basic Writing* 19.1 (2000): 113–23. Print.

—. "Perspectives on Legacies and Literacy in the 1980's." *College Composition and Communication* 32.3 (1982): 252–61. Print.

—. "The Phenomenon of Impact: The CUNY Writing Assessment Test." *WPA: Writing Program Administration* 8.1–2 (1984): 27–36. Print.

Tucker, Marc. "Many U.S. Colleges Are Really Inefficient and High-Priced Secondary Schools." *Chronicle of Higher Education* (5 June 1991): A38. Print.

Tucker, Mark S. "Computers in the Schools: Has the Revolution Passed or Is It Yet to Come?" *Association of American Publishers Annual Meeting*. n.p. 1985. Address.

Uehling, Karen. "The Conference on Basic Writing: 1980–2001." *Histories of Developmental Education*. Ed. Dana Britt Lundell and Jeanne L.

Higbee. Minneapolis: University of Minnesota's Center for Research on Developmental Education and Urban Literacy, 2002. 47–58. Print.

University of Minnesota. "University of Minnesota: Access, Diversity and Success." *Transforming the U.* University of Minnesota, 27 Apr. 2005. Web. 14 Mar. 2008.

Villanueva, Victor, Jr. *Bootstraps: From an American Academic of Color.* Urbana, IL: NCTE, 1993. Print.

Vygotsky, Lev. *Thought and Language.* Cambridge, MA: MIT Press, 1978. Print.

Wall, Susan, and Glynda Hull. "The Semantics of Error: What Do Teachers Know?" *Writing and Response: Theory, Practice, and Research.* Ed. Chris Anson. Urbana, IL: NCTE, 1989. 261–92. Print.

White, Edward M. "An Apologia for the Timed Impromptu Essay Test." *College Composition and Communication* 46.1 (1995): 30–45. Print.

—. "Holisticism." *College Composition and Communication* 35.4 (1984): 400–09. Print.

—. "The Importance of Placement and Basic Studies: Helping Students Succeed Under the New Elitism." *Journal of Basic Writing* 14.2 (1995): 75–84. Print.

—. "Mass Testing of Individual Writing: The California Model." *Journal of Basic Writing* 1.4 (1978): 18–38. Print.

—. *Teaching and Assessing Writing.* San Francisco: Jossey-Bass, 1985. Print.

Wiener, Harvey S. "The Attack on Basic Writing—and After." *Journal of Basic Writing* 17.1 (1998): 96–103. Print.

—. "Evaluating Assessment Programs in Basic Skills." *Journal of Developmental Education* 13.2 (1989): 24–26. Print.

—. *The Writing Room: A Resource Book for Teachers of English.* New York: Oxford UP, 1981. Print.

Wiley, Mark. "Building a Rose Garden: A Response to John Trimbur." *JAC* 13.2 (1993): 529–34. Print.

Williams, Joseph. "The Phenomenology of Error." *College Composition and Communication* 32.2 (1981): 152–68. Print.

—. "Re-Evaluating Evaluation." *Journal of Basic Writing* 1.4 (1978): 7–17. Print.

Wolfram, Walt, and Ralph W. Fasold. *The Study of Social Dialects in American English.* Englewood Cliffs, NJ: Prentice-Hall, 1974. Print.

Yancey, Kathleen Blake. "Made Not Only in Words: Composition in a New Key." *College Composition and Communication* 56.2 (2004): 297–328. Print.

—. "Outcomes Assessment and Basic Writing: What, Why, and How?" *BWe: Basic Writing e-Journal* 1.1 (1999): n. pag. Web. 20 July 2001.

Ybarra, Raul. "Cultural Dissonance in Basic Writing Courses." *Journal of Basic Writing* 20.1 (2001): 37–52. Print.

Yelin, Louise. "Deciphering the Academic Hieroglyph: Marxist Literary Theory and the Practice of Basic Writing." *Journal of Basic Writing* 2.1 (1978): 13–29. Print.

Young, Richard, A. L. Becker, and Kenneth L. Pike. *Rhetoric: Discovery and Change.* New York: Harcourt, 1970. Print.

Zamel, Vivian. "Engaging Students in Writing-to-Learn: Promoting Language and Literacy Across the Curriculum." *Journal of Basic Writing* 19.2 (2000): 3–21. Print.

Zamel, Vivian, and Ruth Spack. "Teaching Multicultural Learners: Beyond the ESOL Classroom and Back Again." *Journal of Basic Writing* 25.2 (2006): 127–53. Print.

Index

abolition, 35, 37, 69, 73, 171
academic discourse, 10, 26, 55–61, 72, 75, 102, 109–110, 115, 125, 128, 149–150, 152–155, 174
Adams, Peter Dow, 31, 62, 65, 107, 121, 138
Adler-Kassner, Linda, 39, 71–73, 88–89, 131, 161, 173, 189
Anzaldúa, Gloria, 73, 159, 160
apartheid, 33, 36, 118, 169
Apple, Michael, 74
Ashley, Hannah, 115, 116
assessment, 11, 19–20, 22, 32, 35, 50, 62, 66, 68, 80, 90–97, 108–109, 115–116, 120, 123, 127, 131–142, 194
Attewell, Paul, 183–186
August, Bonne, 98, 173, 174

Bartholomae, David, 22, 26, 30–32, 54–61, 65, 68, 76, 86–87, 89, 105–110, 116, 123, 126, 138, 150–151, 153, 156–157, 169–170
basic writing: intensive model, 175
Bazerman, Charles, xi, 177
Bedford Bibliographies for Teachers of Basic Writing, 189
Belanoff, Pat, 94, 136–137, 139
Berg, Anna, 102, 147–148
Berger, Mary Jo, 31, 63
Berlin, James, 4, 45, 151
Bernstein, Susan Naomi, 98, 191, 195

Berthoff, Ann E., 21, 25, 111, 149, 153, 155
Bérubé, Michael, 122
Bizzell, Patricia, 25–26, 51, 55–56, 65, 72, 111, 149–156
Black and Puerto Rican Student Community (BPRSC), 5–6
Blum, Melissa, 37, 73
Board of Higher Education (CUNY), 5, 15–16
Board of Trustees (CUNY), 5, 34, 93, 167, 180
Borough of Manhattan Community College (CUNY), 93
Bousquet, Marc, 122
Braddock, Richard, 123, 132
Bradford, Annette, 19, 148
Brereton, John, 4, 44
Brodkey, Linda, 157
Brown, Rexford, 90–91, 133, 135, 137
Bruffee, Kenneth, xi, 9

Cannon, Sally, 67, 94
Carter, Shannon, 114–116, 174, 191
Chomsky, Noam, 124
City University of New York (CUNY), xi–xii, xvii–xviii, 3–6, 8–9, 15, 20–21, 23, 32–36, 62, 69–70, 92–95, 117, 134–135, 139–141, 162–165, 167, 172–175, 183–184, 186
Coleman, Gerald, 102, 147–148

221

College Assessment Program Evaluation, 93
College Composition and Communication, 14, 17, 18, 19, 21, 30, 33, 36, 66, 69, 83, 85, 92, 96–97, 109, 114, 119, 130, 142, 151, 153, 161, 189, 191, 192, 193
College English, 18, 29, 64, 92
Collins, Terence, 34, 37–38, 70, 73, 169
CompPile, 189–190
computer-assisted instruction, 9, 23
Conference on Basic Writing (CBW), 21, 33, 189, 191–192
Conference on College Composition and Communication, 21, 33, 96–97, 139, 142, 191–193; *Position Statement on Writing Assessment*, 139
Connors, Robert, 4, 24, 47, 55, 128–129
Council of Writing Program Administrators, 33, 92, 174, 193
Crouch, Mary Kay, 75, 98
Crowley, Sharon, 35, 66–70
CUNY Association of Writing Supervisors, 9, 15, 163
CUNY Graduate Center, xviii
CUNY Writing Assessment Test (WAT), 92–94, 141

Deans, Thomas, 176
DeGenaro, William, 38, 73
Dewey, John, 111
Diederich, Paul, 132, 135–136
DiPardo, Anne, 114
Douglas, Wallace, 45

Elbow, Peter, 94, 109, 110
Eliot, Charles W., 13, 44, 46
Emig, Janet, 17, 85, 100, 143–144, 150

English as a Second Language (ESL), xvii, 41, 85, 94, 125, 126, 177
English Language Learning, 41
Enos, Theresa, 52, 54–55, 57, 85, 104; *A Sourcebook for Basic Writing Teachers*, 52, 85
error, 12–15, 17, 22, 29, 41, 50, 55, 72–73, 80–82, 84–89, 99–100, 102, 108, 116, 119, 121, 123, 125–132, 137, 187
error analysis, 72, 85–89, 125–127, 130, 137
Essex Community College, 62–63

Faigley, Lester, 113
first-year composition, 35, 41–42, 44, 46–47, 78, 94, 108, 173, 175, 180
Fish, Stanley, 79–80, 106, 111
Fishman, Judith, 92, 94, 104
Fishman, Stephen M., 76, 120
Fitzgerald, Sallyanne, 38, 99
Flower, Linda, 18, 21, 25, 101, 103, 144–145, 150–151
Fox, Tom, 31, 37, 61, 75, 158–160; *Defending Access*, 75, 159, 160
Freire, Paolo, 111–113, 155, 159
freshman composition, xi, 44–45, 62
Fund for the Improvement of Postsecondary Education (FIPSE), 93

Gibson, Michelle, 167, 171, 187
Gilles, Roger, 98, 139, 175
Gillotte-Tropp, Helen, 39
Gilyard, Keith, 28, 30, 36–37, 59–60, 73, 110, 119, 157, 160
Giuliani, Rudolph, 34, 93
Glau, Gregory R., 39, 117, 121, 175, 189
Glazer, Nathan, 165

Gleason, Barbara, 35, 69, 95, 117, 139–140, 172, 175
Goen, Sugie, 39, 167, 179–180
Goen-Salter, Sugie, 39, 167, 179–180
Goto, Stanford, 75
grammar, 22, 24, 46, 62, 81, 83, 85, 87, 90, 104, 116, 124–125, 127, 131
Gray-Rosendale, Laura, 39, 104, 119, 160, 173
Greenberg, Karen, xi, 31–34, 55, 62, 64–65, 70, 134, 169
Greene, Nicole Pepinster, 113, 119, 136, 167–168, 171
Grego, Rhonda, 35, 69, 117, 120, 139, 161, 175
Groden, Suzy Q., 114, 160
Grubb, W. Norton, 119
Gunner, Jeanne, 17, 31, 63, 64

Hairston, Maxine, 17, 151, 153
Harkin, Patricia, 79
Harley, Kay, 67, 94
Harrington, Susanmarie, 39, 71–73, 88–89, 131, 173
Harris, Joseph, 65
Harris, Muriel, 18
Hartwell, Patrick, 83–84, 127
Harvard University, 4, 44–46, 66, 69, 146, 169, 182
Haswell, Richard, 161
Hayes, John R., 19, 101, 103, 144–145, 150
Hays, Edna, 44
Hays, Janice N., 25, 50, 149
Hilgers, Thomas, 66, 96, 142
Hillocks, George, 97, 142
Hirsch, E. D., 17, 56
Hoggart, Richard, 157
Horner, Bruce, 29, 33, 38, 72–73, 88, 161, 166–167, 170–172

Horner, Bruce, and Min-Zhan Lu: *Representing the "Other,"* 33, 166, 170, 172
Hourigan, Maureen, 51
Hull, Glynda, 14–15, 17, 87, 126, 128, 130–132, 160
Hunter College, xvii, 6, 9, 32, 70
Hunter, Paul, 29
Hyllegard, David, 119, 186

Initiation, 56, 58, 61, 68, 76, 109, 132, 154–156
Instructional Resource Center, 92–93, 134

Jensen, George H., 22–23, 25, 51–52
Jones, William, 31, 61, 134
Journal of Basic Writing (JBW), 13–14, 21, 23–24, 29, 31, 34, 36, 53, 61–64, 66–67, 69, 72–75, 78, 81, 90–91, 103, 105, 114, 127, 134, 136–138, 147–148, 150, 169, 173, 179, 193
Journal of Developmental Education, 189, 194

Kitzhaber, Albert, 7, 41, 46
Kogen, Myra, 25, 148–150
Kraemer, Don J., 176
Kroll, Barry, 85–86, 126
Kuhn, Thomas, 151–153
Kutz, Eleanor, 111, 114, 160

Labov, William, 82, 123
Lalicker, William, 76, 174, 176
Lamos, Steve, 75
Larson, Richard, xi, 9, 132
Lavin, David E., 6, 119, 183–186
Leary, Chris, 116
Lederman, Marie Jean, 92–93
Lloyd-Jones, Richard, 20, 96, 123, 134–135

Long, Bridget Terry, 6, 182, 186
lore, 79–80, 90, 116, 119
Lu, Min-Zhan, 29, 33, 59, 60, 72–73, 110, 113, 159–161, 166, 170–172
Lunsford, Andrea, 19, 22, 50–51, 86–87, 102–103, 116, 124, 128–130, 146–147, 149
Lynch, Kim, 38, 74
Lyons, Robert, xi, 8, 9, 10, 12, 17, 84, 123

Maher, Jane, 5–7, 11, 15, 17, 29
Mainstreaming, 35, 37–39, 62, 68, 75–76, 98, 117–118, 139–140, 161, 170, 172, 175
Maxson, Jeffrey, 115
McAlexander, Patricia J., 119, 167–168, 171
McCarthy, Lucille, 76, 120
McCrary, Donald, 115
McNenny, Gerri, 38, 69, 75, 98, 170; *Mainstreaming Basic Writers*, 38, 69, 99, 170
McQuade, Donald, 8
Meem, Deborah T., 167, 171, 187
Miraglia, Eric, 139
Mlynarczyk, Rebecca, 160, 161, 173, 174, 178, 194
Modern Language Association, 9, 10, 17, 19
Murray, Donald, 21
Mutnick, Deborah, 8, 32–34, 37, 60, 73, 95, 121, 139, 161, 169; *Writing in an Alien World*, 33–34, 37, 60, 95, 139, 161
Myers-Briggs, 22, 51

National Assessment of Educational Progress, 90, 133, 137
National Association for Developmental Education (NADE), 189, 194
National Association of Scholars, 67, 69
National Council of Teachers of English (NCTE), 64, 83–84, 85, 125, 191, 193
National Survey of Basic Writing Programs, 192
National Testing Network in Writing (NTNW), 31, 93, 134
North, Stephen, 79–80, 112
Nystrand, Martin, 136

Obama, Barack, 181
Odell, Lee, 19, 50, 65
open admissions, xi, xv, xvii, 3–8, 29, 33, 44–45, 47, 55, 69, 98, 120, 141, 162, 167, 181–184, 186
Otte, George, 33, 37, 72, 88, 97–98, 141, 165–166

Parisi, Hope, 173, 194
Perl, Sondra, xi, 9, 18, 23, 100–101, 116, 144
Petrosky, Anthony, 26, 32, 54–56, 87, 105–109, 151, 157
Piaget, Jean, 18, 102, 146–148
Pike, Kenneth, 124
Pine, Nancy, 177
Ponsot, Marie, 8, 20, 78
Pratt, Marie Louise, 28, 32, 60, 65, 158
process, 15, 17–18, 24–25, 28, 33, 42, 50, 70, 84–87, 99–101, 103–104, 116, 119, 121, 123–125, 128, 130, 143–145, 147, 150, 176

Raimes, Ann, 9
Rich, Adrienne, 3, 5, 7, 17
Richards, I. A., 111, 125, 153
Ritter, Kelly, 46
Rodby, Judith, 37, 75, 161

Rodriguez, Richard, 157
Rose, Mike, 18–19, 25–28, 30, 36, 50–52, 59–60, 65, 110–111, 150–151, 157, 187–188; *Lives on the Boundary*, 27–28, 36, 59, 110, 157
Roskelly, Hephzibah, 111
Rouse, John, 79
Royer, Daniel, 98, 139, 175

Schafer, John, 85–86, 126
Scholes, Robert, 46
Schor, Sandra, 104
Scott, Jerri Cobb, 31, 61, 113
SEEK (Search for Education, Elevation, and Knowledge) Program, 4–7, 47, 80
self-directed placement, 139
Shaughnessy, Mina, xi, xv–xvi, 3, 5–22, 26–27, 29–30, 32, 36–37, 39, 41–43, 45, 47–51, 56–57, 59–60, 78–82, 84–86, 92–93, 99–100, 102, 110, 116, 122–126, 142–144, 152, 163, 166, 172, 183, 195; *Errors and Expectations*, xvi, 9, 11, 14–16, 26, 43, 47–48, 57, 80, 82, 84, 88, 99–100, 116, 122–123, 126, 142–143, 166, 172, 183
Shen, Fan, 157–158
Shor, Ira, 33–35, 37, 47, 69–70, 73, 111, 113, 118, 169, 170
Shuy, Roger, 82
Sledd, James, 127–128
Smoke, Trudy, 31, 33, 37, 64, 72
Soliday, Mary, 35, 40, 69, 76, 113, 117–118, 139–141, 161, 165, 171–172, 175; *The Politics of Remediation*, 40, 76, 118, 140, 165
Sommers, Nancy, 21, 23
Spack, Ruth, 39, 76, 120
Spellmeyer, Kurt, 95
Standard English, 50, 83, 104, 127, 154

Sternglass, Marilyn, 36, 38, 76, 141, 160, 172; *Time to Know Them*, 36, 38, 141, 160, 172
Stewart, Donald, 46
Stygall, Gail, 34, 74, 171
Sullivan, Patricia, 51

Thompson, Nancy, 35, 69, 117, 120, 139, 161, 175
Tinberg, Howard, 161
Trachsel, Mary, 45
Traub, James, 33–34, 164–165; *City on a Hill*, 33–34, 164–165
Trimbur, John, 28
Trimmer, Joseph, 24, 31, 69
Troyka, Lynn Quitman, xi, 21, 23, 25, 31, 37, 51–54, 73, 92–93, 105, 142, 148, 150

Uehling, Karen, 21, 33, 190

Villanueva, Victor, 28, 30, 36, 59, 110, 157
Vygotsky, Lev, 102, 146, 148

WAC (Writing Across the Curriculum), xviii, 9, 11, 176–177, 189, 195
WAC Clearinghouse, xviii, 189, 195
White, Edward M., 35, 38, 66–68, 73, 127, 134–135, 138–139
WID (Writing in the Disciplines), 176
Wiener, Harvey, xi, 9, 20, 68, 92, 134–135
Wiley, Mark, 27–28
Williams, Joseph, 130, 133–134
Wolfram, Walter, 82, 123

Yale University, 46
Yancey, Kathleen Blake, 96, 114

Zamel, Vivian, 39, 76, 114, 120, 161

About the Authors

For much of his academic life, George Otte was an English professor and a director of writing programs. Currently member of the doctoral faculty at the CUNY Graduate Center (in the PhD Programs in English, Urban Education, and Interactive Technology & Pedagogy), he was coeditor of the *Journal of Basic Writing* from 1996 to 2002. In the late 1990s, while still at Baruch College, he served as Baruch College's Executive Director of Enrichment Programs, which included presiding over high school outreach and communication-across-the-curriculum programs. In 2006, he became Academic Director of the CUNY Online Baccalaureate, CUNY's first fully online degree, and is now the chief academic officer of the CUNY School of Professional Studies, where that Online BA has been joined by an Online BS and an Online MS in Business. In 2008, he was named University Director of Academic Technology for CUNY, a modulation in the title of CUNY Director of Instructional Technology, a position he has held since 2001.

Rebecca Williams Mlynarczyk has taught basic writing at the City University of New York since 1974. She is currently Professor of English at CUNY's Kingsborough Community College, where she codirects the ESL program, and the Graduate Center, where she works with doctoral students in the composition and rhetoric area group. She is the author of *Conversations of the Mind: The Uses of Journal Writing for Second-Language Learners* (Erlbaum) and *In Our Own Words: Student Writers at Work* (coauthored with Steven Haber and published by Cambridge University Press). She has served as coeditor of the *Journal of Basic Writing* since 2003.

www.ingramcontent.com/pod-product-compliance
Lightning Source LLC
Chambersburg PA
CBHW030135240426
43672CB00005B/133